# SERVICING

*Facsimile Machines*

# SERVICING
## *Facsimile Machines*

## MARVIN HOBBS

**Prentice Hall**
Englewood Cliffs, New Jersey 07632

*Library of Congress Cataloging-in-Publication Data*

HOBBS, MARVIN
    Servicing facsimile machines / Marvin Hobbs.
        p.  cm.
    Includes bibliographical references and index.
    ISBN 0-13-805649-8
    1. Facsimile transmision—Equipment and supplies—Maintenance and
repair. I. Title.
    TK6710.H63  1992           91-42304
    621.382'35'0288—dc20       CIP

Editorial/production supervisor and interior designer: **Karen Bernhaut**
Cover designer: **Wanda Lubelska Design**
Prepress buyer: **Mary McCartney**
Manufacturing buyer: **Susan Brunke**
Acquisitions editor: **Bernard M. Goodwin**

© 1992 by Prentice-Hall, Inc.
A Simon & Schuster Company
Englewood Cliffs, New Jersey 07632

The publisher offers discounts on this book when
ordered in bulk quantities. For more information, write:

> Special Sales/Professional Marketing
> Prentice-Hall, Inc.
> Professional & Technical Reference Division
> Englewood Cliffs, New Jersey 07632

FAXSIM is a trademark of Yamaha Corp. of America; IBM is a trademark of IBM Corp.; IBM XT and AT
are trademarks of International Business Machines Corp.; Panafax and Panasonic are trademarks of Matsushita Electric Co.; Rapicom is a trademark of Ricoh Corp.; Turbo C is a trademark of Borland Corp.

No liability is assumed with respect to the use of information herein. Service personnel and others should
comply with all caution and safety-related notes located on or inside fax machines, on their components, and
in manufacturer's service manual and data.

Printed in the United States of America
10  9  8  7  6  5  4  3  2  1

ISBN  0-13-805649-8

Prentice-Hall International (UK) Limited, *London*
Prentice-Hall of Australia Pty. Limited, *Sydney*
Prentice-Hall Canada Inc., *Toronto*
Prentice-Hall Hispanoamericana, S.A., *Mexico*
Prentice-Hall of India Private Limited, *New Delhi*
Prentice-Hall of Japan, Inc., *Tokyo*
Simon & Schuster Asia Pte. Ltd., *Singapore*
Editora Prentice-Hall do Brasil, Ltda., *Rio de Janeiro*

# Contents

## PART I—SERVICING

## PART II—TECHNOLOGY

# *Preface*

This book is divided into two parts. The first part, extending from chapters 2 through 8, is related to the servicing of facsimile (fax) machines. The second part, extending from chapters 9 through 14, is devoted to the technology that has made modern high-speed facsimile transmissions possible.

Chapter 1 covers the background leading up to digital facsimile equipment capable of transmitting documents in a matter of seconds.

Chapter 2 describes the local and remote diagnostics, which are peculiar to facsimile equipment, and gives a new perspective on the diagnosis of faults from remote locations.

Chapter 3 covers general maintenance and the procedures for the disassembly of major parts and personal computer (PC) boards. The cleaning and replacement of these parts are described. The necessary adjustments required after some replacements are outlined.

Chapter 4 describes the circuit operation of a typical desktop machine.

Chapter 5 outlines test procedures and provides flow charts for the troubleshooting of various situations, which arise when the equipment does not perform properly.

Chapter 6 gives an overview of the Consultative Committee for International Telephone and Telegraph (CCITT) standards for facsimile transmission and the modems that hand them to the public telephone lines. The protocol of steps taken to send and receive facsimiles are described in detail.

Chapter 7 describes the components of a high-end fax machine employing a laser printer and their operations. The description is based on a patent granted to the manufacturer. The details given in this chapter can be useful to service personnel in understanding the internal structure and operation of a top-of-the-line machine.

Chapter 8 covers the use of fax boards with PCs, and describes in detail an arrangement by which a PC and a facsimile machine may be associated locally to an advantage. Here again the detailed description is based on a patent.

Chapter 9 outlines the basis for the adoption of both one-dimensional and two-dimensional coding, one as the standard and the other as the option, by the CCITT. The use of dither coding to permit the transmission of halftones is also covered.

Chapter 10 provides detailed descriptions of charge coupled device (CCD) and contact-type scanners. One of the early patents relating to a contact-type scanner using amorphous silicon is described. The details of two later patents covering different approaches to the design of contact-type scanners are presented.

Chapter 11 covers four types of printers—two of which are used extensively in facsimile equipment and two of which are used to lesser degree.

Chapter 12 deals with the unique problems that have plagued paper cutters in fax machines and describes patents aimed at correcting such problems.

Chapter 13 describes in detail a patent that covers the implementation of the error correction mode (ECM), which the CCITT has defined in its T.30 ECM recommendation.

Chapter 14 covers the function of modems as applied to facsimile transmissions and outlines the evolution of their development leading to the use of digital signal processing.

## ACKNOWLEDGMENTS

The author thanks Charlie Howard of the Matsushita Service Company for his valuable input in the writing of this book. Service information was also furnished by Richard Bulko of the Ricoh Corporation and by the Sharp Corporation. The author also thanks the Institute of Electrical and Electronics Engineers for permission to use certain material from their publications.

During the past decade practically all of the technical publications in the facsimile field have been in Japanese; before that time some technical publications were in English. Because of the lack of recent technical publications in English, the author has found it necessary to depend on the information in U.S. patents granted to Japanese inventors showing the advances in facsimile technology.

# SERVICING

*Facsimile Machines*

# CHAPTER 1

# *Introduction*

At least four major factors have affected the development and availability of modern high-speed facsimile machines and services.

1. • Elimination of barriers to transmission of nontelephone signals over public-switched telephone network
2. • Application of digital compression techniques to facsimile transmission to increase speed
3. • Standardization of facsimile transmissions to achieve compatible interworking of facsimiles on both a national and international basis
4. • Development of component technology leading to high-speed, high-quality transmission, as well as reduction in size and cost of equipment

Regarding the first factor, the "Carter Phone" decision is well known and need not be elaborated upon here. It may be noted, however, that a ten-year period elapsed between that decision and the time when direct connections could be made to the telephone line. From 1967, when the "Carter Phone" decision was handed down and 1977, it was necessary to connect through a coupling device provided by the Bell System. The alternative was to use an acoustic coupler, which most facsimile people preferred to use. The Bell coupler was in effect a modem, which to a degree duplicated the one already built into the facsimile equipment. Nevertheless, the acoustic coupler was not an ideal solution. The acoustic coupling could introduce room noise and distortion. Either approach increased the cost of the installation.

1

## ANALOG MACHINES

From the 1950s on there was considerable activity in fax equipment of the nondigital type. First, in the 1950s several models could send an 8 1/2" × 11" page in 6 min. Some of these types carried over into the 1960s and 1970s. In these periods the earliest types of equipment used double-sideband FM modulation of an audio signal suitable for transmission over ordinary telephone lines. By going to a form of AM modulation, called AM-PM-VSB, equipment that could transmit the 8 1/2" × 11" document in 3 min. appeared in the 1970s. Even at a transmission cost of about $3/page at these speeds, considerable interest developed in fax machines. It was estimated that about 100,000 fax machines of the nondigital type were in use in the United States in 1975.

Magnavox, using nondigital FM techniques, was a leader in the 1960s. In 1965 Xerox purchased 25,000 Magnavox units for resale and offered them under the name of Telecopier in 1966. With its own modem this machine could be coupled to the telephone line either acoustically or through the Bell System's model 602 data set. By either method baseband scanner output was converted to a continuously shifting audio frequency for transmission over standard telephone lines. White portions of the transmitted pages were represented by a frequency of 1500 Hz, and the black or darkest portions by a frequency of 2450 Hz. At that time the Electronic Industries Association in the United States issued a Message Fax Standard covering these basic frequency shift parameters.

Although it was thought at that time that FM was essential to cope with noise for transmission over telephone lines, a company known as Graphic Sciences, Inc., introduced in 1967 its DEX-1 model employing amplitude modulation. Using carrier frequencies of 1800 to 2000 Hz this method was not affected by noise as much as had been anticipated, and it helped to lay the groundwork for the Group 2 standard that was to be promulgated later by the CCITT.

Analog fax machines of the types described earlier usually employed drum scanners and depended on a single photoelectric transducer to pick up the signal. After acquiring a signal from the photocell relatively little processing of the signal was done as compared with that done in digital fax machines. An oscillator-modulator prepared the signal for transmission over the telephone line. Send-receive logic controlled the send and receive modes. A data-access modem linked the machine to the telephone line. Most terminals were synchronized through built-in precision power supplies but were first phased with the aid of start of line to ensure against split images. Phasing was accomplished automatically by pulse comparison during the first few seconds of transmission. The interconnected terminals ran at different speeds until local and remote pulses occurred simultaneously, at which time the speeds were automatically equalized. For the remainder of the transmission, continuing synchronization depended on the closeness of the frequencies of the separate power supplies from which the motors in the fax machines operated. Printing of the received copy was sometimes done by varying the pressure of a stylus against carbon paper. This principle was applied in the Magnavox machine mentioned earlier. A functional block diagram of a typical analog fax machine is shown in Figure 1–1.

The AM analog technique in its final form as combined with phase modulation (PM) and vestigial sideband (VSB) resulted in the Group 2 standard and permitted the transmission of 8 1/2″ × 11″ documents in 3 min. Another technique to shorten the transmission time was to alternate the baseband polarity of black signal peaks so signals appeared to be at only half of their actual frequencies. This bandwidth compression technique is shown in Figure 1–2.

By the end of the 1960s it had become apparent that facsimile as practiced up to that time could not compete without high-speed digital data techniques. It was realized that the main problems were redundancy and resolution. Too much electronic effort was going into reproducing areas of identical data. As an entire page was transmitted, up to 90% of the transmission could be wasted. When digitized, an average A4 document (8 1/2″ × 11″) could result in about 2 million b of data. To transmit this digitized image at 9600 b/s, in less than 30 s, required a data compression of about 10:1. Resolution is determined by how closely the facsimile scanner inspects the document to be transmitted. The transmission time is proportional to the product of horizontal and vertical resolution. Data compression offered a solution to both the redundancy problem and the transmission of higher-quality resolution.

## DIGITAL DATA COMPRESSION

One of the first companies to apply digital compression techniques to facsimile machines was DACOM. Using an adaptive run-length (RL) encoding algorithm patented by Donald Weber, the code length was continuously variable in accordance with the source document information content. The scanned data from the original document was associated with two possible states. In scanning a typewritten page the scanner would sense and identify as black elements those elemental areas representing the printed type, and sense and identify as white elements those elemental areas representing the unmarked surface of the paper. When a major portion of a scanned line was either all black or all white, the code used to transmit the data was simplified by compressing the data required to transmit the long stretches of either type. At that time the primary advantage of the DACOM system was that it provided a new family of adaptive codes that could reduce the total number of bits required to describe a scanned document, and the adaptive codes would be applied to both single and multiple scan lines.

Facsimile machines that could send a page in less than a minute were called subminute machines. Dacom, Inc., and Comfax Communications Industries as competitors introduced subminute fax machines in the early 1970s. Later during the 1970s Burroughs, Panafax, 3M, and Xerox offered this class of machine. Before 1980 the Dacom patents had been transferred to a company called Rapicom Corporation.

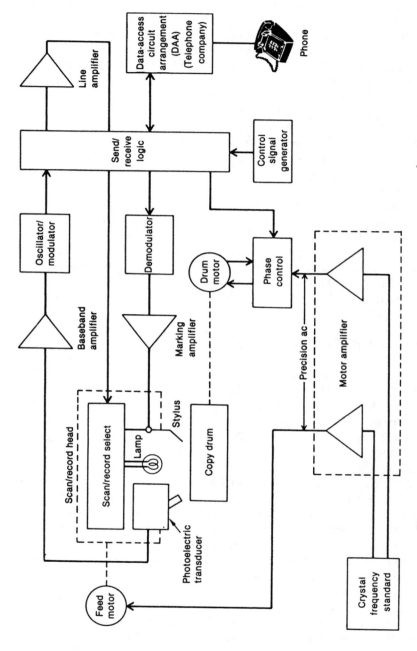

**Figure 1–1** Functional Block Diagram of Typical Analog Fax Transceiver © 1980 IEEE [3]; *reprinted with permission.*

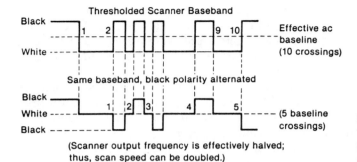

**Figure 1–2**  Bandwidth Compression Technique Used in Some Analog Fax Systems © *1980 IEEE [3]; reprinted with permission.*

## ACTIVITY IN JAPAN

During the 1970s there was intense activity in the study of applying digital data compression to facsimile transmission as well as actual application of facsimile coding schemes. The Japanese had a strong incentive to replace teletypewriters with facsimile equipment so that the typing of Japanese and Chinese characters would no longer be necessary. With facsimile machines, handwritten copies could suffice for their telecommunication needs.

A variety of coding schemes were studied. In an article titled "Overview of Digital Facsimile Coding Techniques in Japan" by Yasuhiko Yasuda, published in the *IEEE Proceedings* in 1980, more than fifty articles written by Japanese authors and published only in Japanese were listed as references. The conversion of some of the coding schemes to practice was indicated by papers presented by personnel of Fujitsu, Ricoh and Toshiba. Under rather similar titles of "High Speed Facsimile Equipment," all three presented papers describing their versions of a product at a technical conference in Japan in September 1977. Companies appeared to be jockeying for position in implementing a code that would give them a competitive edge. The variations in codes, however, emphasized the need for standardization to provide compatibility and to allow machines of different manufacturers to work together.

### Data Compression Encoding

Among the digital encoding transmission systems, most have focused on the continuity length of black and white signals, namely the statistical nature of the run length (RL). Because RL depends on the image data, the encoded digit number has a wide temporal variation, and a buffer memory is necessary to smooth the transmission bit rate. To reduce the size of this memory, subscanning is performed intermittently with a stepping motor, thus controlling memory overflow and underflow.

Many proposals have been issued regarding the method of encoding, but they can be divided into one-dimensional and two-dimensional systems. In the one-dimensional system, encode processing is performed within each scanning line, whereas with the two-dimensional system, encode processing is spread over more than one line.

The CCITT has recommended the Modified Huffman (MH) coding scheme as a one-dimensional method. Figure 1–3 is an explanatory diagram of the principle of one-dimensional RL encoding. When a document like that shown in Figure 1–3a is scanned, the picture signal is like that shown in Figure 1–3b. The RL of the white signals and black signals in this case are indicated in Figure 1–3c. The system used for converting this RL in code and transmitting it is the RL encoding system; one such system uses the MH code table and is called the MH Coding Scheme. Figure 1–3d illustrates a coded signal using an MH code table.

By assigning short code words to RLs frequently generated during encoding, a high compression rate can be achieved. From this perspective, the coding assignment achieved by Huffman is theoretically superior. If individual code assignment were performed in response to the occurrence frequency for all kinds of RLs, however, the preparation of an immense and unrealistic coding scheme would be needed. For this reason, MH coding makes the following code configuration: In general, because short RLs have a high rate of occurrence, individual codes are assigned for

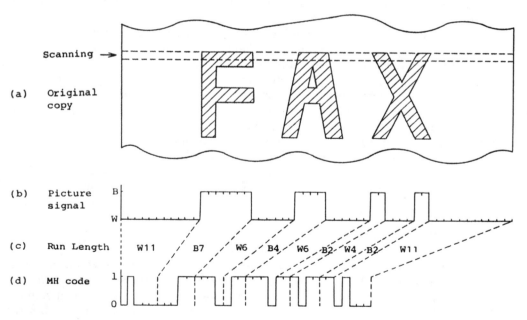

**Figure 1–3**   Principle of Run-Length Encoding (W = White; B = Black) © *1985 IEEE [11]; reprinted with permission.*

RLs from 0 to 63 in response to their occurrence frequency, and these are called terminating codes. Also, 64 integral multiple codes are prepared for run lengths of 64, 128, . . . , and these are called makeup codes. With respect to run lengths above 64, coding is performed by a combination of terminating code and makeup code. Table 1–1 shows a part of the MH code table.

**TABLE 1–1**   MODIFIED HUFFMAN CODE TABLE

| White run length | Code word | Black run length | Code word |
|---|---|---|---|
| | | Terminating codes | |
| 0 | 00110101 | 0 | 0000110111 |
| 1 | 000111 | 1 | 010 |
| 2 | 0111 | 2 | 11 |
| 3 | 1000 | 3 | 10 |
| 4 | 1011 | 4 | 011 |
| 5 | 1100 | 5 | 0011 |
| 6 | 1110 | 6 | 0010 |
| 7 | 1111 | 7 | 00011 |
| 8 | 10011 | 8 | 000101 |
| 9 | 10100 | 9 | 000100 |
| 10 | 00111 | 10 | 0000100 |
| 11 | 01000 | 11 | 0000101 |
| . | . | . | . |
| . | . | . | . |
| . | . | . | . |
| 62 | 00110011 | 62 | 000001100110 |
| 63 | 00110100 | 63 | 000001100111 |
| | | Makeup codes | |
| White run length | Code word | Black run length | Code word |
| 64 | 11011 | 64 | 0000001111 |
| 128 | 10010 | 128 | 000011001000 |
| 192 | 010111 | 192 | 000011001001 |
| 256 | 0110111 | 256 | 000001011011 |
| . | . | . | . |
| . | . | . | . |
| 1664 | 011000 | 1664 | 0000001100100 |
| 1728 | 010011011 | 1728 | 0000001100101 |
| EOL* | 000000000001 | EOL* | 000000000001 |

*EOL = End of line. This code word follows each line of data.

© 1985 IEEE [11]; reprinted with permission.

Each encoded scan line is followed by an end-of-line (EOL) code. This is a unique code word that can never be found in a valid line of data, so that resynchronization after an error burst is possible.

As a two-dimensional encoding method, CCITT has recommended the Modified Relative Element Address Designate (READ) coding scheme as an option. The Modified READ (MR) system refers to the image signal of the preceding scanning line while encoding the image signal of the next scanning line. The image signals of adjacent scanning lines are closely interrelated, with little shift in relative address data, thus allowing an increase in encoding efficiency. If an error is generated in decoding, however, the error will be propagated. To prevent this propagation, one-dimensional encoding is performed on every $K$th scanning line, thus reducing errors to a minimum. According to the recommendation, $K$ is set equal to 2 (at 3.85 lines/mm) and 4 (at 7.7 lines/mm).

Encoded signals are transmitted by using a data modem. If transmission errors are generated, a reproduced image will be distorted. With respect to errors, calculation of the pixel number for each scanning line after decoding is made at the receiving side; if this number does not agree with a designated value, its line data is judged to be in error. Usually this data is then discarded, and the previous scanning-line data is substituted.

The compression rate varies depending on the coding scheme and also on the contents of the document to be transmitted. When the MH coding scheme with a 4800-b/s modem is used, a typically typescript A4-size document at 3.85-lines/mm definition can be transmitted in about 1 minute.

If the MR coding scheme is applied under the same conditions, the transmission time can be reduced by 10% to 20% at 3.85 lines/mm and by 30% to 40% at 7.7 lines/mm compared with the MH coding scheme. The MR coding scheme is especially effective in the high-definition mode.

## INTERNATIONAL STANDARDIZATION

One of the problems in the 1950s and most of the 1960s was a lack of standards in the fax industry. Machines of different manufacturers were incompatible and there was little flexibility beyond a system using only equipment of the same maker. The need for standards was paramount to establishing fax as a viable means of communication. It remained for the CCITT, a specialized agency of the United Nations, to undertake the standardization of fax transmissions on an international basis.

The CCITT standards for facsimile equipment and transmission have been issued as T-series recommendations. They are newly drafted or amended every four years. In 1976, the CCITT classified document facsimiles for use over the public telephone network into three groups (G1 to G3). G1 apparatus used double-sideband FM modulation without any band-compression technique, which transmits a document of ISO A4 size in about 6 min. G2 apparatus exploits band-compression techniques, transmitting the same size document in about 3 min. G3 apparatus uses redundancy reduction techniques that transmit a document of A4 size in about 1 min. In contrast to G1 and G2, which use analog techniques, G3 uses digital techniques.

With respect to standardization of G1, even before the establishment of the aforementioned classification (in 1968), a recommendation was defined, and this was amended in 1972 and 1976. Recommendations for G2 and G3 standardization were made in 1976 and in 1980, respectively.

In addition, in 1980, a Group 4 of error-free apparatus for use over public data networks was defined, and standardization of this continues to be studied. Standards for G4 were recommended near the end of 1984. G4 apparatus is divided into three classes, depending on whether they are capable of interworking with a teletex terminal or with a mixed-mode terminal (teletex and facsimile). The outlines of the standardization recommendations for these four groups (G1 to G4) are shown in Table 1-2.

Figure 1-4 shows a typical block diagram of G3 apparatus. For transmission, the original document is focused on the image sensor by an optical lens system and converted to a picture signal at the photoelectric converter section. The picture signal undergoes shading compensation, automatic background control (ABC), conversion to binary form, and is then sent to the redundancy reduction section.

In the redundancy reduction section, signals are temporarily stored in the line memory, which keeps an equivalent of about two to three scanning lines, after which encoding occurs. The coded signal is connected to the modem via the buffer mem-

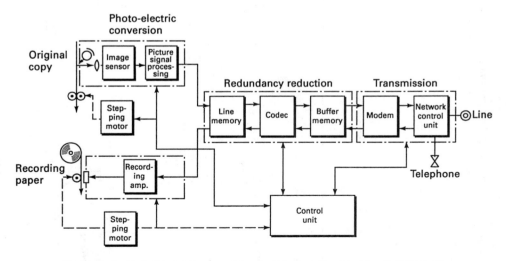

**Figure 1-4**    Basic Block Diagram of Group 3 Desktop Fax Machine © *IEEE 1985*
*[11]; reprinted with permission.*

**TABLE 1–2** OUTLINE OF STANDARDIZED PARAMETERS FOR EACH GROUP APPARATUS

| Apparatus / Parameter | Group 1 | Group 2 | Group 3 | Group 4‡ Class 1 | Group 4‡ Class 2 | Group 4‡ Class 3 |
|---|---|---|---|---|---|---|
| Apparatus recommendation | T.2 | T.3 | T.4 | T.5 | T.5 | T.5 |
| Network | PTN | PTN | PTN | PDN (PTN.ISDN)§ | PDN (PTN.ISDN)§ | PDN (PTN.ISDN)§ |
| Transmission time/A4 (min) | 6 | 3 | Approx. 1 | — | — | — |
| Number of pels along a scan line | — | — | 1728 | 1728, 2074* 2592*, 3456* | 1728, 2074† 2592, 3456* | 1728, 2074* 2592, 3456* |
| Scanning density | 3.85 (1 p/mm) | 3.85 (1 p/mm) | 3.85, 7.7* (1 p/mm) | 200, 240† 300,* 400* (1 p/i) | 200, 240† 300, 400* (1 p/i) | 200, 240† 300, 400* (1 p/i) |
| Modem | FM (1700±400Hz) | AM-PM-VSB (fc: 2100Hz) | PM (V.27ter), AM-PM (V.29)* | — | — | — |
| Data rate (k b/s) | — | — | 2.4, 4.8, 7.2*, 9.6* | 2.4, 4.8, 9.6, 48 | 2.4, 4.8, 9.6, 48 | 2.4, 4.8, 9.6, 48 |
| Coding scheme | — | — | MH MR* | Modified MR (T.6) | Modified MR (T.6) | Modified MR (T.6) |
| Control procedure, protocol, recommendation | T.30 | T.30 | T.30 | T.62, T.70 T.71, T.73 | T.62, T.70, T.71, T.72, T.73 | T.62, T.70, T.71, T.72, T.73 |
| Remarks | | | | | Reception only for teletex and mixed mode | Transmission and reception for teletex and mixed mode |

*Option; †required for teletex and mixed-mode reception; ‡recommended end of 1984; §further study.

© 1985 IEEE [11]; reprinted with permission.

ory, and is then sent out over the transmission line through the network control unit. The encoded signal is a variable-length code, and the buffer memory is provided to make this code a uniform bit stream on the transmission line. To prevent overflow or underflow of this memory, a stepping motor is used to control the feed of the document in units of single scanning lines. The bit rate of the modem is 4800/2400 b/s (CCITT recommendation V.27 ter.) or 9600/7200 b/s (CCITT recommendation V.29).

To verify compatibility and assure operation, a preliminary information interchange between two facsimile apparatuses is required. In the case of the G3 apparatus, these handshaking signals are transmitted by a 300 b/s modem (CCITT recommendation V.21).

Most of the codec, modem, and control functions are realized in a combination of custom large-scale-integration (LSI) circuits and a general-purpose microprocessor. As previously stated, G3 apparatus is becoming more and more dominant, but, to interwork with the former G2 apparatus, many multimode machines, combining the function of G2 and G3, have appeared in the marketplace.

From the standpoint of function, one reason that G3 apparatus has become predominant is its high-speed transmission and stable image quality. Furthermore, technical advances in semiconductor technology and digital processing are helping to ameliorate the cost-function ratio of the G3 apparatus.

## READING AND RECORDING OF DOCUMENTS

The classical construction of analog facsimile machines was arranged as shown in the block diagram of Figure 1–5. The original copy to be transmitted was wrapped around a drum and scanned with a single photocell by rotating the drum and moving the photocell. The paper to receive copies was also wrapped around a rotating drum to be scanned by a recording head fed by the incoming signal. In the construction of modern digital facsimile machines what is called flat-bed scanning, as shown in Figure 1–6, is used. Although the document may move through the machine in anything but a flat path, the scanning is done by moving it across a line of photosensi-

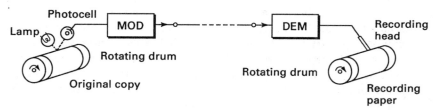

**Figure 1–5** Typical Arrangement of Analog Fax Scanner and Recorder © *1985 IEEE [11]; reprinted with permission.*

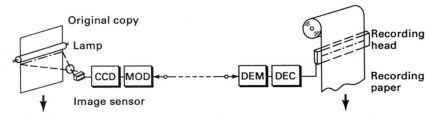

**Figure 1-6**  Typical Arrangement of Digital Group 3 Fax Scanner and Recorder
© *1985 IEEE [11]; reprinted with permission.*

tive elements. The received copy is also made by moving the blank paper across heads that thermally or otherwise form an imprint on the paper.

## Reading the Original Document

During the 1970s when modern facsimile techniques were being formulated, CCD sensors appeared on the scene and offered a new approach to reading a document. A linear array of CCD elements could easily be arranged so that the document could be scanned by moving it past the array. One drawback existed, however. Most of the documents to be transmitted are 8 1/2" (216 mm) wide, but the widest linear CCD array was only 1.02" (26 mm) in width. To use the CCD array it was necessary to reduce the image size of the copy by about 8.33 times by a lens arrangement. If such an optical system is arranged without mirrors, it obviously affects the size of the facsimile machine in which it is incorporated. By using a number of mirrors, it is possible to overlap the path effectively and make the scanner more compact. Equipment designers sought a scanner that was still smaller than any "CCD plus mirrors" approach could provide, however.

To produce the most compact construction much effort has been put forth to develop "contact-type image sensors." They stretch out along the entire width of the document and do not require an optical system to reduce the size of the image that impinges on them. They usually contain amorphous silicon with light-emitting diode (LED) arrays to light the document and optical lens arrays to focus the reflected light onto the photosensitive material in unit magnification.

Today facsimile machines incorporate either a CCD scanner or a contact-type scanner (Figure 1-7). Generally the latter has been preferred to realize the most compact construction of the machine. It has been more expensive, however, by a factor of about 1.5:1. Much effort has been put forth to reduce the cost of contact-type scanners, and it is thought that by depositing the switching elements on the same substrate as that of the photosensitive material, they may finally be made competitive with CCD scanners. Although compactness in a fax machine is certainly desirable, the competitive nature of the business emphasizes the need for cost reduction.

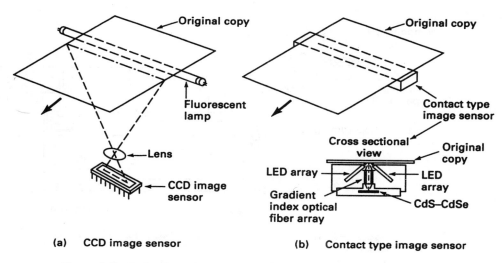

**Figure 1–7** Comparison of CCD and Contact Type Sensors Used in Fax Machines © *1985 IEEE [11]; reprinted with permission.*

## Recording the Received Copy

Many recording methods have been used in facsimile machines. In early analog types, spark recording and electrolytic recording have been used. In modern machines, thermal recorders and laser recorders have been used most widely, with the latter mainly in high-end machines. Thermal-transfer and ink-jet recording have found limited application and may have more application when more color facsimile machines become available.

With the thermal recording method, the recording paper has a coating of a print-developing emulsion of two components that remain separated under normal temperatures. When sufficient heat is applied, these components react to produce a dark printing. Thermal recording heads use a row of heating resistors spaced at minute intervals on an insulating board. Various means have been used to fabricate the thermal head. Thin-film, thick-film, and semiconductor technology have been applied, but thin-film technology is used most widely.

In early thermal recording systems, the thermal head and its recording amplifier were separated. Also, to reduce the number of recording amplifiers, diode matrix circuits were used, so that a single recording amplifier could drive multiple heating elements time divisionally. Recently, as shown in Figure 1–8, the shift registers and recording amplifiers have been integrated and mounted on the board of the thermal head. As a result, the size of such facsimile devices has been reduced, and higher operation speed has been achieved by simultaneous recording.

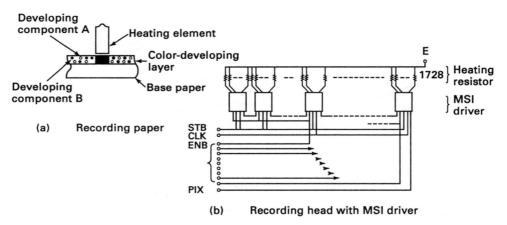

**Figure 1-8**   Thermal Recording Method © *1985 IEEE [11]; reprinted with permission.*

## BASIC MACHINE CONSTRUCTION

From the mechanical viewpoint the main sections of a facsimile machine are the scanning or reading section, and the recording or writing section. By 1983 they were combined into desktop machines typically, as shown in Figure 1-9. There all of the basic parts of a digital fax machine are shown together with a document feeder and a paper cutter. It is seen that with a CCD scanner, the light path runs practically the full length of the machine. More recent designs reduce the length of the path considerably by using more mirrors and overlapping the path, or they use contact-type scanners. The remainder of a fax machine consists of the printed boards (not shown in Figure 1-9) on which solid state components are mounted to provide for data compression, the modem, and control circuits for the signal to be transmitted and the reconstructor circuits for the received signals as well as the common units, such as power supplies.

In this basic design, the facsimile apparatus was arranged to have a read system unit in an upper portion thereof and a write system unit in a lower portion. The read system unit included a table (number 10 in Figure 1-9) on which a stack of documents is laid. Separator rollers (12) and a separator plate (14) constituted in combination an automatic document feeder adapted to pull out the documents one by one of the stack on the table (10). The document was fed by conveyor rollers (16 and 18) toward a tray (20). While moving along a target glass (22) that is interposed between the conveyor rollers (16 and 18), the document reflected light that was emitted from a light source (24). The reflected light has an intensity that varied in accordance with image data. A mirror (26) and a lens unit (28) sequentially steered the reflected light toward a photoelectric transducer element (30), which then converted the incident light into an electric signal.

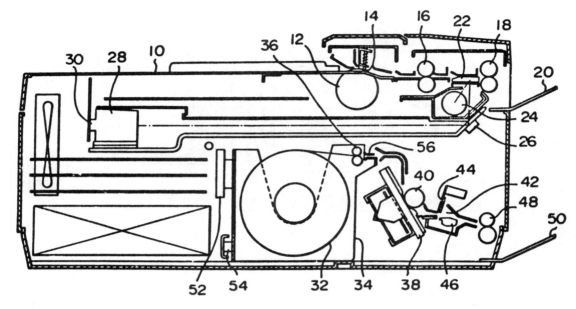

**Figure 1–9**  Typical Mechanical Construction of Group 3 Desktop Fax Machine (ca. 1983).

The write system unit, conversely, included a roll paper unit (34) in which a paper (32) in the form of a roll was received. The paper (32) was paid out of the roll and fed by a manual roller (36) to a recording station. A thermal head (38) is disposed in the recording station to write image data into the paper. A platen roller (40) drove the paper (32) while pressing it against the thermal head (38). The paper (32) coming out from the platen roller (40) was cut by a cutter (42) that is made up of a movable cutting edge (44) and a stationary cutting edge (46); the cut length of the sheet (32) was fed by discharge rollers (48) to a tray (50). The roll paper unit (34) was movable out of the body of the facsimile apparatus, guided by rails (52) and (54). Such a construction allowed one to put a paper roll (32) in the unit (34) after pulling the unit (34) out of the apparatus body, cause the manual rollers (36) to nip the leading end of the sheet (32), cut a needless leading portion of the sheet (32) by means of a manual cutter (56), and then push the unit (34) into the apparatus body.

## MODERN FACSIMILE MACHINES

Considering the size of an 8 1/2″ × 11″ sheet of paper, it is obvious that the fax machine in Figure 1–9 was at least 18″ in length and about 9″ high. By 1990, it was possible to perform all of the basic functions in a fax machine about 12″ in length and 4 1/2″ high. The internal construction of this type, such as Canon's Model 15,

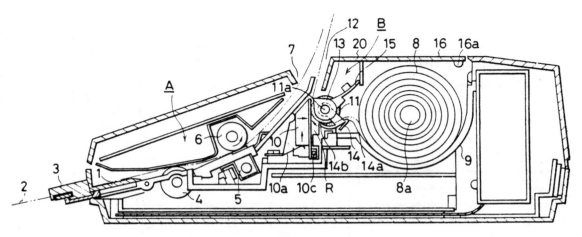

**Figure 1–10**  Internal Construction of Compact Fax Machine (ca. 1990; Circuit Boards Not Shown)

is shown in Figure 1–10. Its weight is about one-third that of the earlier machine. The operation of the 1990 machine is described as follows: In the Figure 1–10, *A* denotes the original conveyance and reading section. A plurality of sheet-shaped originals (number 2 in Figure 1–10) are put on an original setting base (1). Both ends of the originals are guided by a sheet guide member (3) and are separated one by one by a separating feed roller (4) and fed to the reading system. The originals (2) are conveyed at a constant speed by the rotation of a conveying roller (6) onto a reading contact-type sensor (5).

During this conveyance, the information on the surface of the original is read by the read sensor (5). After the image information of the original (2) is read by the sensor (5), the original (2) is ejected upward from an ejecting port (7). In the case of the facsimile mode, the image information read by the sensor (5) is transmitted to the recording system of another facsimile apparatus. In the copy mode, the image information is transmitted to its own recording system.

Conversely, in Figure 1–10, *B* indicates the recording section. A recording sheet (8) consisting of a thermal sheet wound in a roll around a winding core (8a) is detachably set to a roll holder (9). The recording sheet (8) is conveyed at a constant speed by the rotation of a platen roller (11). Further, a thermal head (10) having a plurality of heat-generating elements is brought into pressure contact with the platen roller (11). When the head (10) generates heat in accordance with the image signal as the recording sheet (8) is conveyed through the gap between the platen roller (11) and the thermal head (10), a predetermined image is recorded on the recording sheet (8). After the image is recorded, the recording sheet (8) is ejected upward from an ejecting port (12).

The miniaturization of this unit is due in part to a retractable recording head, which facilitates the loading of the thermal paper in a minimum space. Parts labeled

(a)

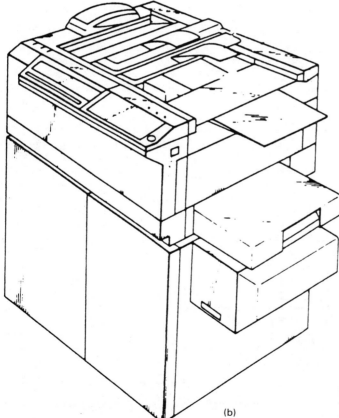

(b)

**Figure 1–11** Range of Modern Fax
Machines: (a) Compact Fax Machine
Suitable for Home-Office or Personal
Use; (b) Large Office Fax Machine with
Laser Printer

(13) to (20) refer to this construction. This machine is packaged with its controls and display together with a telephone handset within the dimensions mentioned earlier. A range of facsimile machines available today is shown in Figure 1–11; this machine, ideal in size for home office or private use, is seen together with a large office fax machine of the type described in detail in chapter 7.

## ELECTRONIC CIRCUITRY

Typically, the electronic circuitry of most facsimile machines now on the market is placed on a main PC board, and other PC boards containing circuitry for operations, the sensor, the switching power supply, and LCD displays. The integrated circuitry of such machines generally consists of LSI (large scale integrated) chips as follows (see Figure 1–12):

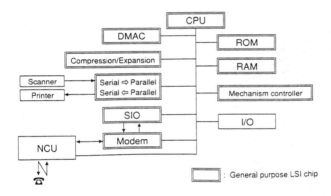

**Figure 1–12**  Application of LSI Chips to Fax Machine Circuitry © *1991 IEEE [5]; reprinted with permission.*

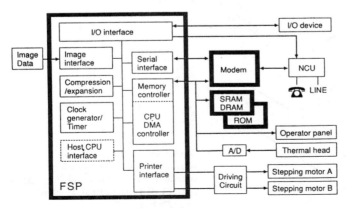

**Figure 1–13**  Further Development Combines Most LSIs in One Chip © *1991 IEEE [5]; reprinted with permission.*

1. A serial-parallel converter reading image data from the scanner
2. A chip that compresses and decompresses image data
3. A DMA controller that controls data transfer
4. A CPU that controls a series of operations and handles protocols
5. Modem and interface chips that control high level data link procedures (HDLC communication protocol)
6. A chip that controls transmission and reception motors and provides other peripheral interfaces
7. Random access memory (ROM) containing program instructions for unit operations
8. Random access memory (RAM) in the form of dynamic access memory (DRAM) for image processing and static RAM for parameter working storage.

A number of less complex integrated circuits are associated with these LSIs. To simplify the construction and reduce the cost and size of facsimile machines, development toward the incorporation of most of the above functions into a single LSI chip (called a facsimile standard processor -FSP) has been pursued. An example of the application of such a chip to a fax machine is shown in Figure 1–13. Here only a few additional LSI chips, such as the memories and the modem, are required to provide the major circuits for facsimile signal processing.

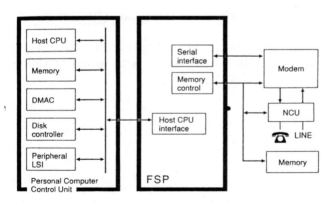

**Figure 1–14** Application of Combined LSI (FSP) to Personal Computer for Fax Transmission and Reception © *1991 IEEE [5]; reprinted with permission.*

Such a chip can also be applied to a personal computer for facsimile operation. In such an application, shown in Figure 1–14, the single LSI chip FSP is controlled by the host CPU through the data bus with specified control signals. The host CPU can use the facsimile functions by simple command/response processing and data transfer. The FSP uses firmware stored in its bus memory to analyze the CPU commands from the host computer to perform the specified operation.

## SERVICING PHILOSOPHY

The philosophy of servicing facsimile equipment can be viewed in a somewhat different way than the servicing of consumer electronic products. At this time, facsimile machines are used primarily in office environments. Although the failure of consumer products is usually an inconvenience, failure of office equipment can be very expensive. For this reason facsimile machines are usually equipped with diagnostic capabilities, which enable the service person to locate the problem very quickly. In servicing consumer electronic products, the service person may proceed through the use of test equipment to locate defective components on a board and replace them. In servicing facsimile equipment in an office, the service person will work at the board level, replacing defective boards or other major components indicated to be at fault by the diagnostics information.

Because of these differences, one could be a competent fascimile service person by being very familiar with symptoms and diagnostics, and adept at changing boards or other major components as well as assembly and disassembly. The use of test equipment would be limited to a few adjustments.

Most of the internal technology of the fax machines, such as data compression and reconstruction, scanning, recording, error correction, and modems, is largely locked in and not subject to anything more than replacements of board or major components. One probably could be a competent service person without in-depth technical knowledge about facsimile. Nevertheless, many may wish to have a greater in-depth knowledge of the technology and think that they can do a better job with such knowledge, even if they do not use much of this information in their day-to-day activities.

Because of the preceding considerations, this book has been divided into two parts—one that deals with servicing procedures and one that deals with the technology in greater depth.

**PART I**

# *Servicing*

# CHAPTER 2

# *Local and Remote Diagnostics*

Most facsimile machines provide a service feature, not found in many electronic products. Provision is made for automatic diagnosis of many service-related conditions by simply pressing buttons on the control panel to enter a service mode. The diagnosis can be seen on a display at the machine. With certain designs a service call will be sent automatically to a service station. Following such action it is also possible to conduct further diagnosis from the service station or other locations to further explore the condition of the equipment. This feature is made possible through the use of bit switches, which are related to each condition to be diagnosed. These switches may be manipulated from a local or remote location to provide local or remote diagnostics.

## LOCAL DIAGNOSTICS

In local diagnostics both test modes and troubleshooting modes can be entered, and displays relating to various conditions are provided. Test modes are used in setting various functions affecting the operation of the unit and in running tests that tell the condition of the unit. In troubleshooting modes tests are run, and the condition of various parts of the machine are displayed. Because the way in which these modes are entered and displayed vary with different designs of facsimile machines, it is necessary to refer to the service manuals of specific models for instructions regarding their operation.

Typically, local diagnostic modes provide for checking panel operation, copy pattern, fluorescent lamp lighting of the sensor, and such components as the ROM and RAM, the automatic document feeder, the modem, the printer, and other important elements of the facsimile machine. Error codes corresponding to various problems are established. Service personnel may display these error codes on the panel of the machine and refer to the service manual for suggested causes of the problem and the action to be taken to correct it. With some designs error codes of problems encountered in the past may be displayed to give the machine's service history. In a final step in this mode, a printout of a service report may be provided. An example describing the service mode of a large facsimile machine employing a laser printer is described below.

### Service Mode

Entering and exiting the service mode

To enter the service mode, press 1, 2, 3, 4, and 5 simultaneously.
  To exit the service mode, press 6, 7, 8, and 9 simultaneously.

*Note:* After entering the service mode, the service mode is disabled automatically if the keypad is not touched for 3 minutes.

Function Table

| Number | Function |
| --- | --- |
| 90 | Bit switch programming |
| 91 | ROM/RAM display, local RAM rewrite |
| 92 | System report |
| 93 | ROM/RAM printout |
| 94 | Error code display |
| 95 | Service report |
| 96 | CCITT and maker codes |
| 97 | Service station telephone number |
| | Recovery from printer system crashes |
| 98 | NCU parameter programming |
| 99 | Maximum address limitation |
| | (Europe only; do not use in USA models) |

The functions are briefly described below.

1. *Bit Switch Programming*—This allows you to change the bit switch settings. While you are changing a bit switch, the factory settings for the bit switch are displayed along with the current settings.
2. *ROM/RAM Display, RAM Rewrite*—This allows you to check the local terminal memory and change RAM addresses if necessary.

3. *System Report*—This report lists counter totals, programmed parameters, bit switches, ID codes, and other items.

4. *ROM/RAM Printout*—This function allows you to print a table of the current contents of the desired range of addresses in local terminal memory.

5. *Error Code Display*—This function displays the most recent 32 error codes. All types of error are included.

6. *Service Report*—This gives a list of the most recent communication errors, listing the RTI and other details. The Error Code column lists communication errors, and the Error Code List area gives all types of error codes (the most recent 32 codes only).

7. *CCITT and Maker Codes*—This allows you to program the CCITT and maker codes, if you ever need to. If incorrect codes are entered, communication using NSF(S) is disabled and proprietary functions such as confidential communication are disabled.

8. *Service Station Telephone Number*—If bit 6 of bit switch 1F is 0, the machine will send an Auto Service Call to the service station on the following occasions:

    LD power control failure
    Master home position sensor failure
    Pentagonal mirror motor lock failure
    Main motor lock failure
    Lower paper feed motor lock failure
    Fusing lamp failure
    Transfer corona leak
    Tonor overflow
    Time to replace the master

    If the Auto Service Call function will be used, enter the service station's fax number using this function. Auto Service Calls will be sent to this number.

    *Note:* If any of the above mentioned conditions occurs, reception (including reception into SAF memory) is disabled.

9. *Recovery from Printer System Crashes*—If the printer software crashes and makes the machine inoperable, this function allows you to return the machine to standby. It is not possible to do a printer reset using remote RAM read/write, but if the power is switched off and back on, the machine will reset.

10. *NCU Parameter Programming*—This allows you to change NCU parameters which affect dialing and ringing detection.

Note that it is possible to change the master belt counter reset function into a service function by setting bit 3 of bit switch 1D to 0. Also, you can use function 75 (when in service mode) to print out confidential files. This is useful when the user has had his/her password over-ridden by the sender and that password cannot be found. (The user's own password can be found on the system report.) The procedure is as follows.

1. Enter the service mode.
2. Select function 75.
3. Enter #0 and press Copy.
   Files are printed but none are erased. The machine will have to be switched off to clear the confidential files.

## Test Mode

The machine has the following tests.

- Model test (G3 and G2 signal transmission).
- Operation panel test.
- Fluorescent lamp lighting (for adjusting the scanner).
- DTMF tone transmission.

## SERVICE CALL CONDITIONS

If the Call Service indicator is lit, one of the following errors has occurred.

- LD power control failure
- Master home position failure
- Pentagonal mirror motor lock failure
- Laser main scan synchronization failure
- Main motor lock failure
- Lower paper feed motor lock failure
- Fusing lamp failure
- Transfer corona leak
- FCU-UIB handshake error
- FCU-LIB handshake error
- Master unit needs replacing

To find out which error has occurred, check the error code memory. To clear the Service Call condition, do one of the following:

- Switch the power off, wait a few seconds, then switch back on
- Execute function 97.

If the problem is not cleared, proceed as follows:

| Symptom | Action |
|---------|--------|

LD power control failure

Does the FCU receive −12V, +24VS, and +5V from the PSU?
Y        N
|         |
|         Replace the PSU.
Does the master set sensor component on the upper unit pass +12V?
Y        N
|         |
|         Replace the sensor.
Replace the master unit, LDDR, UIB, or FCU

Master home position failure

- Clean the sensor patch on the master belt.
- Replace the master unit if it cannot be cleaned.
- Check the master belt drive mechanism.
- Does the master belt motor work?
Y        N
|         |
|         Does the UIB output +24V to the DSB?
|         Y        N
|         |         |
|         |         Replace the UIB or FCU.
|         Does the DSB output the motor drive phases?
|         Y        N
|         |         |
|         |         Replace the PSB, UIB, or FCU.
|         Replace the motor.
- Does the UIB receive a signal from the sensor?
Y        N
|         |
|         Does the sensor receive +5V?
|         Y        N
|         |         |
|         |         Trace the +5V supply line and replace defective board (PSU, FCU, or UIB).
|         Replace the sensor.
Replace the UIB or FCU.

Pentagonal mirror motor lock fail, or laser main scan synchronization fail

- Does the FCU receive +24VD at CN17-1?
Y        N
|         |
|         Does 1POWON go high after Copy is pressed?
|         Y        N
|         |         |
|         |         Replace the FCU.
|         Replace the PSU, upper unit interlock switch, or right cover interlock switch.
If the FCU does not output +24V at CN9-1, replace the FCU.
- Replace the pentagonal mirror motor or the SMDR.
- Replace the LSD or LDDR.
- Replace the UIB or FCU.

(*continued*)

| Symptom | Action |
|---------|--------|
| Main or lower paper feed motor lock fail (Error code 9-24) | If the main motor caused the problem: <br>• Check the $+24$VD supply from the PSU to the main motor as for the previous procedure (check output at CN18-7 instead of CN9-1). <br>• Replace the main motor assembly or the FCU. <br>If the lower paper feed motor caused the problem: <br>• Trace the $+24$VD supply from the PSU through to the motor similarly to the main motor procedures. Replace the defective board. <br>• Does the motor return a low at CN5-4 (on the LIB)? <br>   Y          N <br>   │          │ <br>   │          Replace the LIB or FCU <br>   Replace the motor |
| Fusing lamp failure | • Is the fusing unit thermistor open or shorted? If so, replace it. Otherwise, clean it. <br>• Replace the fusing lamp if it is open-circuit. <br>• Replace the FCU or UIB. <br>• Replace the PSU. <br>• Replace the upper unit interlock switch or right cover interlock switch. |
| Transfer corona power leak | • Clean the transfer corona unit, wire, endblocks, etc. <br>• Check that the development bias is correct ($-225 \pm 10$V). If not, replace the power pack. <br>• Check that the FCU outputs power and trigger signals to the power pack for bias and transfer corona. <br>• Replace the power pack or the transfer corona unit if the problem still occurs. |
| Handshake errors | Replace the FCU, UIB, or LIB. |

## REMOTE DIAGNOSTICS

Users demand that the facsimile apparatus be readily available at virtually any time. Facsimile, however, can experience transmission and other types of problems, as with any other type of communications equipment. It becomes increasingly important, therefore, to provide a diagnostic capability for the facsimile apparatus for a particular user(s). The facsimile apparatus is typically located at an office, and it becomes very inefficient for a user to have to rely on a diagnostic service to come to the particular office to determine any required repairs. If a visit is necessary to restore the equipment to proper operation, advance preparation will yield the most expeditious results. Often a visit is not necessary to restore operation, if adequate diagnosis can be made remotely at a service station and corrective signals are transmitted.

In other technologies, some approaches have used remote diagnostic systems. The first remote diagnostic system was introduced in general by computer makers to provide checks for the current and prior status of the computer system by running diagnostic programs.

The next sophisticated remote diagnostic system introduced a capability using what can be characterized as expert knowledge. Only one such system or unit, however, is generally not enough to support large numbers of field-installed machines. In a facsimile environment, the dramatic expansion can at times demand concurrent diagnostics.

In view of the foregoing, it would be very desirable to provide a remote diagnostic system that can provide remote diagnostics for one or more remotely located facsimile apparatus. A remote facsimile diagnostic system covered by U.S. patent #4,965,676 granted to the Ricoh Corporation on October 25, 1990, is described below. Briefly, this facsimile remote diagnostic system comprises one or more facsimile apparatuses connected to a conventional telephone line. The system further includes remote diagnostic means for communicating with the facsimile apparatus. The remote diagnostic means includes software control means for providing remote diagnostics for the facsimile apparatus, and communication adapter means for controlling communications between the software control means and the facsimile apparatus. The software control means can provide suitable diagnostics for the facsimile apparatus from a remote location, thereby eliminating the need for service personnel to go to the particular location where the facsimile apparatus requires diagnostic services.

This remote diagnostic system provides remote diagnostics for one or more facsimile apparatus, such as those manufactured by the Ricoh Corporation. Reference will be made to facsimile models of Ricoh Corporation, although the aspects of the present invention would apply to all types of facsimile.

The system (10) shown in Figure 2–1, comprises the following units: 1. one or more facsimiles' (12–1,. . . . . . . 12–N) communication history of which is stored in memory accessible by remote way; 2. communication control adapter (CCA) (20), which can communicate with the fax (12) and computer (50) through serial interface (RS232C) (22); and 3. PC (50) (including an expert system).

**1.** *Facsimile*—The target facsimile is the G3 standard facsimile with the following additional functions: (1) buffer memory that can store communication histories including some image pattern; (2) bit switches that control the functions and mode by remote means; and (3) sensor status stored in the buffer memory.

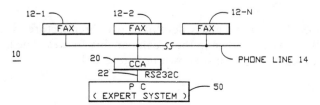

**Figure 2–1**  Block Diagram of Remote Fax Diagnostic System

**2.** *CCA*—This unit has the same function as facsimile, network control unit (NCU), modem, and protocol processor. Image communication with other fax is possible. A block diagram of the CCA is shown in Figure 2-2. It depicts a block diagram of the CCA (number 20 in Figure 2-2). The CCA (20) includes a NCU (26), which controls data communication through a public telephone line (14). The main functions of the NCU (26) are startup of the unit, resetting or sendout of selected signals, calling signal detection, and loop status maintenance (keep loop mode).

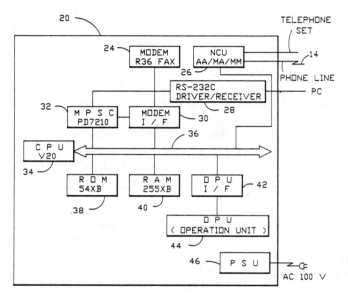

**Figure 2-2**  Block Diagram of Communication Control Adapter

The CCA (20) includes a modem (30), which provides data signal conversion to the transmission of analog signals and also provides the reverse inversions in a known fashion. The CCA further includes a multiple page signal controller (MPSC) (32), which detects the end of the page in image signal. The CCA also includes an operation port unit (OPU) (44), which controls the operation panel and keyboard. Finally, the CCA includes a power supply unit (PSU) (46), which provides suitable power as necessary.

The CCA (20) has all the necessary functions of facsimile and digital interfaces to the PC (50) of Figure 2-1. It can communicate with both current G3 facsimiles and computers, and includes enough memory (RAM) (40) to store two-page document images.

**3.** *PC (expert system)*—This part is newly developed with architecture as seen in Figure 2-3. Details of the flow are shown in the accompanying figures. The main function flow of the fax diagnostic system is shown in Figure 2-4.

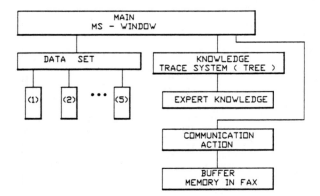

**Figure 2-3**  Block Diagram of PC Expert System

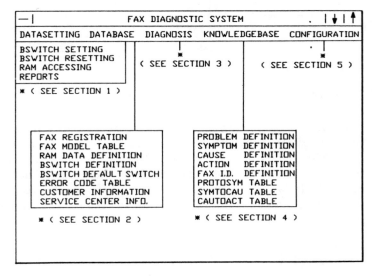

**Figure 2-4**  Main Function Flow of Fax Diagnostic System

## BIT SWITCH SETTING

This function will allow the user to read all bit switch values from a remote fax machine and then, if necessary, rewrite the new data back to the remote fax machine. The key is the customer name or customer fax number. The screen will display as in Figure 2-5.

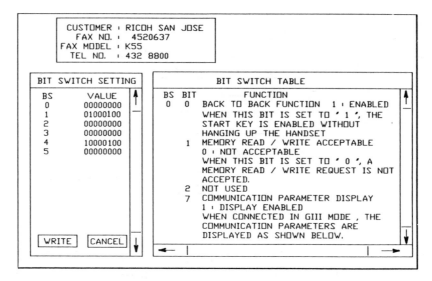

**Figure 2–5**  Screen Display of Bit Switch Setting

## BIT Switch Resetting

If bit switch values read from a remote fax are not clear, this function will reset bit switch values for the remote fax, based on the default values of the particular fax model. After default values have been displayed on the screen, the user can modify any bit switch value and then rewrite all bit switch values back to remote fax. The screen will display as in Figure 2–5. The only difference between these two functions is the former read data from remote fax and the latter read data from bit switch default data base instead.

## RAM ACCESSING

This function will allow the user to read a specific portion of RAM data from a remote fax, and also easily modify those data on the screen and then rewrite the new data back to the remote fax. The screen will display as in Figure 2–6.
    The RAM definition window can have the following two displayed options:

   **1.** *Priority*—Display information on screen started from specified priority
   **2.** *Address*—Display information on screen started from specified address

    The user selects "start address" and "end address" directly from the RAM definition table.

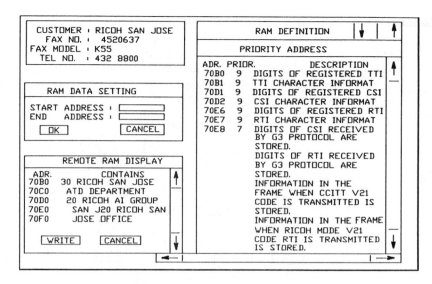

**Figure 2–6** RAM Access Screen Display

If the specified addresses are correct, the user clicks the "OK" button on the RAM data setting window. Then the system will start to access the remote RAM, and then display the retrieved data on the remote RAM display window.

Users will be allowed to modify the data displayed on the remote RAM display window (except for the address column) and then, if necessary, the new data will be rewritten back to the remote fax.

## REPORTS

This function will supply various reports output and allow the user to examine the important information through the screen display. The names of reports are the following:

Transaction Confirmation Report

Service Report

Transmission Report

Transfer Report

Error Report

System Report

Polling File List

Program List

Telephone List

## DATA BASE

The Fax Data Base structure is shown in Figure 2–7. Data Base Entry is covered by Figures 2–8 to 2–15. Figure 2–16 shows the general flow of Diagnosis followed by Knowledge Base Representation, Data Files, and Model Data.

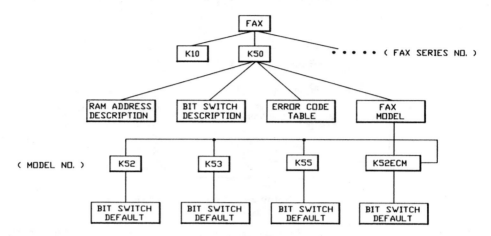

**Figure 2–7**   Fax Data Base (Prestructure)

## Data Base Entry

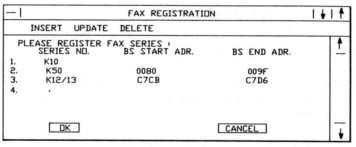

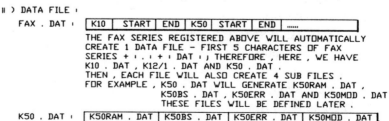

**Figure 2–8**   Fax Registration Window Image

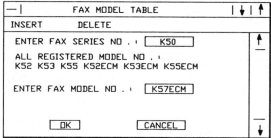

```
─|              FAX MODEL TABLE              |↓|↑|

INSERT       DELETE

    ENTER FAX SERIES NO . ፡ [  K50  ]              ↑
                                                   ─
    ALL REGISTERED MODEL NO . ፡
    K52 K53 K55 K52ECM K53ECM K55ECM


    ENTER FAX MODEL NO . ፡   [ K57ECM ]


                                                   ─
          [ OK ]          [ CANCEL ]               ↓
```

NOTE ፡ FUNCTION  –
        INSERT ፡ REGISTER A NEW FAX MODEL .
        DELETE ፡ DELETE A SPECIFIED FAX MODEL .

ɪɪ ) DATA FILE ፡ THIS PARTICULAR FAX SERIES MUST HAVE BEEN REGISTERED
                DURING FAX REGISTRATION STEP . A FAX MODEL FILE NAME
                IS DEFINED AS THE FIRST 5 CHARACTERS OF FAX SERIES +
                ' MOD ' + ' DAT ' ፡ ALSO THOSE FAX MODELS WHICH REGISTER
                ABOVE WILL AUTOMATICALLY CREATE 1 DATA FILE – THE
                FIRST 5 CHARACTERS OF FAX MODEL + ' DEF ' + ' . ' + ' DAT ' ፡
                THEREFORE , HERE , WE HAVE K52DEF . DAT , K53DEF . DAT AND
                K55DEF . DAT . THESE FILES WILL BE DEFINED LATER .
                FOR EXAMPLE ፡ FAX K50 SERIES WILL GENERATE A DATA
                                FILE CALLED K50MOD . DAT .

K50MOD . DAT ፡ | K52 | K53 | K55 | K52ECM |  . . . . . .  |

**Figure 2–9**  Fax Model Table Window

```
─|          RAM DATA DEFINITION         |↓|↑|

INSERT   SEARCH    DELETE
ADR . PRIOR TYPE       DESCRIPTION       REMARK    ↑
0402    5    0     TELINF CONTROL HEADER            ─
0602    5    0     RAM FOR TELEPHONE NUMBER
                   REGISTER .
1002    4    0     TELOS INPUT PARAMETER
                   STORING RAM .
1102    4    0     TELOS OUTPUT DATA STORING
                   RAM
1202    5    0     ONE TOUCH DIAL PROPER NOUN
                   REGISTERING AREA .
140F    5    0     GROUP PROPER NOUN REGISTERING
                   AREA .
14A2    6    0     TOP ADDRESS OF EMPTY AREA OF
                   TELINF ( LOW ) .
14A3    6    0     TOP ADDRESS OF EMPTY AREA OF
                   TELINF ( HIGH ) .
                                                    ─
       [ UPDATE ]        [ CANCEL ]                 ↓
```

NOTE ፡
PRIORITY WILL BE RATED BETWEEN
10 TO 1 ( HIGH TO LOW ).
TYPE – 0 ፡ HEX DATA TYPE.
        1 ፡ DECIMAL DATA TYPE.
        2 ፡ ASCII DATA TYPE. ( UPPER CASE )

FUNCTION –
INSERT   ፡ INSERT A NEW RECORD TO THE DATA FILE .
SEARCH   ፡ SEARCH A PARTICULAR RECORD BASED ON ADDRESS .
DELETE   ፡ DELETE A SPECIFIED RECORD .
ɪɪ ) DATA FILE  ፡ NAME IS DEFINED AS THE FIRST 5 CHARACTERS OF FAX
                 SERIES + ' RAM ' + ' DAT '
                 FOR EXAMPLE ፡ K50RAM . DAT WHICH MUST HAVE BEEN
                 CREATED DURING FAX REGISTRATION STEP .
K50RAM . DAT ፡ | ADRS | PRIOR | TYPE | DESCRIPTION | REMARK |
                ( 4 )  ( 1 )   ( 1 )   ( 120 )      ( 100 )

**Figure 2–10**  RAM Data Definition Window Image

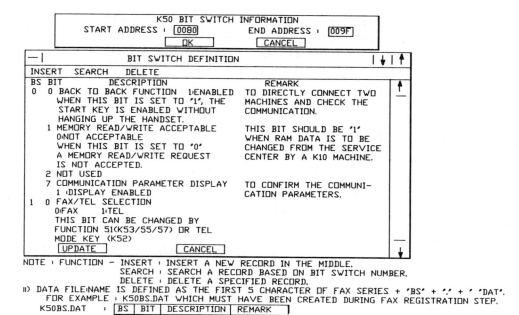

NOTE ι FUNCTION – INSERT ι INSERT A NEW RECORD IN THE MIDDLE.
                          SEARCH ι SEARCH A RECORD BASED ON BIT SWITCH NUMBER.
                          DELETE ι DELETE A SPECIFIED RECORD.
 ιι) DATA FILEιNAME IS DEFINED AS THE FIRST 5 CHARACTER OF FAX SERIES + 'BS' + '.' + ' 'DAT'.
        FOR EXAMPLE ι K50BS.DAT WHICH MUST HAVE BEEN CREATED DURING FAX REGISTRATION STEP.

K50BS.DAT    ι | BS | BIT | DESCRIPTION | REMARK |
                  (2)   (1)      (120)        (100)

**Figure 2–11**  Bit Switch Definition Window Image

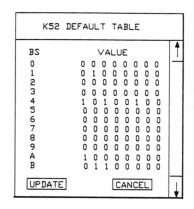

ιι ) DATA FILE ι
NAME IS DEFINED AS FAX MODEL + 'DEF' + '.' + 'DAT'
FOR EXAMPLE ι
K52DEF.DAT WHICH MUST HAVE BEEN
CREATED DURING FAX MODEL TABLE STEP.

      K52DEF.DAT ι | BIT SWITCH | 'VALUE |

**Figure 2–12**  Bit Switch Default Table
Window Image

```
┌─┬──────────────────────────────────────────────────┬───────┬─┐
│─│            K50 ERROR CODE TABLE                   │↓ │ │↑│
├─┴──────────────────────────────────────────────────┴───────┴─┤
│ INSERT   UPDATE    DELETE                                      │
├───────────────────────────────────────────────────────────┬──┤
│ PREFIX  CODE           DESCRIPTION                        │↑ │
│   0      00    INITIAL ID SIGNAL UNDETECTED               │  │
│   0      01    RECEIVED 'DCN FRAME' FROM REMOTE FAX       │──│
│   0      03    MODEM INCOINCIDENCE                        │  │
│   0      04    FAIL TO RECEIVE THE TRAINING RESPONSE      │  │
│                 'CFR/FTT'                                 │  │
│   0      05    TRAINING FAILURE AFTER SHIFTDOWN TO 2400   │  │
│                 BPS.                                      │  │
│   0      06    REMOTE-FAX-FAIL TO RECEIVE THE 'DCN' FRAME │  │
│   0      07    FAIL TO RECEIVE THE RESPONSE,'MCF/RTP/RTN/ │  │
│                 PIP/PIN' AFTER MESSAGE EXCHANGE.          │  │
│   0      08    RECEIVED COPY NG(RTN/PIN)                  │  │
│   0      14    RECEIVED UNKNOWN CODE AFTER MESSAGE        │  │
│                 EXCHANGE.                                 │  │
│   0      15    THE REMOTE FAX HAS NO FUNCTION OF          │  │
│                 'CONFIDENTIAL' OR 'RELAY-TRANSMISSION'    │  │
│   0      16    FAIL TO RECEIVE THE RESPONSE (CFR/FTT) FOR │  │
│                 'CONFIDENTIAL' OR 'RELAY-TRANSMISSION'    │  │
│   0      52    SIGNAL TURNED OVER                         │  │
│   4      01    LINE CUT (ELECTRIC CURRENT CUT) DETECTED.  │──│
│            ┌────────────┐        ┌────────────┐           │  │
│            │  UPDATE    │        │  CANCEL    │           │↓ │
└────────────┴────────────┴────────┴────────────┴──────────┴──┘
```

NOTE ⦂ FUNCTION – INSERT ⦂ INSERT A NEW RECORD IN THE MIDDLE.
                 SEARCH ⦂ SEARCH A RECORD BASED ON THE PREFIX.
                 DELETE ⦂ DELETE A SPECIFIED RECORD.
      ‖ ⟩ DATA FILE ⦂ NAME IS DEFINED AS THE FIRST 5 CHARACTERS OF FAX
                 SERIES + 'ERR' + '.' + 'DAT'
                 FOR EXAMPLE ⦂ K50ERR.DAT WHICH MUST HAVE BEEN CREATED
                      DURING FAX REGISTRATION STEP.

R50ERR.DAT ⦂ | PREFIX | CODE |    DESCRIPTION    |

**Figure 2–13**  Error Code Table Window Image

```
┌────┬──────────────────────────────────┬───┬──┬──┐
│────│     CUSTOMER INFORMATION         │ ↑ │  │↓ │
├────┴──────────────────────────────────┴───┴──┴──┤
│ CUSTOMER NAME    ⦂                            │↑ │
│ FAX TEL NO.      ⦂ 1.                         │  │
│                  ⦂ 2.                         │  │
│ DEPARTMENT CODE ⦂                             │  │
│ FAX MODEL        ⦂                            │  │
│ TEL NUMBER       ⦂                            │  │
│ FAX SERIAL NO.  ⦂                             │  │
│  - ERROR REPORT HISTORY ( UPTO 100 )         │  │
│  -                                           │  │
│  - BIT SWITCH STATUS CHANGE HISTORY (UPTO 100)│ │
│  -                                           │  │
│  - CDD THRESHOLD HISTORY ( UPTO 30 )         │  │
│  -                                           │  │
│  - PULSE WIDTH HISTORY   ( UPTO 30 )         │  │
│  -                                           │  │
│  - ANALYSIS RESULT HISTORY ( UPTO 30 )       │  │
│  -                                           │  │
│  - DIAGNOSIS HISTORY     ( UPTO 30 )         │  │
│  -                                           │  │
│ ┌──────┐              ┌────────┐             │  │
│ │  OK  │              │ CANCEL │             │↓ │
└─┴──────┴──────────────┴────────┴─────────────┴──┘
```

NOTE ⦂ FUNCTION –
       INSERT ⦂ ADD A NEW CUSTOMER RECORD.
       UPDATE ⦂ UPDATE A SPECIFIED CUSTOMER RECORD.
       DELETE ⦂ DELETE A SPECIFICM CUSTOMER RECORD.
   KEY ⦂ CUSTOMER NAME
        OR
        FAX TEL NO.

**Figure 2–14**  Customer Information
Window Image

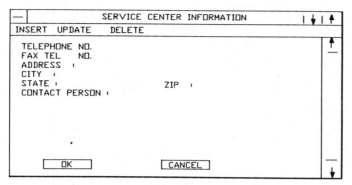

NOTE ⫶ FUNCTION  –

    INSERT ⫶ ADD A NEW SERVICE CENTER RECORD.
    UPDATE ⫶ UPDATE A SPECIFIC RECORD BASED ON
             ZIP CODE , STATE OR CITY.
    DELETE ⫶ DELETE A SPECIFIC RECORD BASED ON
             ZIP CODE , STATE OR CITY.

**Figure 2–15** Service Center Information Window Image

## DIAGNOSIS

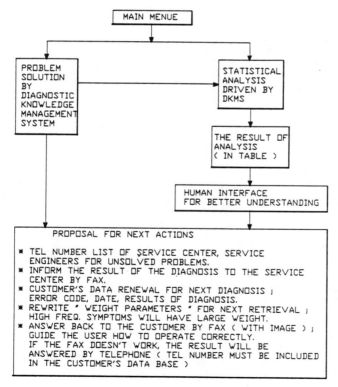

**Figure 2–16** General Flow of Diagnosis

| | * | | | * | |
|---------|---------|--------|---------|---------|---------------------|
| ADDRESS ID | SUCCESS TIMES | WEIGHT | NEXT NODE ID | SUCCESS TIMES | CONDITIONAL BIT PATTERN |
| P0001 | 0 | 10 | S0010 | 0 | BIT ( 1101000.. ) |
| | | 9 | S0011 | 0 | BIT ( 1110111.. ) |
| P0002 | 0 | 10 | S0020 | 0 | BIT ( 1101000.. ) |
| .. | | .. | .. | .. | .. |
| .. | | .. | .. | .. | .. |

SymToCau

| | * | | | * | |
|---------|---------|--------|---------|---------|---------------------|
| ADDRESS ID | SUCCESS TIMES | WEIGHT | NEXT NODE ID | SUCCESS TIMES | CONDITIONAL BIT PATTERN |
| S0001 | 0 | 9 | C0101 | 0 | BIT ( 1101000.. ) |
| | | 10 | C0102 | 0 | BIT ( 1110111.. ) |
| S0011 | 0 | 10 | C0103 | 0 | BIT ( 1101000.. ) |
| .. | | .. | .. | .. | .. |
| .. | | .. | .. | .. | .. |

CauToAct

| | * | | | * | |
|---------|---------|--------|---------|---------|---------------------|
| ADDRESS ID | SUCCESS TIMES | WEIGHT | NEXT NODE ID | SUCCESS TIMES | CONDITIONAL BIT PATTERN |
| C0101 | 0 | 10 | A1001 | 0 | BIT ( 1101000.. ) |
| | | 10 | A1002 | 0 | BIT ( 1110111.. ) |
| | 0 | 10 | A1003 | 0 | BIT ( 1101000.. ) |
| .. | | .. | .. | .. | .. |
| .. | | .. | .. | .. | .. |

NOTE : (*) THESE COLUMNS WILL BE INITIALIZED TO 0 FIRST, AND THEN EACH TIME, AFTER FINISHING DIAGNOSIS, IT WILL AUTOMATICALLY INCREASE 1 TO THE SUCCESS TIMES OF FOUNDED PROBLEM, SYMPTOM, CAUSE AND ACTION.

**Figure 2-17** Knowledge Base Representation

```
┌─────────────────────────────────────────────────────────────────┐
│ PROBLEM                                                           │
├─────────────────────────────────────────────────────────────────┤
│                                                                   │
│ P0001  ' LINE FAIL ' AFTER 30 - 40 SEC WITHOUT DOCUMENT           │
│          SCANNING                                                 │
│ P0002  ' LINE FAIL ' AFTER 5 SEC                                  │
│                                                                   │
└─────────────────────────────────────────────────────────────────┘
```

(1)

```
┌─────────────────────────────────────────────────────────────────┐
│ SYMPTOM                                                           │
├─────────────────────────────────────────────────────────────────┤
│                                                                   │
│ S0010  ' CED ' NOT DETECTED IN AUTO DIALING MODE                  │
│ S0011  ' DIS ' OR ' NSF ' NOT DETECTED FROM REMOTE FAX            │
│ S0012  TRAINING FAILURE WITHOUT RESPONSE FROM REMOTE              │
│          TERMINAL                                                 │
│                                                                   │
└─────────────────────────────────────────────────────────────────┘
```

(2)

```
┌─────────────────────────────────────────────────────────────────┐
│ CAUSE                                                             │
├─────────────────────────────────────────────────────────────────┤
│ C0101    TOO LONG DELAYED SIGNAL                                  │
│          OR EXCESSIVE WHITE NOISE ON TEL LINE                     │
│ C0102    POSSIBLY, THE LOCAL TERMINAL CAN'T DETECT CED            │
│ C0103    POSSIBLY, NSF/DIS SIGNAL DOESN'T COME FROM REMOTE        │
│          TERMINAL                                                 │
│ C0104    SN RATIO IS TOO LOW                                      │
│                                                                   │
└─────────────────────────────────────────────────────────────────┘
```

(3)

```
┌──────────────────────────────────────────────┬──────────────────┐
│ ACTION                                        │                  │
│                                               ├──────────────────┤
│                                               │ CONDITIONS       │
├───────────────────────────────────────────────┼─────────────────┤
│ A1001   ECHO COUNTERMEASURES                   │ FX3300          │
│         INSTALL A CARRIER-ON RETROFIT ROM      │ RAPI3300        │
│ A1002   SET THE ECHO COUNTERMEASURE SW2 BIT    │ FX5000          │
│         #6 ON                                  │ I6500, R5000    │
│         IF MACHINE IS NOT GROUNDED, REMOVE     │                 │
│         CAPACITORS C1, C2, C3 ON AA-NCU1       │ FX5000          │
│ C0103   CHANGE CED TO 2100Hz                   │ FX5000          │
└────────────────────────────────────────────────┴────────────────┘
```

(4)

**Figure 2-18**  Representation of Data Files

| MODEL ID | NAME    | BIT POSITION |
|----------|---------|--------------|
| F0001    | R600s   | 0            |
| F0002    | R700    | 1            |
| F0003    | RX5000  | 2            |
| F0004    | Rapi600 | 3            |
| F0005    | FX3300  | 4            |

| BIT PATTERN          |
|----------------------|
| 0000000 00000001     |
| 0000000 00000010     |
| 0000000 00000100     |
| 0000000 00001000     |
| 0000000 00010000     |

**Figure 2-19**  Representation of Model Data

## WAY SYSTEM WORKS

A specific fax model is sometimes important to diagnose because most knowledge is related to that model. In this example, FX3300 is stored in user's data base for initial communication setup. The customer's name is used as a key to connect the remote fax. Another telephone number is necessary in case of fax malfunctions.

Analyses results are reserved for future data analysis. The result of statistical analysis is represented here.

"Line fail," "CED not detected," and "DIS . . ." are part of the stored expert knowledge listed in the manual. Tables 3 and 4 in Figure 2–18 are the example already stored in Ricoh. The result of this diagnosis is service "ACTION." This should be connected to the small data base of service engineers. The result of the diagnosis will be sent to the customer or service center via fax or telephone (if fax does not work).

Another window "DATA for FX3300" is connected to the specific data concerning FX3300. Tables 1 and 2 in Figure 2–18 are the example.

A description of the operation of the facsimile diagnostic system is now provided (Figure 2–20). To run the system, a user will need a configuration such as depicted in Figure 2–1, which includes a control system such as a PC/AT, XT, or IBM PS2, which runs DOS operating systems. In addition, a hard disk and a double-sided disk drive is recommended. Two double-sided disk drives can be used, however. The user will need a serial cable, a CCA, a mouse, an analog telephone line and two serial ports, or a serial and a mouse port. The software is typically one such as Microsoft Windows version 2.0 or a later version, and DOS 2.0 or a later version.

The hardware interconnection is as depicted in Figure 2–1, in which a telephone line is connected to the CCA socket, which indicates line side. The user connects a serial cable to both the CCA and computer serial port, and connects the mouse to the serial or mouse port.

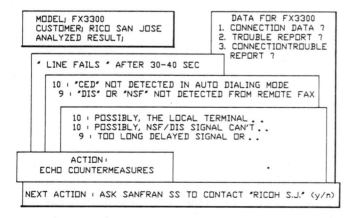

**Figure 2–20** Illustration of System Operation

The "DTE/DCE" switch is set to "DCE." In starting up, the operation is as follows:

1. Copy "*.*" to the windows' working directory.
2. When in DOS enter "WIN FAXSET" and then press < Return >, or do the following.
3. Select and run FAXSET.EXE in the MS-DOS executive window. Starting FAXSET automatically creates an empty window where the user can select various commands. Before running the program, Microsoft Windows is usually already installed.

The main menu on the display of PC of Figure 2-1 is depicted in Figure 2-21. To choose a command from a menu, proceed as follows:

1. If using the mouse, the user chooses a command from a menu.
   a. Click the menu name on the menu bar.
   b. Click the command name.
2. If using the keyboard, then follow these steps.
   a. Press the ALT key.
   b. Press the underlined letter in the menu name.
   c. Press the underlined letter in the command name.

To cancel a menu, proceed as follows:

1. If using the mouse and deciding after selecting the menu that the user does not want to choose a command, the menu can be canceled by pressing ESCAPE.
2. if using the keyboard and deciding after selecting the menu that the user does not want to choose a command, the menu can be canceled by clicking anywhere outside the menu. Clicking in a blank area of the window is best, so that the user does not select something else in the window without meaning to.

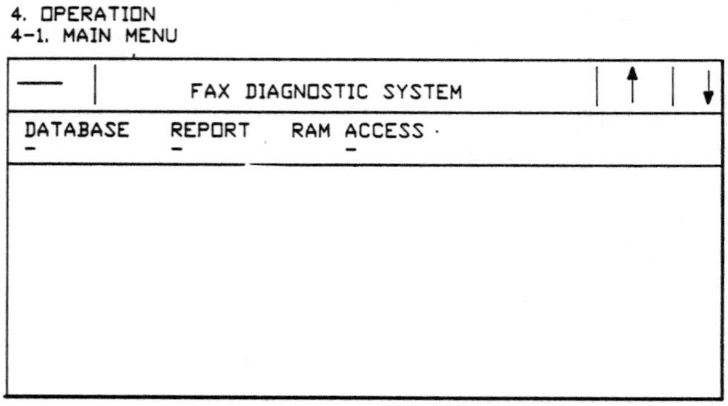

```
4. OPERATION
4-1. MAIN MENU
```

**Figure 2-21**  Main Menu Display

4-4. THE RAM ACCESS MENU

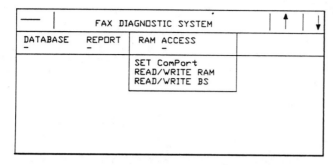

**Figure 2–22** RAM Access Menu Display

Figure 2–22 depicts a RAM access menu on the display of the PC of Figure 2–1.

To set up a communications port, the set comport command provides this function, as seen in Figure 2–23. The user does this only if the port connection to CCA is different from default—COM1.

The user should use the mouse to select the right serial port that will communicate with CCA.

1. Click "OK" to make some changes.
2. Click "CANCEL" if no changes or discarding those changes.

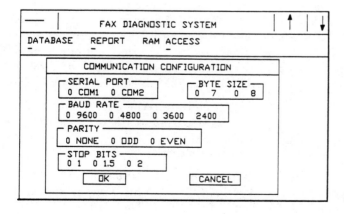

**Figure 2–23** Set Comport Command

Figure 2–24 depicts the display of RAM accessing.

1. If the user receives a message "error in opening com port" after selecting RAM accessing command, then reset communications port.
2. Input target fax telephone number to telephone number blank field.

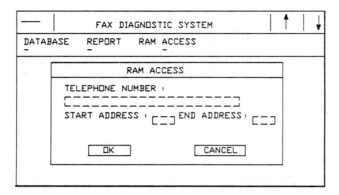

**Figure 2–24**   Display of RAM Access

3. Input the starting and ending address of RAM where the user is going to retrieve data from target facsimile. If the command menu selected is "read/-
   write BS" then input the starting and ending address of whole bit-switch-table
   basing on target machines' models. For example, if target machine is R50 series, then enter "0080" for starting address field, and enter "009F" for ending
   address field.

4. Click "OK" if input information is correct.

   Then the application program will automatically dial the telephone number entered and retrieve the remote fax information which is stored in the
   RAM just entered above. If the RAM address specified is larger than 256
   bytes, the application program will need to dial another call to get the rest of
   the data from remote target facsimile. The RAM accessing will not succeed,
   however, if the telephone number entered is incorrect, the target facsimile is
   busy, the target facsimile does not power on, or CCA does not power on.

   For each of these causes, the application program will pop up a related
   message on the screen. Here are some actions that should be followed.

   a. Reexamine the information entered on the screen.
   b. Check the target facsimile's current status—power is off or machine is
      still busy.
   c. Check CCA's connection and power switch.

5. Click "CANCEL" if it is decided not to continue the program.

   After data has been retrieved successfully from the target facsimile, the
   user needs to input data type for each address group. The window will display
   as seen in Figure 2–25. For example, if retrieving the remote RAM from 70b0
   to 70fa out of R50 series machines, the corresponding information will be TTI
   counter, TTI, CSI counter, CSI, RTI counter, and RTI.

   As defined, all three counters are HEX types, and all three identifica-
   tions are ASCII (uppercase) types. Therefore, the input sequence will be as
   above table, which means the following:

| | |
|---|---|
| Address 70b0 stores a HEX data | (TTI counter) |
| Address from 70b1 to 70d0 stores ASCII (uppercase) data | (TTI) |
| Address 70d1 stores a HEX data | (CSI counter) |
| Address from 70d2 to 70e5 stores ASCII (uppercase) data | (CSI) |
| Address 70e6 stores a HEX data | (RTI counter) |
| Address from 70e7 to 70fa stores ASCII (uppercase) data | (RTI) |

Click ''OK'' if input information is correct, and click ''CANCEL'' if it is decided not to continue the application program.

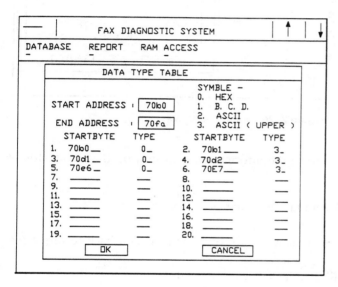

**Figure 2–25** Data-Type Table Display

## RAM DATA DISPLAY

After clicking ''OK'' on the data type table window, the user can check the target facsimile information on the remote RAM display window as seen in Figure 2–26. In this case,

| | |
|---|---|
| TTI counter | is 20 (HEX) |
| TTI | is RICOH SAN JOSE ATD DEPARTMENT |
| CSI counter | is 14 (HEX) |
| CSI | is 94520637 |
| RTI counter | is 14 (HEX) |
| RTI | is RICOH SAN JOSE BULD2 |

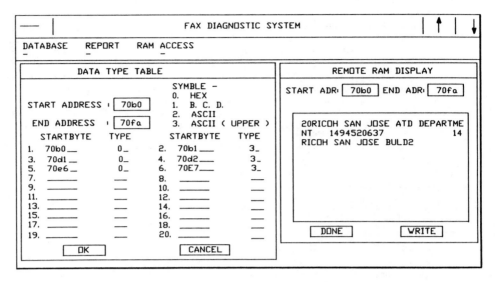

**Figure 2-26**   RAM Data Display

   If the user needs to rewrite the information displayed on the screen, follow these steps.

1. Use mouse and click on that particular position.
2. Type in new data.
3. Click "WRITE" if the user wants to write the new data back to target facsimile.
4. Click "DONE" if all data have been examined.

Because the maximum digits that can be entered for TTI is 20 (HEX), which is 32 (decimal), the user should not overtype new data to the next field, which will be a counter of CSI; also, the same as CSI, RTI, and some other similar cases applies.
   If the size of retrieved data is larger than the size of the display window, the window will offer a vertical scroll bar on the right margin of the window. Then the user can use the scroll bar to review all of the data.
   If the user needs to modify some data and rewrite back to target facsimile, then the application program will only rewrite those data that show on the current window.
   After data have been retrieved successfully from the target facsimile, the user can check the target facsimile bit switch information on the bit switch display window in Figure 2-27. If the user needs to rewrite the information displayed on the screen, follow these steps.

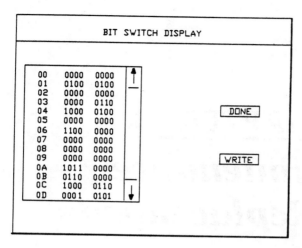

**Figure 2-27**  Bit Switch Display

1. Use mouse and click on that particular position.
2. Type in new data.
3. Click "WRITE" if the user wants to write the new data back to target facsimile.
4. Click "DONE" if all the data have been examined.

# CHAPTER 3

# *Maintenance and Replacements*

## GENERAL MAINTENANCE

Several general maintenance items, aside from diagnostics, need to be observed to keep a facsimile machine in good working order. The following points need to be observed:

1. *Perform periodic maintenance*—Inspect the equipment periodically and, if necessary, clean the contaminated parts.
2. *Check for breakdowns*—Look for signs of trouble and consider how the problems arose. If the equipment can still be used, perform a copying, self-testing, or communications testing.
3. *Check equipment*—Perform a copying, self-testing, or communications testing to determine if the problem originates from the transmitter, receiver, or telephone line.
4. *Determine causes*—Determine the causes of equipment troubleshooting on the basis of the DIP switch (S1, S4) settings.
5. *Make equipment repairs*—Repair or replace the defective parts and take appropriate measures at this stage to ensure that the problem does not recur.
6. *Confirm normal operation of the equipment*—After completing the repairs, conduct copying, self-testing, or communications testing to confirm that the equipment operates normally.

**7.** *Keep records*—Make a record of the measures taken to rectify the problem for future reference.

Outline drawings of the interiors of three models of Panasonic machines are shown in Figures 3–1 to 3–3. The first machine (the model KX-F80) is the simplest of the group. It has been called a "bare-bones fax," but at the same time it is described as a fabulous bargain because of what it does. The machine in Figure 3–2 (the model KX-F120) is more fully featured, whereas the machine in Figure 3–3 (the KX-F220)

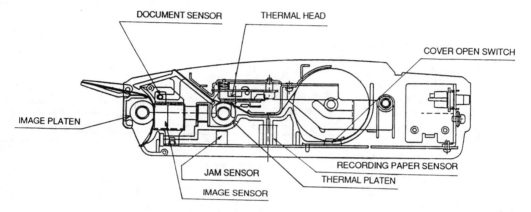

**Figure 3–1**  Interior of Panasonic's KX-F80 Fax Machine

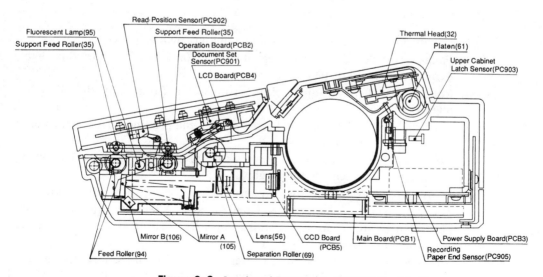

**Figure 3–2**  Interior of Panasonic's KX-F120 Fax Machine

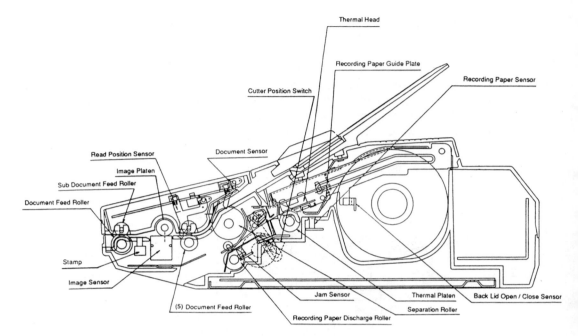

**Figure 3-3**  Interior of Panasonic's KX-F220 Fax Machine

is a full-featured office machine. The general maintenance steps to be taken for these machines is as follows:

1. *Document path*—Remove any foreign matter, such as paper.
2. *Platen*—If the platen is dirty, clean it with a damp cloth, then dry thoroughly. Remove any piece of paper.
3. *Rollers*—If rollers are dirty, clean them with a damp cloth then dry thoroughly.
4. *Thermal head*—If the thermal head is dirty, clean printing surface with a damp cloth and dry thoroughly.
5. *Image sensor*\*—If the image sensor is dirty, clean the glass surface with a damp cloth and then dry thoroughly.
6. *Mirrors and lens*†—If mirror and lens are dirty, clean with a dry cloth.
7. *Operation of other sensors*—Document Set Sensor, Read Position Sensor, Upper Cabinet Latch Censor, Recording Paper End Sensor, Back Lid/Close Sensor. Confirm operation of sensors.
8. *Switches*—Cover Open Switch, Cutter Position Switch‡. Check operation of switches. Cutter and cutter position switch have a life of about 300,000 times.

9. *Stamp‡*—The ink life is about 50,000 times. The stamp (plunger) life is about 200,000 times. Replace accordingly.

10. *Abnormal wear and tear or looseness of parts*—Exchange the part. Check tightness of screws on each part.

The preceding steps can be applied to any desktop or portable fax machine. Larger machines employing laser printers would require the checking and care of several additional parts. The complexity of such machines can be appreciated by reading the description of one in chapter 7. In general all smaller machines incorporate the same basic parts as those referred to earlier. Of course, their placement within the machine will vary because of the decisions of different engineers and mechanical designers.

Once the diagnostic steps, outlined in the service manual (supplied by the manufacturer), have been taken, it may be necessary to replace certain parts, such as PC boards, scanners, or thermal heads. The policy of manufacturers in general is that field service should be kept at the PC board level and that individual electronic components, such as ICs, resistors, and capacitors, be replaced only at service centers. If any replacement of electronic components is undertaken in the field it should not go beyond those of the switched power supply and telephone answering machine, which is often part of the fax machine package. The disassembly and exchange procedures for a typical machine (the Panasonic KX-F120) are described subsequently.

## REMOVAL OF MECHANISM PARTS

### Upper Section

Figure 3–4 shows how to remove the upper section parts.

1. Push the latch knob (number 122 in Figure 3–4) to open the cover.
2. Remove the four screws (A).
3. Remove the thirteen screws (B).
4. Remove the upper document guide (45).

### Support Feed Roller and Support Roller

Figure 3–5 shows how to remove the support feed roller (35) and support roller (25).

---

*Applies to KX-F80 and KX-F220; †KX-F120 only; ‡KX-F220 only.

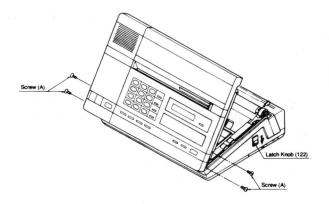

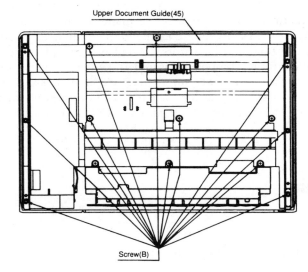

**Figure 3–4**  Removal of Upper-Section Parts

## Cleaning

1. If the feed (35) and support (25) rollers are dirty, clean them with a damp cloth and then dry them thoroughly.
2. If the white level plate (44) is dirty, clean it with a dry cloth.

## Replace

1. Remove the six screws (A).
2. Remove the bracket.

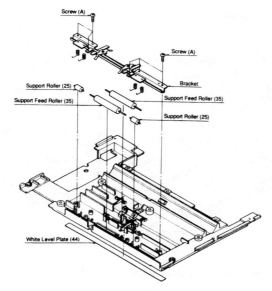

**Figure 3-5** Removal of Support Feed and Support Rollers

3. Remove the rollers (25, 35).
4. To reassemble, reverse this procedure.

## Operation and LCD Boards

1. Remove the two screws (A) from the operation board (PCB2).
2. Remove the operation board (PCB2).
3. Remove the four screws (B) from the LCD board (PCB4).
4. Remove the LCD board (PCB4).
5. To reassemble, reverse this procedure.

## Thermal Head

Figure 3-6 shows how to remove the thermal head.

1. Remove the two screws (A).
2. Pull out the connector (33).
3. Remove the four screws (B).
4. Remove the head guides R (29) and L (30), and exchange the thermal head (32).

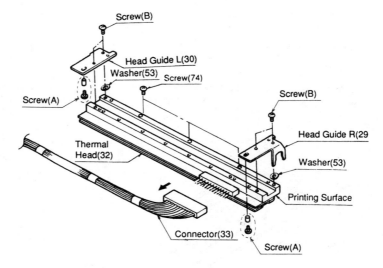

**Figure 3-6**  Removal of Thermal Head

5. Remove the three screws (74) from the old thermal head (32), and attach the three screws (74) to the new thermal head (32).
6. To reassemble, reverse this procedure.

### Cleaning

If the thermal head (32) is dirty, clean the printing surface with a damp cloth and then dry thoroughly.

## Lower and Rear Cabinets

Figure 3-7a shows how to remove the lower (121) and rear (120) cabinets.

1. Remove the three screws (A).
2. Remove the seven screws (B).
3. Pull out the latch knob (122). (See Figure 3-7b.)
4. Remove the lower cabinet (121).
5. Remove the rear cabinet (120).
6. To reassemble, reverse this procedure.

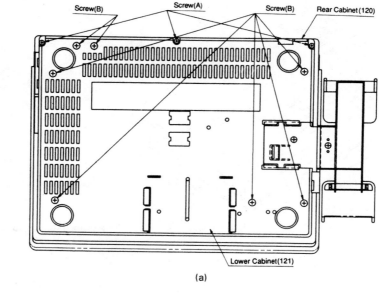

(a)

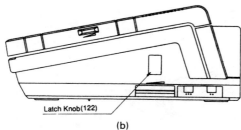

(b)

**Figure 3-7** (a) Removal of Lower and Rear Cabinets; (b) Part of Removal Procedure of (a)

## Main Board

Figure 3-8 shows how to remove the main board.

1. Remove the two screws (A).
2. Remove the main board (PCB1).
3. To remove the main board (PCB1) completely, pull out the nine connectors.
4. To reassemble, reverse this procedure.

*Note:* After removing the main board (PCB1), be careful not to handle the unit (Figure 3-9), because the mirrors will be damaged.

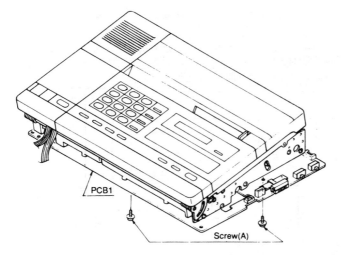

**Figure 3-8**  Removal of Main Board

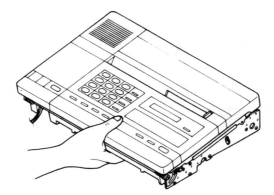

**Figure 3-9**  Precaution about Handling Unit after Removal of Main Board

## Switching Power Supply Board, Inverter Board, and Mirrors

Figure 3-10 shows how to remove the switching power supply board (PCB3), inverter board (100), and mirrors (105, 106).

Switching power supply board

1. Remove the four screws (A).
2. Remove the switching power supply board (PCB3).

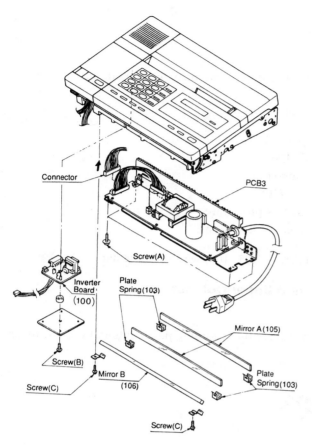

**Figure 3-10**  Removal of Switching Power Supply Board, Inverter Board, and Mirrors

**3.** To remove switching power supply (PCB3) board completely, pull out the two connectors.

**4.** To reassemble, reverse this procedure.

## Inverter board

**1.** Remove the screw (B).

**2.** Remove the inverter board (100).

**3.** To remove the inverter board (100) completely, pull out the two connectors.

**4.** To reassemble, reverse this procedure.

Mirror

*Cleaning*

If the mirrors A (105) and B (106) are dirty, clean with a dry cloth.

*Replace*

1. Remove the two screws (C).
2. Replace the mirror B (106).
3. Remove the plate spring (103).
4. Exchange the mirror A (105).
5. To reassemble, reverse this procedure.
6. CCD adjustment (see later discussion).

*Note:* Do not touch the mirrors (105, 106) with the bare hand.

## Recording Paper End and Upper-Cabinet Latch Sensor Boards

Figure 3–11 shows how to remove the recording paper end and upper-cabinet latch sensor boards.

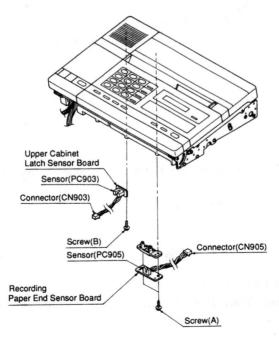

Upper Cabinet
Latch Sensor Board

Sensor(PC903)

Connector(CN903)

Screw(B)

Sensor(PC905)

Connector(CN905)

Recording
Paper End Sensor Board

Screw(A)

**Figure 3–11**  Removal of Recording Paper End and Upper-Cabinet Latch Sensor Boards

## Recording paper end sensor board

1. Remove the two screws (A).
2. Remove the sensor board.
3. To remove the sensor board completely, pull out the connector (CN905).
4. Exchange the sensor (PC905).
5. To reassemble, reverse this procedure.

## Upper-cabinet latch sensor board

1. Remove the screw (B).
2. Remove the sensor board.
3. To remove the sensor board completely, pull out the connector (CN903).
4. Exchange the sensor (PC903).
5. To reassemble, reverse this procedure.

# REPLACEMENT OF MECHANISM PARTS

## Platen Gear and Platen

Figure 3–12 shows how to remove the platen gear, and Figure 3–13 illustrates how to remove the platen.

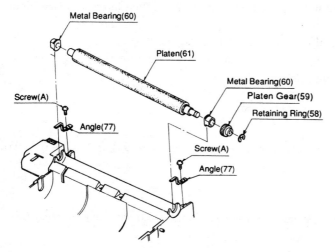

**Figure 3–12**  Removal of Platen Gear

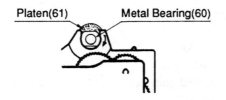

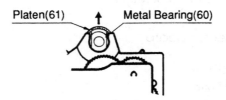

**Figure 3-13**  Removal of Platen

### Cleaning

If the platen (61) is dirty, clean it with a damp cloth and then dry thoroughly.

### Replace

1. Remove the upper cover (see Figure 3-4).
2. Remove the rear cabinet (see Figure 3-7).
3. Remove the retaining ring (58).
4. Remove the platen gear (59), and exchange it.
5. Remove the two screws (A).
6. Rotate the two metal bearings (60) 90° and remove the platen (61) (see Figure 3-13).
7. Remove the two metal bearings (60) from the platen (61).
8. Exchange the platen (61).
9. To reassemble, reverse this procedure.

## Rollers and Gears

Figures 3-14 and 3-15 show how to remove the rollers (69, 94) and gears (62, 93).

### Cleaning

1. If the rollers are dirty, clean them with a damp cloth then dry thoroughly.
2. If the glass is dirty, clean it with a dry cloth.

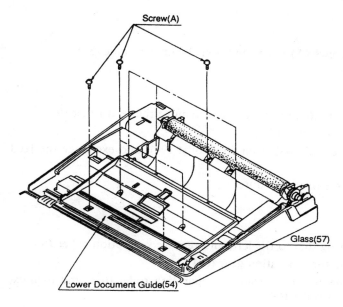

**Figure 3–14** First Steps in Removal of Rollers and Gears

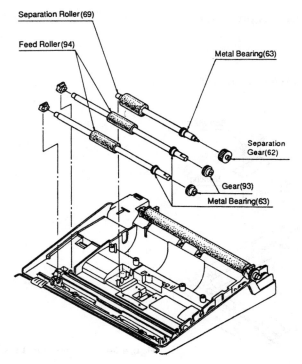

**Figure 3–15** Further Steps in Removal of Feed Roller-Gear and Separation Roller-Gear

*Replace*

**1.** Remove the eight screws (A) from the lower document guide (54).

## Feed roller-gear

**1.** Slide the metal bearing (63) to the left, and remove the feed roller (94).
**2.** Remove or exchange the gear (93).
**3.** Remove the metal bearing (63) from feed roller (94), and exchange the feed roller (94).
**4.** To reassemble, reverse this procedure.

## Separation roller-gear

**1.** Slide the metal bearing (63) to the left, and remove separation roller (69).
**2.** Remove or exchange the separation gear (62).
**3.** Remove the metal bearing (63) from the separation roller (69), and then exchange the separation roller (69).
**4.** Attach the metal bearing (63) and separation gear (62) to the new separation roller (69).
**5.** To reassemble, reverse this procedure.

## Lens

Figure 3–16 shows how to remove the lens.

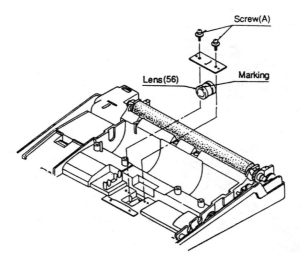

**Figure 3–16**   Removal of Lens

*Replace*

1. Remove the two screws (A).
2. Exchange the lens (56).
3. Make CCD adjustment (see later discussion).

*Note:* When replacing the lens (56), pay attention to the markings on the lens, which may be white, yellow, or orange. The number of the CCD spacers to use differs depending on the markings as follows: Two CCD spacers are provided with the lens (56). Refer to Figure 3–20 for the location of the CCD spacers.

| Marking on lens | Number of CCD spacers |
|---|---|
| Orange | 0 (not used) |
| White | 1 |
| Yellow | 2 |

1. Install the lens (56) so that the marking (white, yellow, or orange) is on the upper side.
2. Do not touch the glass face of the lens (56) with the bare hand.

*Cleaning*

If the lens (56) is dirty, clean it with a dry cloth.

## Gear, Belt, Fluorescent Lamp, Motors, and CCD Board

Gear and belt

Figure 3–17 shows how to remove the gear and belt.

1. Remove the lower cabinet (121) (see Figure 3–7a).
2. Remove the seven screws (A) from the gear chassis (88).
3. Remove the gear chassis (88).
4. Remove the gear (82 to 85) or timing belt (87), and exchange it.

*Note:* The order of installation of the gear is shown by numbers 1, 2 and 3.

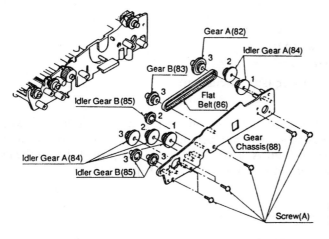

**Figure 3-17** Removal of Gear and Belt

## Fluorescent lamp

Figure 3-18 shows how to remove the fluorescent lamp.

1. Remove the two screws (B) from the main board (PCB1).
2. Pull out the nine connectors, and remove the main board (PCB1).
3. Pull out the two connectors from the inverter board (100).
4. Remove the two screws (C) from the fluorescent lamp (95), and exchange the fluorescent lamp (95).
5. Make CCD adjustment (see later discussion).

## Motor

Figure 3-19 shows how to remove the motor.

1. Remove the two screws (D) from motor (87).
2. Remove the motor (87), and replace it.

## CCD board

Figure 3-20 shows how to remove the CCD board.

1. Remove the two nuts (E).
2. Remove the CCD board (PCB5) with CCD board holder (109).
3. Remove the two screws (F) from the CCD board (PCB5).

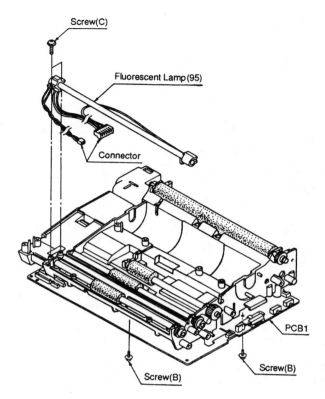

Screw(C)

Fluorescent Lamp(95)

Connector

PCB1

Screw(B)

Screw(B)

**Figure 3–18** Removal of Fluorescent Lamp

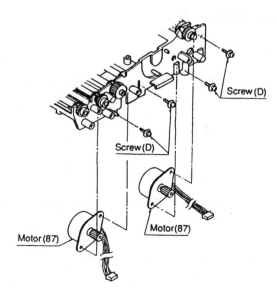

Screw (D)

Screw (D)

Motor(87)

Motor(87)

**Figure 3–19** Removal of Motors

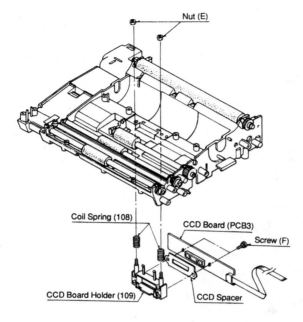

**Figure 3-20**　Removal of CCD Board

4. Remove the CCD board (PCB5).
5. To reassemble, reverse this procedure.
6. Make CCD adjustment (see later discussion).

## ADJUSTMENTS AFTER PARTS REPLACEMENTS

### Facsimile Transmission Level

Perform the following adjustment after replacing fax transmission system (modem board, T1, and VR4).

Test equipment—loop simulator and vacuum tube voltmeter (VTVM)

Figure 3-21 shows the circuitry of a loop simulator.

1. Connect the unit to loop simulator. (Set the selector switch to "TX.")
2. Service switch (S4) ON (Figure 3-22).
3. Press the FUNCTION button.
4. Press the 5 and 3 buttons (on front panel of machine).
5. Display "MODEM = OFF" on LCD.

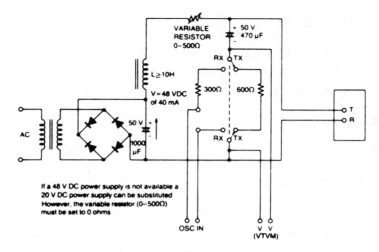

**Figure 3-21**  Circuit Diagram of Loop Simulator

**Figure 3-22**  Location of Service Switch on Panasonic KX-F120

6. Press the START/COPY button.
7. Display "MODEM = 462Hz" on LCD.
8. Adjust VR4 for a reading of $-10.5 \pm 0.5$ dB on the VTVM.
9. Press the STOP/CLEAR button.
10. Service switch (S4) OFF.

## Clock

Perform the following adjustment after replacing IC4, X1, and CV1.

1. Connect the frequency counter.
   a. + Side—test point T.
   b. − Side—test point U.
2. Connect the AC cord of the unit to AC outlet.
3. Set the power switch of the unit to ON.
4. Adjust CV1 for a reading of msec on the frequency counter.

| Room temperature for adjusting (°C) | Period value (msec) | Room temperature for adjusting (°C) | Period value (ms) |
|---|---|---|---|
| 14–14.9 | 15.624943 ($\pm 0.00001$) | 20–20.9 | 15.624880 ($\pm 0.00001$) |
| 15–15.9 | 15.624933 ($\pm 0.00001$) | 21–21.9 | 15.624876 ($\pm 0.00001$) |
| 16–16.9 | 15.624922 ($\pm 0.00001$) | 22–27.9 | 15.624870 ($\pm 0.00001$) |
| 17–17.9 | 15.624910 ($\pm 0.00001$) | 28–28.9 | 15.624876 ($\pm 0.00001$) |
| 18–18.9 | 15.624899 ($\pm 0.00001$) | 29–29.9 | 15.624880 ($\pm 0.00001$) |
| 19–19.9 | 15.624888 ($\pm 0.00001$) | | |

## CCD

Figure 3–23 shows the preparation for CCD adjustment. Perform this adjustment after replacing lens (56), mirrors (105, 106), fluorescent lamp (95), and CCD board (PCB5).

Test equipment: Oscilloscope

*Preparation*

1. Make oscilloscope connection as shown in Figure 3–23.
2. Turn service switch ON.
3. Fit the unit at the table jig (see Figure 3–23).
4. Turn power switch ON.
5. Press the FUNCTION button.

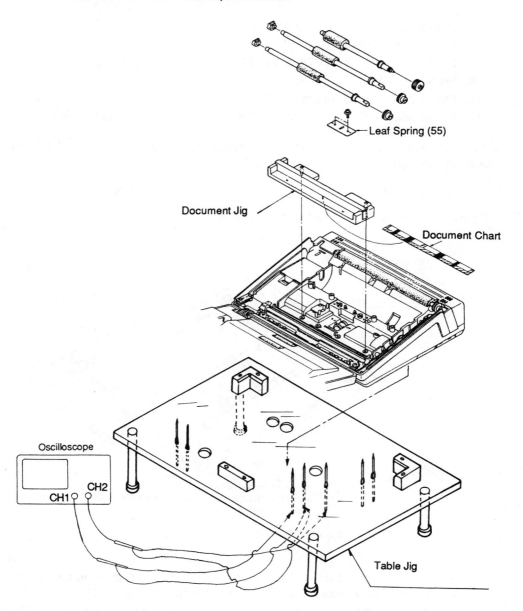

**Figure 3–23** Preparation for CCD Adjustment

6. LCD will show; "SERVICE MODE".
7. Press the 5 button twice.
8. LCD will show; "READOUT TEST".
9. Press the START/COPY button.
10. Fluorescent lamp (95) lights.
11. Fit the document jig at the mechanism chassis. (Refer to Figure 3–23)

*Note:* Do not touch the glass face of the document jig, glass face of the lens (56) and mirrors (105, 106) with the bare hand.

### Adjustment

Figure 3–24 shows the CCD adjustment points.

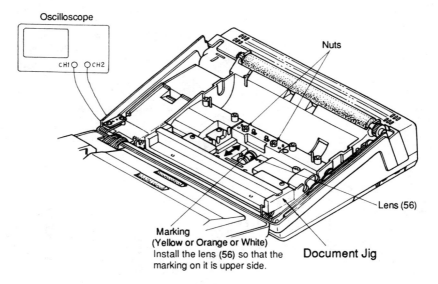

**Figure 3–24**  CCD Adjustment Points

1. Move the lens (56) back and forth, and adjust the nut tightening amount so that one of video signals (A), (B), or (C) is output (Figure 3–25).
2. Move the lens (56) back and forth to a position such that the amplitude of the moire of the video signal is maximum. In this case, with moire 1 and 4 about the same, adjust so that moire 2 and 3 become about the same, adjust so that moire 2 and 3 become larger than moire 1 and 4, and adjust so that the amplitude overall becomes a maximum. The left-right symmetry shall have preference, however.

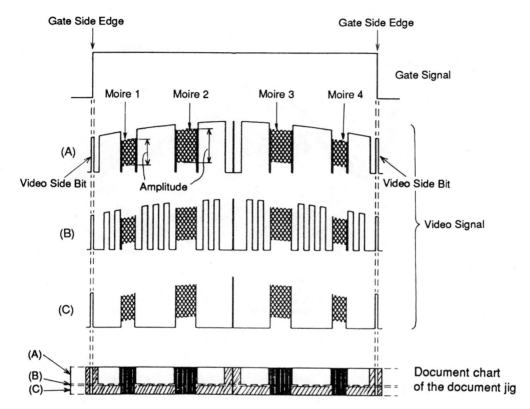

**Figure 3–25**  Adjustment of Moire of Image Signal

3. Tighten the two screws alternately a little bit at a time, so that the amplitude of the moire of the video signal is not reduced, and fix the lens (56) with the leaf spring (55) (Figures 3–26 and 3–27).

4. Fix the two screws with the screw lock.

5. Adjust the nut tightening amount to put out the video signal (B), and adjust so that the amplitude (D) becomes a maximum. In case of the video signal (A) or (C), the reading line has deviated to the document chart (A) or (C), and the nut tightening amount must be adjusted so that the video signal (B) is put out.

6. Confirm that there is no change of the video signal (B), and then fix the two nuts with the screw lock.

7. Exchange the document jig from PQZZ4F120M to PQ224F120M and fit at the mechanism chassis (Figure 3–28).

8. Adjust VR301 on the CCD board so that the waveform becomes 2.5 ± 0.2 V (white-level adjustment) (Figure 3–29).

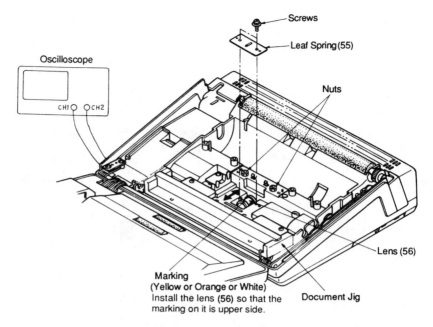

**Figure 3–26**  Fixing of Lens with Leaf Spring

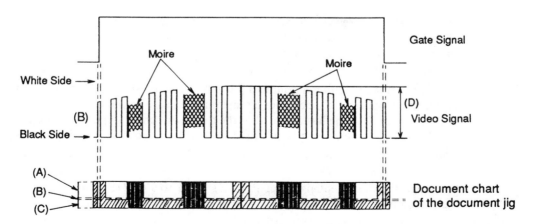

**Figure 3–27**  Confirmation of Moire Adjustment

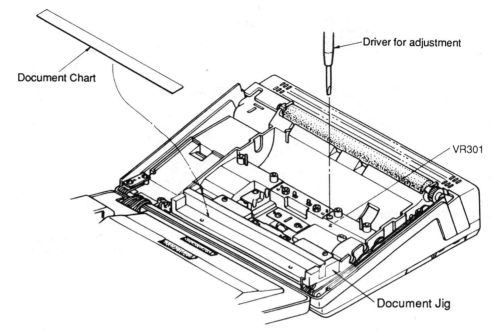

**Figure 3-28** Preparation for White-Level Adjustment

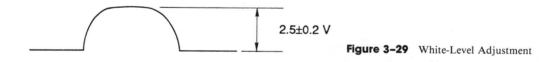

2.5±0.2 V

**Figure 3-29** White-Level Adjustment

9. Press the FUNCTION button.
10. Service switch (S4) OFF (Figure 3–30).

*Adjustment*

Figure 3–31 shows adjustment of document read start position.

1. Copy the document, and confirm the read start position of the document.
2. If it is out of position, adjust the read start position switch (S1).

*Note:* The adjustment indicated in 1 to 5 should be executed within 3 min after lighting of the fluorescent lamp (95). When adjustment is not possible within 3 min, the fluorescent lamp (95) must be switched off for 10 min, and then readjustment must be executed.

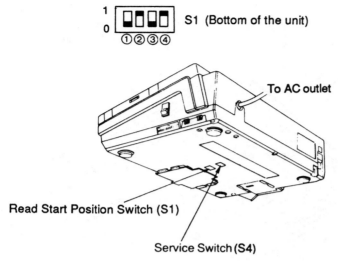

S1  (Bottom of the unit)

To AC outlet

Read Start Position Switch (S1)

Service Switch (S4)

**Figure 3–30**  Preparation for Document Read Start Position Adjustment

| NO. | S1 POSITION | | | |
|-----|----|----|----|----|
| | ① | ② | ③ | ④ |
| 0 | 1 | 1 | 1 | 1 |
| 1 | 0 | 1 | 1 | 1 |
| 2 | 1 | 0 | 1 | 1 |
| 3 | 0 | 0 | 1 | 1 |
| 4 | 1 | 1 | 0 | 1 |
| 5 | 0 | 1 | 0 | 1 |
| 6 | 1 | 0 | 0 | 1 |
| 7 | 0 | 0 | 0 | 1 |
| 8 | 1 | 1 | 1 | 0 |
| 9 | 0 | 1 | 1 | 0 |

← Standard (at NO. 3)

Move the read position of the document to the right.

Move the read position of the document to the left.

* The starting position of the reading shifts 1mm as the numbers changes.

**Figure 3–31**  Adjustment of Document Read Start Position

## Black Level

Figure 3–32 shows the preparation for the black-level adjustment. Perform this adjustment after replacing IC15, IC19, and IC33.

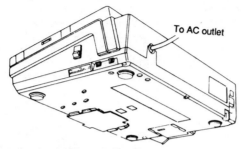

To AC outlet

Fit the unit at the table jig

**Figure 3–32** Preparation for Black-Level Adjustment

Test equipment: Oscilloscope

*Preparation*

1. Make oscilloscope connection as shown in Figure 3–23.
2. Turn power switch ON.

*Adjustment*

1. Confirm the range of oscilloscope (Figure 3–33).

*Image signal (IC32 pin 6)
   DC 500mV/DIV
       20mS/DIV — CH1
   Gate signal (IC8 pin 100)
   DC 5V/DIV . . . CH2

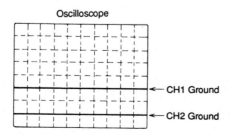

Oscilloscope

← CH1 Ground

← CH2 Ground

**Figure 3–33** Check of Range and Ground Level of Oscilloscope

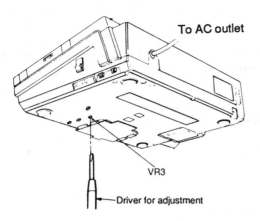

**To AC outlet**

VR3

Driver for adjustment

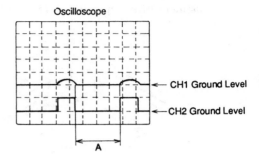

Oscilloscope

CH1 Ground Level

CH2 Ground Level

A

**Figure 3-34** Adjustment of Waveform of Oscilloscope (Equal to Ground Level of CH1 in Figure 3-33)

**Figure 3-35** Confirmation That Waveform (A) of Oscilloscope Does Not Deviate from Ground of CH1 When Document Is Copied

2. Confirm the ground level of oscilloscope.

3. Adjust VR3 so that the waveform (part A) of CH1 of the oscilloscope becomes equal to ground level of CH1 (Figure 3-34).

4. Confirm that when a document is copied, the waveform (Figure 3-35; A) of CH1 of the oscilloscope does not deviate from ground of CH1.

# CHAPTER 4

# *Circuit Operations*

This chapter covers the circuit operations of a typical desktop facsimile machine, the Panasonic KX-F120. The overall block diagram of this unit is shown in Figure 4–1. It may be referred to along with other diagrams throughout the chapter in connection with the various designations given to components and boards.

## CONTROL SECTION FOR MAIN FUNCTIONS

### Function

As shown in the detailed block diagram (Figure 4–2), this control section consists mainly of the following: CPU (IC1), ROM (IC2), RAM (IC3), RAM (IC9), real-time clock (IC4), gate array (IC5) that operates mainly as an address decoder, gate array (IC8) that controls fax section as a whole, gate array (IC29) that controls the Automatic Telephone Answering System (ATAS), Integrated Telephone System (ITS), and NCU section; parallel I/O (IC501) for communication modem board control panel; and LCD controller-driver (IC801). It controls everything pertaining to the unit. The main clock (7.962624 MHz) is input by crystal (X2) to gate array (IC8), where it is divided and becomes the system clock (3.981312 MHz) for CPU (IC1) and clock (10.368 kHz) for modem-gate array (IC5).

In the block diagram, MD0–MD7 denotes the data bus (D0–D7) after passing through bus buffer (IC6). Similarly, LD0–LD7 denotes data bus (D0–D7) after passing through bus buffers (IC6, IC7). A0C–A3C, WRC, RDC, and RDC denote ad-

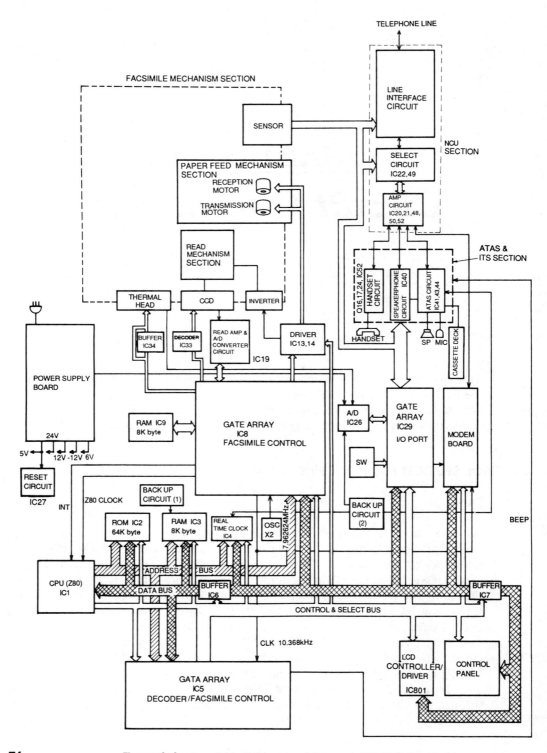

**Figure 4-1** Overall Block Diagram of Panasonic KX-F120 Fax Machine

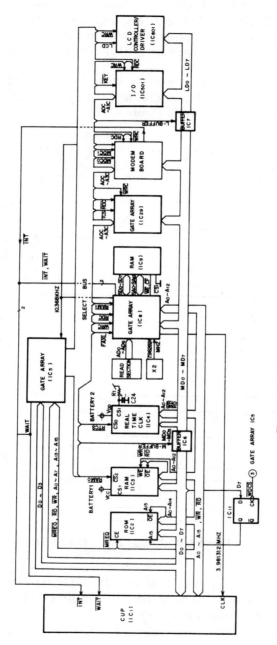

**Figure 4-2** Block Diagram of Control Section

dress bus (A0–A3); WR and RD denote address bus after passing through buffer of gate array (IC5) interior. SD0–SD7 and SA0–SA12 denote data bus and address bus after passing through memory controller in gate array (IC8). ADO–AD6 are buses for image data input to gate array (IC8) from the readout component.

1. *CPU (IC1)*—This is the core of the control section, and it controls all other control sections. The chip is Z80, and the clock operates at 3.981312 MHz. The timing chart is shown in Figure 4–3.

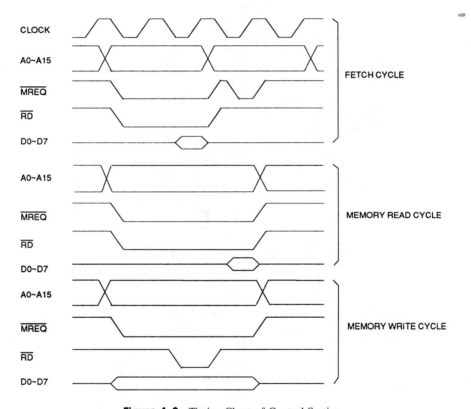

**Figure 4–3**  Timing Chart of Control Section

2. *ROM (IC2)*—This is a 64-kilobyte EP-ROM that stores the program. This component switches to bank via flip flop (IC11). The memory map of the entire system is shown in Figure 4–4.

3. *RAM (IC3)*—This is an 8-kilobyte RAM; 4 kilobytes are used as work area, and the other 4 kilobytes back up such items as auto dial number, sender

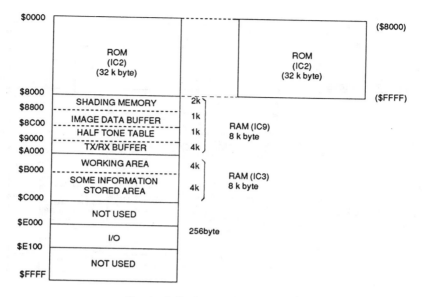

**Figure 4-4** Control Circuit ROM

identification for fax, and details of user setting mode, and so on by means of a lithium battery (Batt 1).

4. *Real-time clock (IC4)*—This is a timer IC for time and date clock. In initial time setting, the preset time is written in from CPU (IC1) via data bus, and, thereafter, the CPU (IC1) goes to read the time once every 1 s. Backup is by the manganese battery (Batt 2).

5. *Gate array (IC5)*—The gate array (IC5) is an original large-scale integration (LSI) that unifies several complex circuits into one integrated circuit (IC) chip. Gate array (IC5) consists of six circuits: address decoder, buffer, LCD interface, counter, stepping motor enable-timing generator, and alarm-beep tone generator (Figure 4-5).

6. *Gate array (IC8)*—The gate array (IC8) is an original LSI that unifies several complex circuits into one IC chip. Gate array (IC5, shown in Figure 4-6), consists of five circuits, central processing unit (CPU) interface, counter-timing controller, memory controller, thermal head controller, and stepping motor controller. This IC controls almost all fax operation.

    a. *CPU interface*—This circuit functions for selecting each circuit and storing the status of each circuit.

    b. *Counter-timing controller*—This circuit generates CCD scanning timing, modem clock, CPU clock, interruption timing, thermal head control timing, and motor control timing.

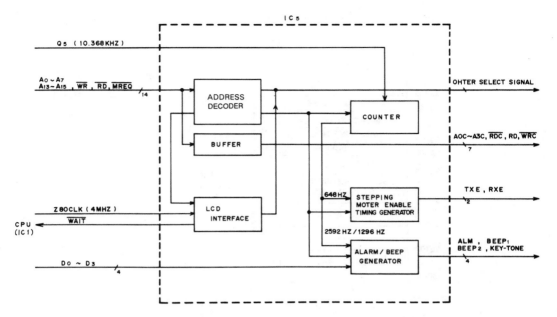

**Figure 4-5**   Block Diagram of Gate Array (IC5)

**c.** *Memory controller*—This circuit controls DMA (RAM [IC9] —> thermal head, A/D converter for CCD —> RAM [IC9])

**d.** *Thermal head controller*—This circuit generates all strobes for the thermal head based on the control timing generated by the counter-timing controller.

**e.** *Stepping motor controller*—This circuit generates a pulse for TX/RX motor based on the control timing generated in counter-timing controller.

**f.** *RAM (IC9)*—This is an 8-kilobyte RAM, and it is used as working area in fax communication. Its breakdown is shown on the memory map in Figure 4-4.

**g.** *Gate array (IC29)*—The gate array (IC29) is an original LSI that integrates several complex circuits into one IC chip. This IC consists of $9 \times 8$ bit input/output (I/O) port (same as three 8255) and controls ATAS/ITS/NCU section.

**h.** *Modem board*—This board facilitates modulation and demodulation for fax communication. Because it conforms to communication sequences stipulated in CCITT, it can be controlled from the CPU (IC1) by writing in instruction commands with chip select signals MDC0 and MDC1 through address buses A0C–A3C to the thirty-two individual registers in ICs of the modem board. Details are discussed later.

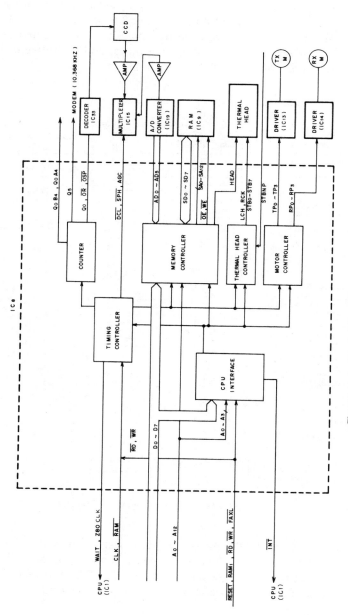

**Figure 4-6** Block Diagram of Gate Array (IC8)

i. *I/O port (IC501)*—IC501 is an I/O port controller containing three 8-b ports. Chip selection is by KEYCS; the three ports are selected via address buses A0C and A1C; write and read are set with WRC and RDC; and data write and read occur along data buses LD0–LD7.

Ports PB0–PB7 are output ports, and each type of LED is driven through Q502 to Q507 (Figure 4–7).

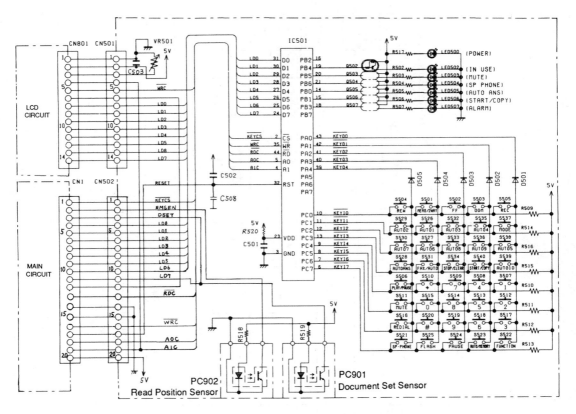

**Figure 4–7**  Circuit Diagram of I/O Port

Ports PA0–PA4 are output ports. From PA0 to PA4, becomes low toggle. PC0 to PC7 are input ports. If a key is depressed when PA0–PA4 are at low level, low level is input. PA0–PA4 and PC0–PC7 form a matrix and using this combination you can determine which key has been depressed.

j. *LCD controller-driver*—This IC is a chip with LCD controller and driver built in (Figure 4–8). The CPU (IC1) need only write ASCII code from the data bus (LC0–LD7).

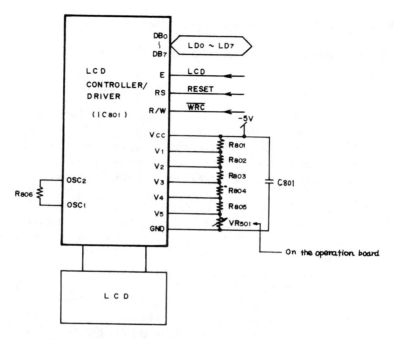

**Figure 4–8**  Circuit Diagram of LCD Controller-Driver (IC801)

V1 through V5 are power supplies for crystal display drive. VR501 is density control volume, and R806 is an externally applied resistance for internal oscillation circuit. This IC is similar with the 6800 type CPU.

Consequently, for control by Z80, in this set the timing (mainly positive clock) is generated by the LCD interface circuitry of the gate array (IC5). The timing chart is shown in Figure 4-9.

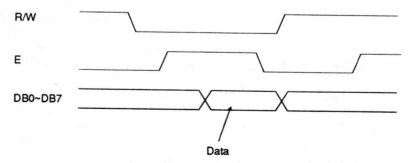

**Figure 4–9**  Timing Chart of LCD Controller-Driver

## CONTROL CIRCUIT FOR OTHER FUNCTIONS

### Reset Circuit and Watchdog Timer Circuit

Function

The reset circuit enables normal system operation to begin and end when the power supply is cycled ON-OFF. A manual reset switch has also been provided on the bottom side. The watchdog timer circuit engages reset to protect the entire system, beginning with memory, in the event that the system malfunctions because of factors such as static electricity, electric noise, or lightning surges.

1. *Reset circuit*—In the reset circuit (Figure 4–10), pin 1 of IC27 for reset becomes high level when the input (+5-V power supply) of pin 2 is 40 V or more. The timing chart of each section from A to E when the power is ON-OFF is as shown in Figure 4–11.

2. *Watchdog timer circuit*—When a software interrupt occurs, gate array IC5 (pin 3, WDCS) becomes low level once every 1.543 ms. A low at the base of Q45 will cause C261 to discharge. IC10 is a timer IC. At the time constant (about 20 ms) determined by R280 and C261, IC10 (3) pin output goes from high level to low level when IC10 (6) pin becomes about 3.3 V or more. In other words, when the system malfunctions and WDCS remains at high level for more than 20 ms, IC10 (3) pin becomes low level, point B falls to low level, and reset is engaged in the system. When reset is engaged in the system, Q44 goes ON, and Q45 goes ON at the same time, C261 discharges, and watchdog timer operation starts once again. The timing chart is shown in Figure 4–12.

### Memory Backup Circuit

Function

This set has two types of batteries. One is a lithium battery that backs up RAM (IC3), which stores auto dial number, sender identification for fax, contents of use setting mode, and so forth. The other is a manganese battery that backs up LSI (IC44) for OGM, D-RAM (IC45, IC46), and real-time clock (IC4).

Circuit operation

1. *RAM (IC3) backup circuit*—When AC power is present, power is supplied through the route from +12 V to R56 to D8 to IC3 (number 28 in Figure 4–13). When AC power is absent, power is supplied from lithium battery to R55 to D9 to IC3 (28). If there is a power failure, reset IC27 pin 1 becomes

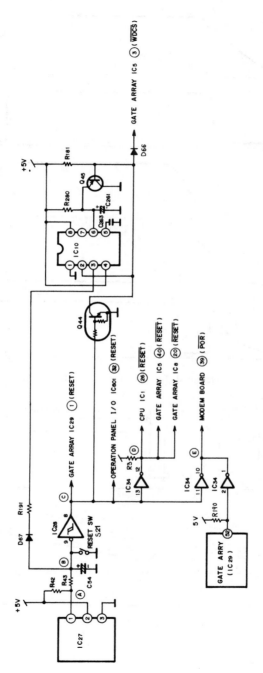

**Figure 4-10** Diagram of Reset-Watchdog Timer Circuit

85

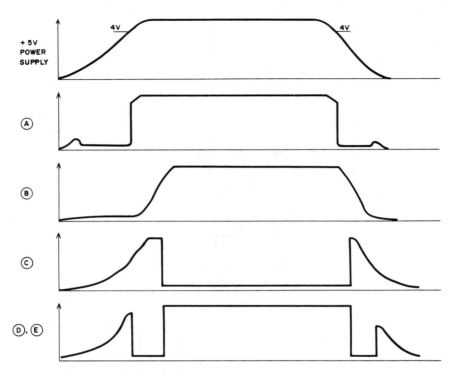

**Figure 4–11**   Timing Chart of Reset Circuit

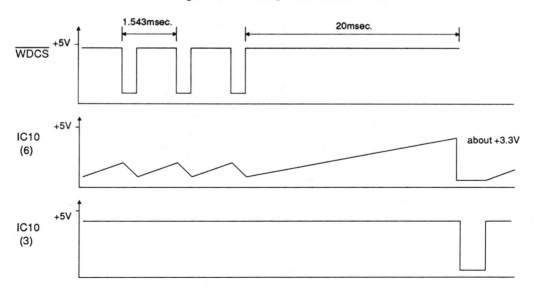

**Figure 4–12**   Timing Chart of Watchdog Timer

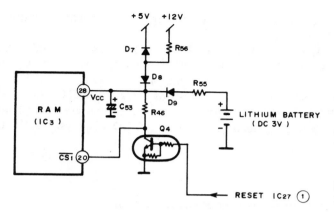

**Figure 4-13** Memory Backup Circuit Diagram

low level, Q4 goes OFF, CS1 of RAM becomes high, and RAM enters backup mode.

2. *LSI, D-RAM for OGM, and real-time clock backup circuit*—When AC power is present, power is supplied to the real-time clock (IC4) through the route +6 V to D60 to D30 to Vcc (number 18 in Figure 4–14); power is supplied to OGM LSI (IC44) and D-RAM (IC45, IC46) through D82 from +6 V. When AC

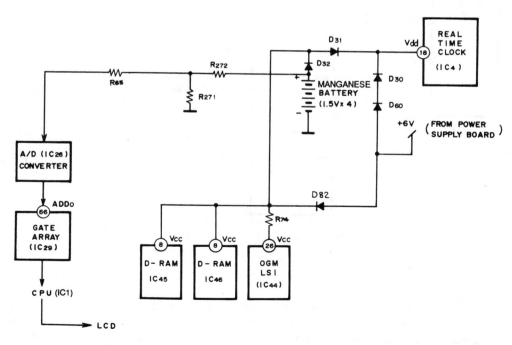

**Figure 4-14** Diagram of LSI, D-RAM for OGM, and Real-Time Clock Backup

power is absent, real-time clock receives power from manganese battery through D32 to D31 to Vcc (18).

OGM LSI (IC44) and D-RAM (IC45, IC46) receive power through D32.

OGM LSI (IC44) and D-RAM (IC45, IC46) cannot guarantee preservation of memory contents when Vcc is less than 4 V. To determine if it has become less than 4 V, the voltage between resistor R272 and R271 is detected by A/D converter IC26. CPU (IC1) learns that manganese battery voltage has become 4V or less through gate array IC29 and LCD displays "CHECK OGM/BATTERY."

## Analog-Digital Converter

Figure 4–15 shows the analog-digital converter circuit diagram.

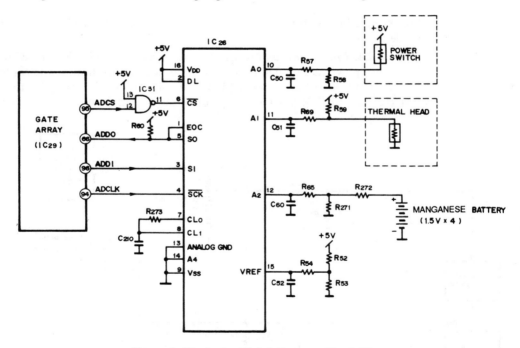

**Figure 4–15**   Analog-Digital Converter Circuit Diagram

## Function

Resistance value of a thermistor for power supply overheat detection, resistance value of thermistor for thermal head temperature detection, and voltage of the manganese battery for OGM backup are converted to digital data; this information is sent to CPU (IC1).

In other words,

1. *At the time of power supply overheating*—The alarm sound rings, and LCD displays "WAIT OVERHEATED" to give warning.

2. *At the time of thermal head temperature detection and overheating*—Impression pulse width is set according to thermal head temperature so that there is no variation in print density with temperature changes. At time of overheating, the same display is given as in the case of power supply overheating.

3. *At the time of voltage detection of battery for OGM backup*—When OGM memory backup voltage drops below 4V, the LCD displays "CHECK OGM/BATTERY."

Voltages input to analog input terminals A0 to A2 (A3 not yet used) and 1/256th increment voltage of Vres voltage (2.5 V) are compared constantly, converted to digital data and to serial data, and input to gate array IC29 (66) from S0. CPU (IC1) reads these values and performs corresponding processing. R273 and C210 are externally applied components for internal clock (internal oscillation is 200 kHz). The timing chart is shown in Figure 4–16.

## DATA FLOW DURING FACSIMILE OPERATION

Figure 4–17 shows the components involved in the transmission and reception of the facsimile signals.

Copy

### Standard, fine mode

1. One line increment (1728 dots) of white-level data is read from the CCD and converted to 64 gradations (6 b) of density data, for each dot, by the A/D converter (IC19).

2. Shading buffer above RAM (IC9) along routes 1 to 5 to 6 during DMA continuous transmission.

3. Through routes 6 to 8 to 10 to 11 to 12, the 65% level of the white-level data stored at 2 is calculated at the CPU (IC1), and this value determines the threshold level for distinguishing black and white.

4. Actual document is read at CCD input is via A/D converter to the comparator along route 2.

    The threshold value calculated in step 3 is input to the comparator along routes 12 to 11 to 10 to 9 to 3; these two values are compared, and if the actual document data is higher than the threshold level, white (0) is input; if it is lower, black (1) is output (Figure 4–18).

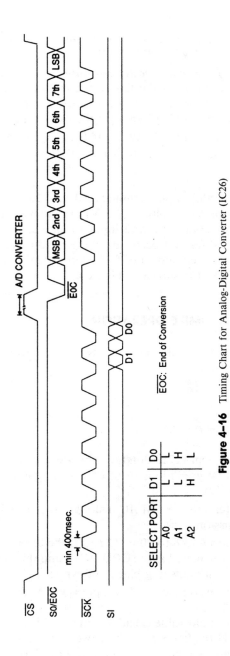

**Figure 4–16** Timing Chart for Analog-Digital Converter (IC26)

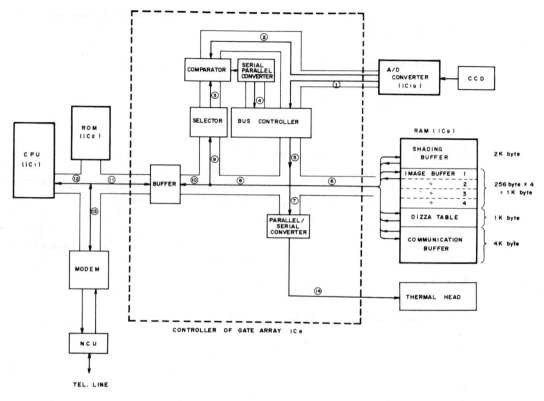

**Figure 4–17** Block Diagram of Components for Fax Transmission and Reception

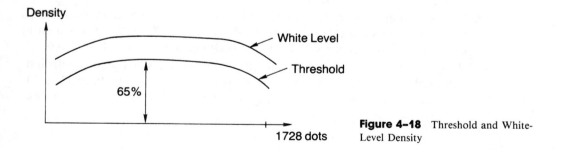

**Figure 4–18** Threshold and White-Level Density

5. Black and white data of step 4 is converted to parallel data by serial-parallel converter and during DMA continuous transmission is stored in image buffer along routes 4 to 5 to 6.

6. Line increment data stored in image buffers 1 to 4 is sent sequentially to parallel-serial converter along routes 6 to 7 during DMA continuous transmission.

Here it is converted to serial data, output to the thermal head, and printed on recording paper.

*Note:* Standard: reads 3.85 lines/mm; fine: reads 7.7 lines/mm.

### Halftone mode

1. Same as step 1 of standard, fine mode.
2. Same as step 2 of standard, fine mode.
3. To create halftones, a dither pattern is used.

   The meaning of the dither pattern (discussed further in chapter 9) follows. It is impossible to change the density of each dot and print it out. Consequently, a 4 × 4 dot matrix is established, and by changing the density (unit number) of black, a printout is obtained that appears to the human eye as halftone. This means that the threshold value for distinguishing each dot of the 4 × 4 dot matrix as white or black is changed.
4. Same as step 4 of standard, fine mode.
5. Same as step 5 of standard, fine mode.
6. Same as step 6 of standard, fine mode.

*Note:* The readout density is 7.7 lines/mm.

## Transmission

1. Same processing at time of copy (steps 1 to 5 in standard, fine mode) and at time of copy halftone mode).
2. Data stored in image buffer is fetched by CPU (IC1) along routes 6 to 8 to 10 to 11 to 12, reduced (MH coding) at table inside RAM (IC2), then stored in communication buffer inside RAM (IC9) along routes 12 to 11 to 8 to 6.
3. While fetching data stored in communication buffer synchronous with modem, CPU (IC1) inputs data to modem along routes 6 to 8 to 10 to 11 to 13, where it is converted to serial analog data and forwarded over telephone lines via NCU section.

## Reception

1. Serial analog image data is received over telephone lines and input to the modem via NCU section, where it is demodulated to parallel digital data. Then the CPU (IC1) stores the data in the communication buffer of RAM (IC9) along routes 12 to 11 to 10 to 8 to 6.

2. CPU (IC1) fetches data stored in communication buffer along routes 6 to 8 to 10 to 11 to 12, restores data to original form inside ROM (IC2), then stores data in image buffer in RAM (IC9) along routes 13 to 11 to 10 to 8 to 6.

3. Same processing at time of copy (step 6 in standard, fine mode).

For details on the read section, see chapter 10. For details on the thermal head, see chapter 11.

## Inverter Circuit

Figure 4–19 shows the inverter circuit diagram.

This circuit is a booster circuit for turning on the fluorescent lamp used in the read section.

When gate array IC29 pin (99) becomes high level, Q72 and Q401 turn ON, and +24 V is impressed between pins 1 and 2 of T401, and pins 2 and 3.

Moreover, the bases of transistors Q402 and Q403 are impressed via R404 and R405. Because of differences in the saturation characteristics of the transistors, Q403 starts to go ON early, and at the same time current passes between 1 and 2 of T401.

This induces voltage between 4 and 5 of T401 (5 is positive), causing Q403 to go ON rapidly. Conversely, Q402 goes OFF rapidly because 4 is negative. When 2 to 3 saturates thereafter, the induced voltage between 4 and 5 drops, and the collector current of Q403 diminishes. The reduction in this collector current induces a reverse bias (4 is positive) between 4 and 5, which causes Q403 to go OFF and Q402 to go ON. When Q402 starts to go ON, current flows between 1 and 2, and voltage is included between 4 and 5, thus going even further in the direction causing ON. In this way, Q402 and Q403 repeatedly go ON-OFF alternately, and through alternate excitation between coils 2 and 3, and 1 and 2, a high voltage is induced in T401 (7 to 10), causing the lamp to turn ON.

In addition to the main discharge tube in the lamp there is a subdischarge tube for activation that supplies voltage through CN403 (2). The line from CN402 serves to light the lamp for activation during nighttime use (when fluorescent lamp is extinguished).

The reason is that when it is pitch dark, discharge cannot begin because of the darkness characteristic of the discharge tube.

Specifications are as follows:

1. Oscillation frequency is 30 kHz.
2. Secondary output voltage is 1200 V (o-p) of sine wave.
3. Secondary output current is 18 mA.
4. Primary current consumption is 300 mA.
5. Life of fluorescent lamp is 3000 hours of consecutive use.

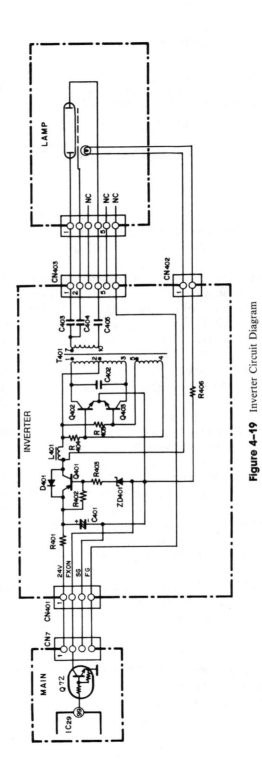

**Figure 4-19** Inverter Circuit Diagram

## Modem Section

Function

The unit uses a modem board that consists of two ICs, enabling it to act as an interface between the control section for fax sending and receiving, and the telephone line. In other words, during a sending operation, the digital image signals are modulated and sent to the telephone line. During a receiving operation, the analog image signals that are received via the telephone line are demodulated and converted into digital image signals. The communication format and procedures for fax communication are standardized by CCITT. This modem board has hardware that sends and detects all of the necessary signals for fax communication.

It can be controlled by writing commands from the CPU (IC1) to the register in the IC on the modem board.

This board also sends dual-tone multifrequency (DTMF) signals, generates a call tone (from the speaker), and detects busy and dial tones.

Circuit operation

The modem board (Figure 4–20) has all the hardware satisfying the CCITT standards mentioned previously. Resistors inside two ICs in the modem board are selected by select signals from gate array IC5, commands are written through data bus, and through readout all processing is controlled at the CPU (IC1) according to CCITT procedures.

Here the interrupt signal INT dispatched from IRQ (1) to the CPU (IC1) is output when preparation for acceptance of transmission data is OK and when demodulation of reception data is complete; the CPU (IC1) implements postprocessing.

This modem has an automatic application equalizer. With training signal 1 or 2 at time of G3 reception, it can automatically establish the optimum equalizer.

With CABS1, the equalizer in the modem can be set up from outside. When the distance to the station is long or transception does not occur properly, correction* of 0.0 km, 1.8 km, 3.6 km, 7.2 km and 13.2 km is possible with user setting. (See port description of gate array IC29.)

The +5-V and −12-V power supply voltages are cut off by relay RLY3 when the modem is not in use to minimize heat dissipation from the modem board. The operation is controlled by IC29 (55).

At time of reception, moreover, there is an equalizer circuit IC21 (2 to 1) for 6 km correction outside the modem, so correction up to 7.2 km + 6 km = 13.2 km is possible.

---

*Correction is the equivalent of this length of 0.4-mm diameter cable in kilometers.

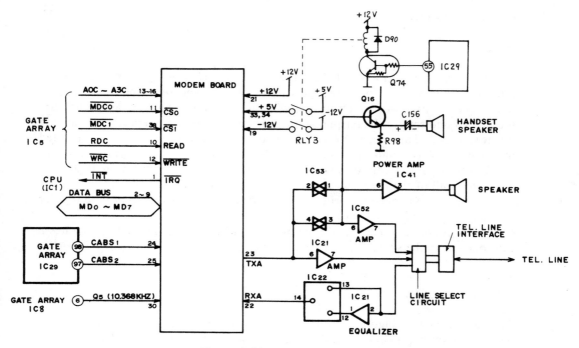

**Figure 4-20**  Circuits Associated with Modem Board

The course of signal travel follows:

1. *Facsimile transmission*—The digital image data on the data bus is modulated in the modem board, and sent from pin 23 via the telephone line to amplifier IC21 (6 to 7) and then to the NCU section.

2. *Facsimile reception*—The analog image data that is received from the telephone line passes through the NCU section and enters pin (22) of the modem board. The multiplexer of IC21 is used to select whether or not to route this data through the equalizer circuit of IC21 (2 to 1). The signals that enter pin 22 of the modem board are demodulated in the board to digital image signals and then placed on the data bus.

   In this case, the image signals from the telephone line are transmitted serially; hence, they are placed on the bus in 8-b units.

   Here, the equalizer circuit reduces the image signals to the long-distance receiving level. It is designed to correct the characteristics of the frequency band centered about 3 kHz and maintain a constant receiving sensitivity. It can be set in the service mode.

3. *DTMF transmission (monitor tone)*—The DTMF signal generated in the modem board is output from pin 23, then passes through the analog switch IC53

(4 to 3), the amplifier IC52 (6 to 7), and the NCU section to the telephone line.

During speakerphone operation, the monitor tone is output from the analog switch IC53 (4 to 3) through the ATAS IC41 (6 to 3) power amplifier to the speaker; during handset operation, it is output from the emitter-follower Q16 to the handset speaker.

4. *Call tone transmission*—The call signal that is generated in the modem board passes through analog switch IC53 (2 to 1) and ATAS IC41 (6 to 3) to the speaker.

5. *Busy and dial tone detection*—The path is the same as for FAX receiving. When it is detected, the carrier detect bit of the register in the IC on the modem board becomes 1, and this status is monitored by the CPU (IC1).

## Motor Drive Circuits

Figure 4–21 shows the transmission motor-drive circuit, and Figure 4–22 shows the receiving motor-drive circuit.

Function

Two individual stepping motors are used for transceiving. They feed paper synchronized for readout and printing.

Circuit operation

During motor drive, gate array IC5 pin (37, TXE; 36, RXE) becomes high, driver IC13/14 pins (5 to 12) turn ON, and Q1/Q2 go ON, as a result, +24 V is supplied to the motor coil.

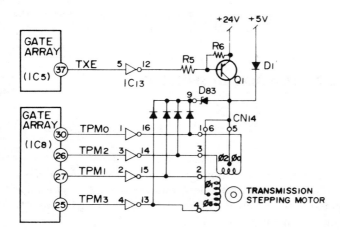

**Figure 4–21** Transmission Motor-Drive Circuit

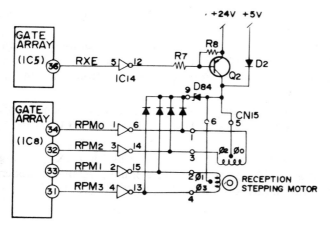

**Figure 4-22** Reception Motor-Drive Circuit

Stepping pulses are output from gate array (IC8), causing driver IC13/14 to go ON. The motor coil is energized sequentially in two-phase increments, which causes a one-step rotation. Rotation of one-step feeds 0.13 mm of recording paper or document paper.

Figure 4-23 shows the timing chart of motor-drive circuits. When the motor is OFF, gate array IC5 pin (37, TXE; 36, RXE) becomes low and driver IC13/14 pins (5 to 12) are OFF. This causes Q1/Q2 also to go OFF, and instead of +24 V, +5 V is supplied through D1/D2 so that the motor is held in place.

**Figure 4-23** Timing Chart of Motor Drive Circuits

## PAPER FEED MECHANISM AND SENSOR CIRCUIT SECTIONS

### Paper Feed

Document feed path

Figure 4-24 shows the document and recording paper feed paths. In the KX-F120 model, the document should be aligned on the left, and the document guide knob (7) is installed on the right side of the document insertion port in such a way that it can slide. The maximum document width is 218 mm.

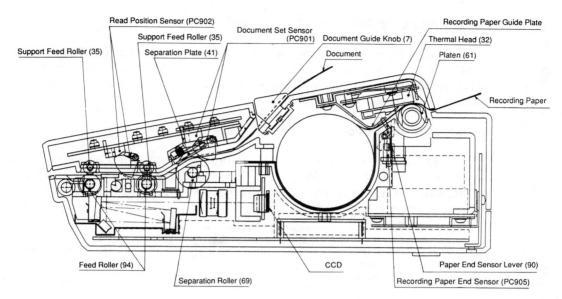

**Figure 4-24** Interior of Panasonic's KX-F120 Fax Machine Showing Document and Recording Paper Feed Paths

The drive side rollers (69, 94) are driven via gears by a stepping motor (87). When the document passes between the separation roller (69) and the separation plate (41), it is separated one sheet at a time.

## Paper feed sequence

1. The operator loads the document by inserting it along the document guide knob (7) to the position where the document set sensor (901) goes ON (beep tone).

2. When the document set sensor (901) goes ON, the separation roller (69) and feed rollers (94) rotate, causing the documents to be fed one at a time. When a document is fed and the read position sensor (902) goes ON, the feed rollers (94) stop feeding the document at the position where the leading edge of the document is to be read.

3. The feed rollers (94) rotate in accordance with the copy command or fax command, causing the document to be fed, and the image is read by the CCD.

4. When the document is fed to the back so that the read position sensor (902) goes OFF, the separation roller (69) and the feed rollers (94) rotate, causing the second document to be fed.

The remaining documents are then fed successively in the same way.

Recording paper feed paths

The recording paper moves along the recording paper guide plate (see Figure 4–24) until it reaches the platen (61) and is then fed by the rotation of the platen (61). The paper end sensor lever (90) rotates about the pivot, causing the recording paper end sensor (905) to detect the recording paper.

## Sensor Circuit Section

**1.** *Document set sensor and read position sensor*—When a document is inserted, the document set sensor (Figure 4–25) blocks the groove in the middle of PC901 with a lever, and the phototransistor of PC901 goes OFF. Related operations are shown subsequently.

|  |  | PC901 Phototransistor | IC28 (pin 1) | IC29 (pin 88) |
|---|---|---|---|---|
| *Document* | No document | ON | L | H |
| *Set sensor* | Set document | OFF | H | L |

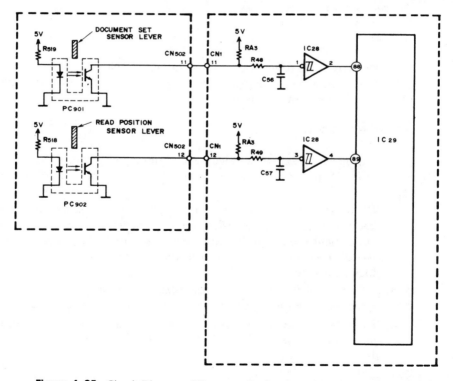

**Figure 4–25**   Circuit Diagram of Document Set Sensor and Read Position Sensor

When the document reaches a read position, the read position sensor blocks the groove in the middle of PC902 with a sensor lever, and the phototransistor of PC902 goes OFF. Related operations are shown subsequently.

|  |  | PC902 Phototransistor | IC28 (pin 3) | IC29 (pin 89) |
|---|---|---|---|---|
| *Read position* | No document | ON | L | H |
| *Sensor* | Set document | OFF | H | L |

**2.** *Upper-cabinet latch sensor*—This sensor detects the open or closed status of the upper cabinet (Figure 4–26). When the cover is closed, the upper-cabinet latch sensor blocks the groove of PC903 on the lower cabinet side with the shelter plate on the upper cabinet side, causing the phototransistor of PC903 to go OFF. Related operations are shown subsequently.

|  |  | PC903 Phototransistor | IC28 (pin 11) | IC29 (pin 67) |
|---|---|---|---|---|
| *Upper cabinet* | Upper cabinet closed | OFF | H | L |
| *Latch sensor* | Upper cabinet open | ON | L | H |

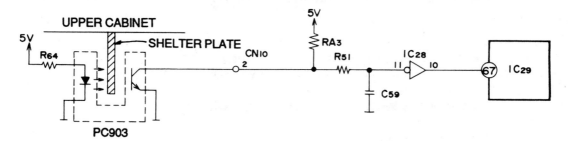

**Figure 4–26**  Circuit Diagram of Upper-Cabinet Latch Sensor

**3.** *Recording paper end sensor*—This sensor detects that the supply of recording paper is exhausted (Figure 4–27). When there is recording paper, the recording paper end sensor blocks the groove in the middle of PC905 with a lever, causing the phototransistor of PC905 to go OFF. Related operations are shown subsequently.

|  |  | PC905 Phototransistor | IC28 (pin 13) | IC29 (pin 92) |
|---|---|---|---|---|
| *Recording paper* | Recording paper set | OFF | H | L |
| *End sensor* | No recording paper | ON | L | H |

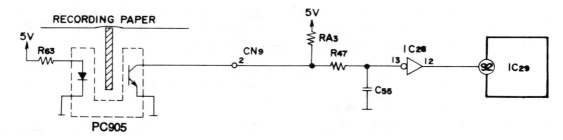

**Figure 4-27**  Circuit Diagram of Recording Paper End Sensor

## NCU MAIN SECTION

Figure 4-28 shows a circuit diagram of the NCU.

### Bell Detection Circuit

Circuit operation

Signal waveforms of each section are indicated in Figure 4-29. Signals (low-level section) input to pin 62 of gate array IC29 are read out at CPU and judged as bell.

*Signal path*

$$T -> L1 -> L3 -> RLY2 -> PC2 -> R202 -> R201 ->$$
$$D24 - > D23 -> RLY2 -> L4 -> L2 -> R$$

### CPC (Calling Party Control) Detection Circuit

Circuit operation

For detection of temporary line disconnection during on-line condition, CPC detection is executed after DC loop formation as shown in Figure 4-30. As the line voltage always is applied between (1) and (2) of photocoupler PC4 during DC loop formation, PC4 (4) always is low level. PC4 (4) momentarily becomes high level by line disconnection. This is read by gate array IC29 (63), and CPC is detected.
As the CPC signal time differs according to the exchange, selection is possible by key input.

|     | A              | B                |
| --- | -------------- | ---------------- |
| OK  | More than 8 ms | More than 600 ms |
| NG  | Less than 5 ms | Less than 350 ms |

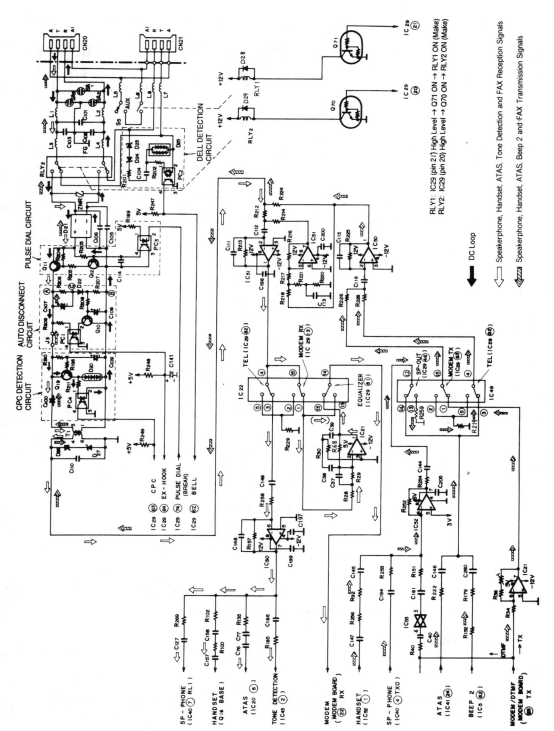

**Figure 4–28**  Circuit Diagram of Network Control Unit

**103**

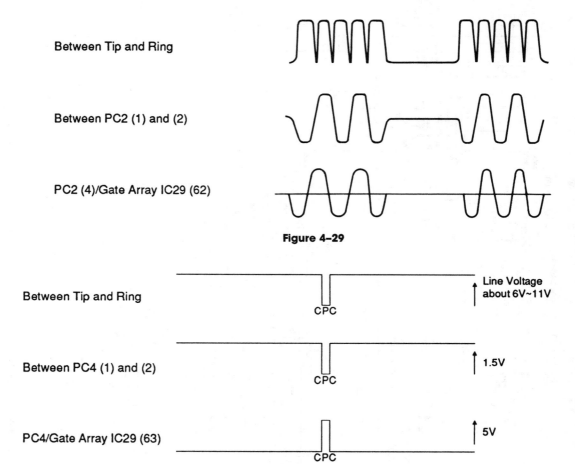

Between Tip and Ring

Between PC2 (1) and (2)

PC2 (4)/Gate Array IC29 (62)

**Figure 4–29**

Between Tip and Ring

CPC

Line Voltage
about 6V~11V

Between PC4 (1) and (2)

CPC

1.5V

PC4/Gate Array IC29 (63)

CPC

5V

**Figure 4–30**

*Signal path*

$$T -> L3 -> RLY2 -> D21 -> Q11 -> Q19 -> R211 ->$$
$$PC4- > D21 -> RLY2 -> L4 -> L2 -> R$$

## Pulse Dial Circuit

Circuit operation

The dial pulses are generated by the IC29 and reach the telephone line via the following path.

*Signal path*

IC29(74) –> low level –> PC3 ON –> Q12 OFF –> Q11 OFF –> telephone line

## Auto Disconnect Circuit

Function

When line recording is occurring in the hold status of an ATAS answer status, this unit will detect the off-hook status of another telephone connected in parallel with the line and then clear the hold status, and stop recording.

Circuit operation

When the unit seizes a line a voltage will be applied between points (A) and (B). At this time a voltage will be applied to the base Q10, causing Q10 to turn ON. As a result, PC1 (4) will go low level, and a low status will be inputted to IC29(64), thus detecting the fact that the unit has seized the line. Then, when parallel-connected telephone goes into an off-hook status, the voltage between (A) and (B) will fall.

However, the charge on C107 causes the previous voltage between (A) and (B) to be retained; hence, the voltage between (C) and (B) falls. Consequently, the base potential of Q10 falls, causing Q10 to turn OFF and PC1 (4) to go high level and IC29 (64) to go high level, thus detecting the fact that the parallel-connected telephone is in an off-hook status.

## SWITCHING POWER SUPPLY SECTION

Figure 4–31 shows a circuit diagram of switching power supply.

Circuit operation

The input from the AC line passes through the line filter composed of across-the-line capacitors (C401, C404), line bypass capacitors (C402, C403, C407, C408), and a common mode choke coils (L401, L402). It is rectified by bridge diode (D401), smoothed by an electrolytic capacitor (C409), and a 160-V DC voltage is obtained. A thermistor (TH401) is used to prevent rush current to the electrolytic capacitor (C409).

Next, the voltage impressed over the electrolytic capacitor (C409) is impressed via the carbon resistor (R410) to the base of the switching transistor (Q401). The switching transistor (Q401) turns ON, and current flows to the main winding of the switching transformer (T401). Voltage is generated at the base drive winding of the switching transformer (T401); this voltage also is applied to the base of the switching transformer (T401) via resistors (R401, R402, R403, R422), capacitor (C413),

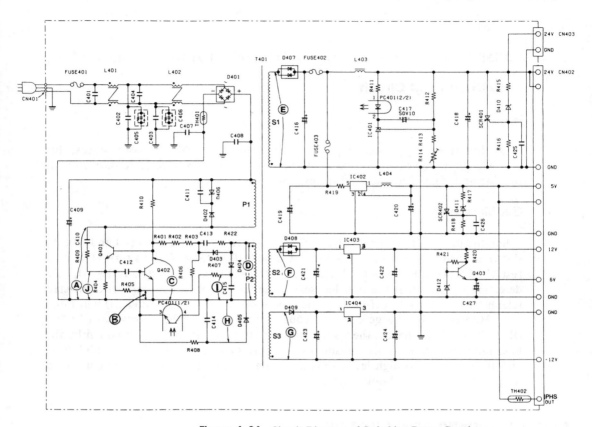

**Figure 4–31**  Circuit Diagram of Switching Power Supply

and rectifying diode (D403). The current flowing through the main winding of the switching transformer (T401) increases.

Next, the voltage generated in the S1 output winding by the current flowing through the main winding of the switching transformer (T401) is rectified by the rectifying diode (D407), and is smoothed by electrolytic capacitors (C416, C418, C419) and choke coil (L403). The smoothed output is subjected to voltage splitting by resistors (R412, R413) and variable resistor (R414); it is impressed to the shunt regulator IC (IC401), and current flowing through the photocoupler (PC401) is controlled by the regulator IC (IC401) by means of this voltage. When here the voltage impressed to the resistor (R415) exceeds the specified voltage (+24 V), the regulator IC (IC401) operates to let current flow to the LED side of the photocoupler (PC401), the phototransistor of the photocoupler (PC401) is turned ON, the voltage rectified by diode (D404) and capacitor (C415) is impressed to the base of the transistor (Q402), this transistor is turned ON, the base current of the switching transistor (Q401), and the current flowing through the main winding of the switching transformer (T401) is limited.

The output voltage is regulated to 24 V by means of the preceding operation. When the current flowing through the resistor (R404) increases, a voltage drop results, so that the transistor (Q402) is turned ON via the resistor (R405), the base current of the switching transistor (Q401) is taken in, and the current flowing through the main winding of the switching transformer (T401) is limited.

The voltage generated in the secondary winding S2 of the switching transformer (T401) is rectified by the diode (D408) and smoothed by the electrolytic capacitor (C421), and +12 V is put out from the regulator IC (IC403). In the same way, the voltage generated in the winding S3 is rectified by the diode (D409) and smoothed by the electrolytic capacitor (C423), and −12 V is put out from the regulator IC (IC404).

The DC voltage of +24 V impressed over the +24-V electrolytic capacitor (C416) is supplied to the switching regulator IC (IC402) via the fuse (F403); it is converted to a voltage of +5 V by means of pulse width control, and +5 V is put out after smoothing by choke coil (L404) and electrolytic capacitor (C420).

When the switching regulator IC (IC402) breaks down, short mode is reached, +24 V is supplied to the +5-V system, and the set is destroyed. For this reason, abnormalities are detected by D411, the thyristor (SCR402) is switched ON, the abnormal output is short-circuited, and the fuse (F403) blows to protect the set.

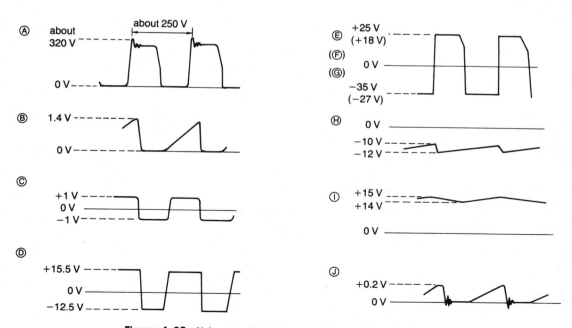

**Figure 4–32** Voltages and Waveforms at Various Points in Power Supply

The applications of the various power supplies are as follows:

+ 24 V     Thermal head power, transmission motor power, reception motor power, and inverter board.

+ 12 V     Modem power, ATAS/ITS telephone line interface power, telephone line interface relay power, and CCD board

− 12 V     Modem power and image sensor power

+ 5 V     FAX control section power, ATAS plunger, and operation board

+ 6 V     ATAS/ITS circuit power

When a completely black document is copied for a long time (abnormal use), the power supply output is highest, resulting in abnormal heating. In this case, the condition is detected by thermistor (TH402) in close contact with the regulating diode of the 24-V system (the resistance value increase), and output (PHS OUT) of pin 1 of CN402 is input to A/D converter inside the main board, thus, operation is stopped to protect the set. Allow unit to cool. Voltages and waveforms may be checked at various points in the switched power supply by referring to Figure 4–32.

# CHAPTER 5

# *Testing and Troubleshooting*

The steps outlined in this chapter are more applicable to machines that do not have a full complement of diagnostic features, and they are the more conventional approaches to testing and troubleshooting of electronic equipment. They can be applied to any machine, however, if its problems have not been solved by other means. The tests and flow charts as detailed are specifically applicable to the Panasonic model KX-F120 machine. They refer to its displays, button operations, and switches. Nevertheless, they can be applied to other machines by relating to components with similar functions even though their designation is different. Some manufacturers furnish service manuals with troubleshooting flow charts even though they may rely on diagnostics features to a considerable extent. Even those with extensive diagnostics, generally list symptoms and outline corrective measures to be taken.

Because manufacturers prefer to change only PC boards and other major components at the field level, whenever changes in electronic components are indicated, it may be preferable to do these at service centers rather than to delve into the equipment to such an extent in the office where the equipment is installed. An exception might be when it is known from the history of a machine that a particular component has been subject to repeated failure and needs replacement with a component of better quality. The troubleshooting flow charts by the causes of difficulties that may arise in long-distance and international communications, and the countermeasures, which may be applied to cope with these problems.

## TESTING MODES

| Test mode | Function | Operation |
|---|---|---|
| 1. Printer test | Print a test pattern and check the thermal head (32) for abnormalities (missing dots, etc.) and also check the operation of the reception motor (87). | 1. Press the FUNCTION button.<br>2. Press the REDIAL or MUTE buttons (several times).<br>3. LCD will show: "PRINTER TEST."<br>4. Press the START/COPY button. |
| 2. Motor test | Rotate the transmission and reception motors (87) to check the operation of the motors. | 1. Press the FUNCTION button.<br>2. Press the REDIAL or MUTE buttons (several times).<br>3. LCD will show: "MOTOR TEST."<br>4. Press the START/COPY button.<br>5. Press the STOP/CLEAR button. |
| 3. Modem test | Send four kinds of fax signals to check the sending function of the modem.<br>1. 462Hz: Consecutive signal of PIS for tonal process<br>2. 1100Hz: Consecutive signal of EOM for tonal<br>3. 2100Hz: G2 carrier signal consecutive of CED signal<br>4. G3, V29 training signal [modulation wave of carrier signal (1700Hz)] | 1. Set the service switch (S4) to ON.<br>2. Press the FUNCTION button.<br>3. Press the 5 and 3 buttons.<br>4. LCD will show: "MODEM =OFF."<br>5. Press the START/COPY button (every time press: 462Hz—> 1100Hz—>2100Hz—>V29).<br>6. Press the STOP/CLEAR button. |
| 4. Readout test | Turn on the fluorescent lamp (95) and operate the read system (there is no need to use paper). Observe the signals obtained to check the read system. | 1. Set the service switch (S4) to ON.<br>2. Press the FUNCTION button.<br>3. Press the 5 button twice.<br>4. LCD will show: "READOUT TEST."<br>5. Press the START/COPY button.<br>6. Press the STOP/CLEAR button. |
| 5. ROM check | Check the ROM (IC2) by means of a check sum to see if the contents have been destroyed and also to check the version. | 1. Set the service switch (S4) to ON.<br>2. Press the FUNCTION button.<br>3. Press the 5 and 2 buttons.<br>4. LCD will show: "VER.XX SUM =XXXX."<br>5. Press the START/COPY button.<br>6. Press the STOP/CLEAR button. |

| Test mode | Function | Operation |
|---|---|---|
| 6. RAM check<br>*Note:* Before servicing, you must print the telephone and system list, and keep the printouts as the memory will be cleared when the RAM is checked. | The read and write operations of the RAMs (IC3 and IC9) can be checked to see whether or not the contents have been destroyed. | 1. Set the service switch (S4) to ON.<br>2. Press the FUNCTION button.<br>3. Press the 5 and 1 buttons.<br>4. LCD will show: "MEMORY CHECK."<br>5. Press the START/COPY button.<br>6. LCD will show: "CHECK = OK." |
| 7. LCD check | Check the LCD (E801) lights. | 1. Set the service switch (S4) to ON.<br>2. Press the FUNCTION button.<br>3. Press the 5 and 4 buttons.<br>4. LCD will show: "LCD TEST."<br>5. Press the START/COPY button.<br>6. LCD will show: ". . . . . ."<br>7. Press the STOP/CLEAR button. |

*Notes:* For further discussion on service switch (S4), refer to page 64. After test and check, turn service switch (S4) OFF (refer to page 66).

## TROUBLESHOOTING FLOW CHARTS

Figures 5–1 and 5–2 are flow charts relating to overall troubleshooting. Figures 5–3 to 5–13 apply to the Facsimile Section. Figures 5–14 and 5–15 relate to the Operation Panel Section while Figures 5–16 to 5–19 apply to the Switching Power Supply Section.

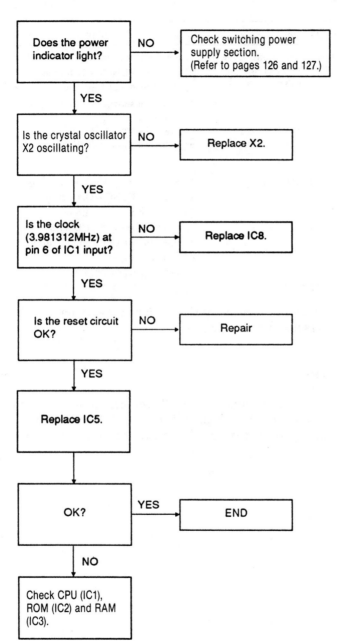

**Figure 5–1** Machine Functions Do Not Operate

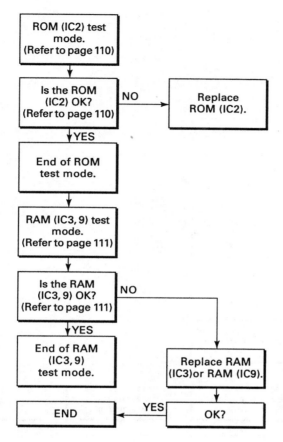

**Figure 5–2** Check of ROM and RAM before Commencing Troubleshooting If Unit Can Operate to Certain Extent

## Facsimile Section

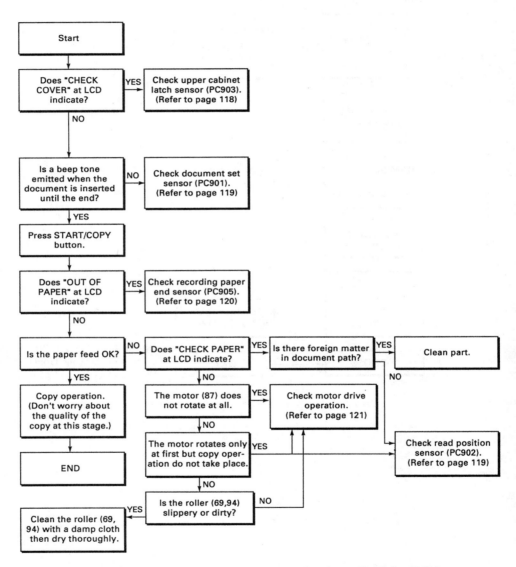

**Figure 5-3**  Check of Abnormality in Paper Feed or Sensor Operation If Either Transmission or Reception Cannot Occur

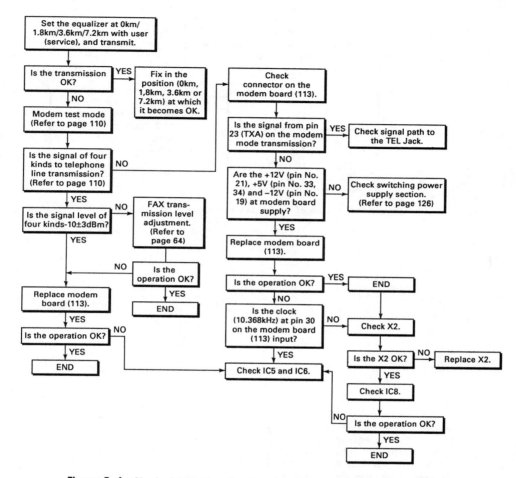

**Figure 5–4** Check of Unit That Can Copy but Cannot Transmit: When START/ COPY Button Is Pressed, START/COPY Indicator Flashes but Does Not Change to Steady Glow, and Unit Does Not Go into Transmission Mode

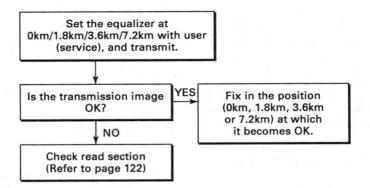

**Figure 5–5**   Check of Unit That Can Copy, but has Incorrect Transmitted Image

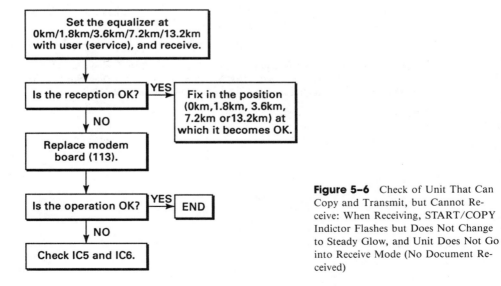

**Figure 5–6**   Check of Unit That Can Copy and Transmit, but Cannot Receive: When Receiving, START/COPY Indictor Flashes but Does Not Change to Steady Glow, and Unit Does Not Go into Receive Mode (No Document Received)

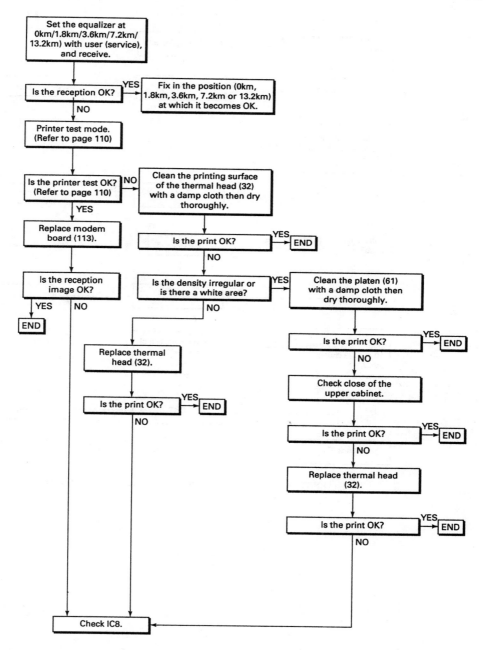

**Figure 5-7**  Check of Unit That Can Copy but Has Received Incorrect Image

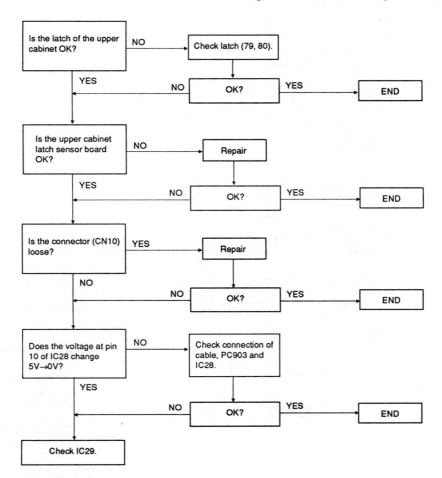

**Figure 5-8**   Check of Upper-Cabinet Latch Sensor (PC903)

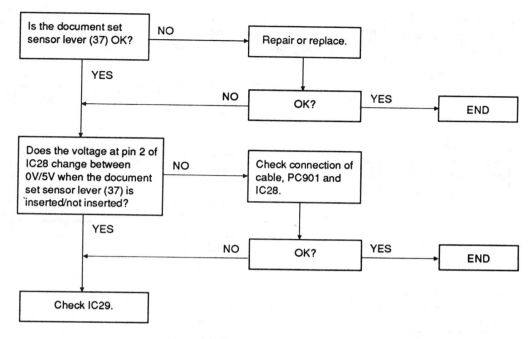

**Figure 5–9** Check of Document Set Sensor (PC901)

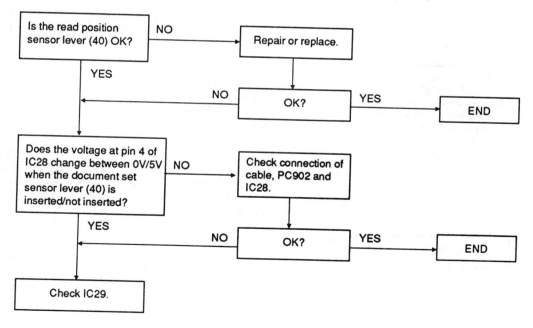

**Figure 5–10** Check of Read Position Sensor (PC902)

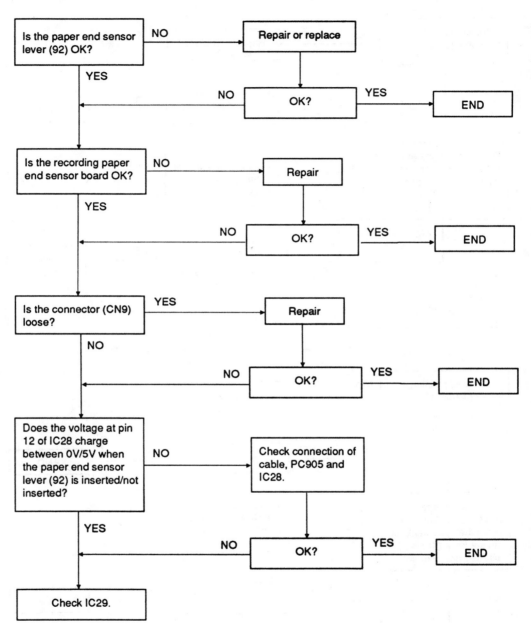

**Figure 5–11**  Check of Recording Paper End Sensor (PC905)

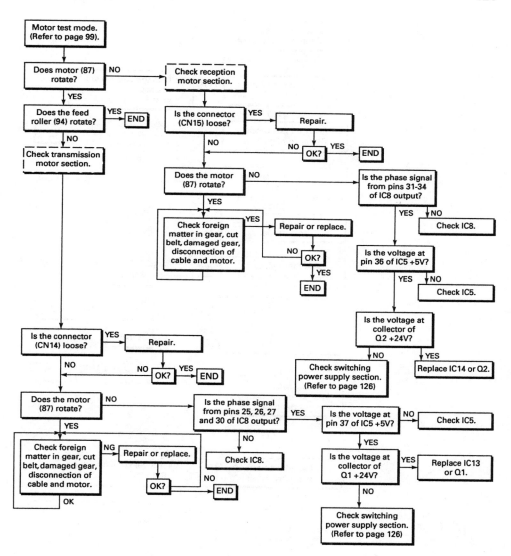

**Figure 5-12** Check of Motor-Drive Operation

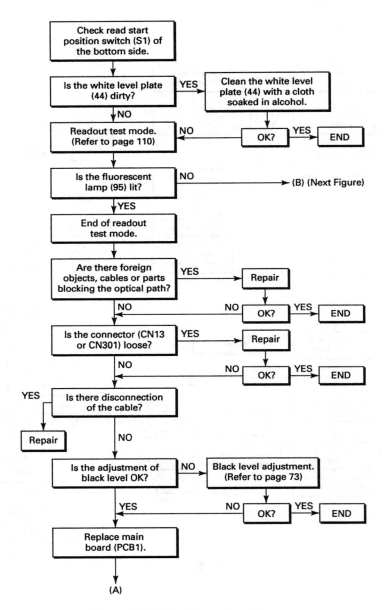

**Figure 5-13 (a)**   Check of Read Section

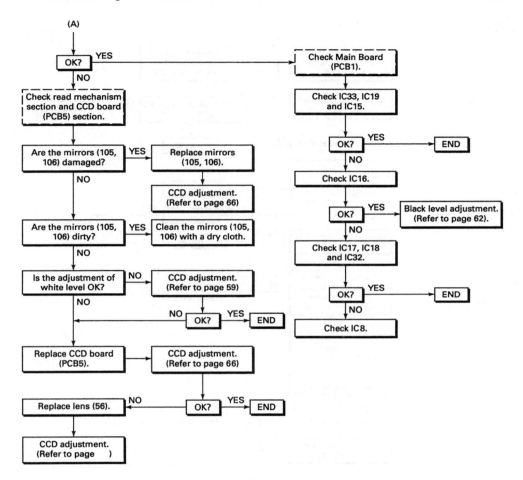

**Figure 5–13 (b)** Check of Read Section (*continued*)

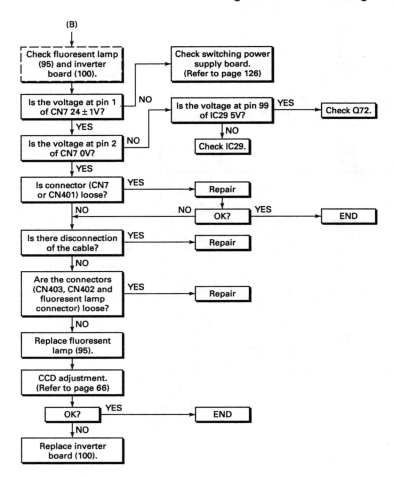

**Figure 5–13 (c)**   Check of Read Section (*continued*)

## Operation Panel Section

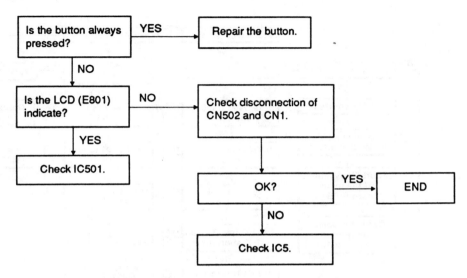

**Figure 5-14**  Diagram Showing No Key Operation

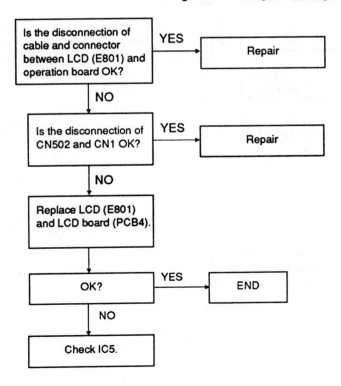

**Figure 5-15**  Diagram Showing No LCD Operation

## Switching Power Supply Section

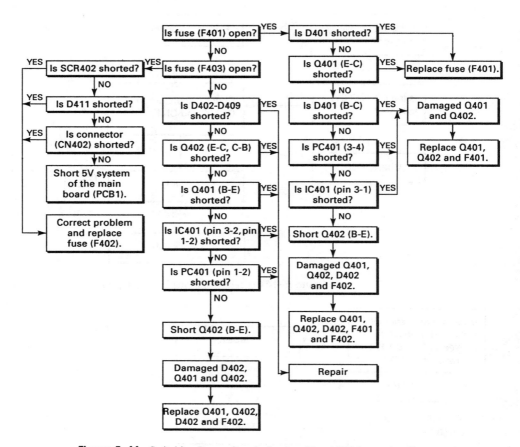

**Figure 5–16**  Switching Power Supply Section; Not All Voltages Are Output

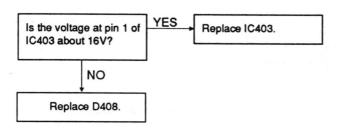

**Figure 5–17**  Correct Voltages Output from 5- and 24-V Systems, but +12 V Not Output

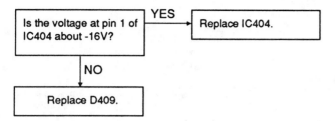

**Figure 5–18** Correct Voltages Output from 5- and 24-V Systems, but − 12 V Not Output

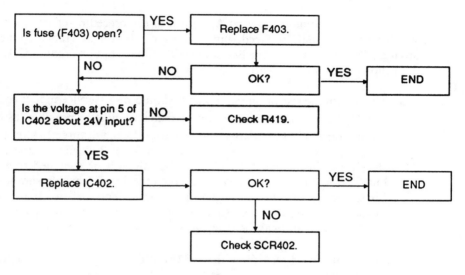

**Figure 5–19** Correct Voltages Output from + 24-V System but + 5 V Not Output

## UNIT CAN COPY, BUT CANNOT TRANSMIT OR RECEIVE
## LONG-DISTANCE OR INTERNATIONAL COMMUNICATION

The following two causes should be considered:

**1.** *Cause 1*—The other party is executing automatic calling, the call has been received by this unit, and the time until response with a CED or digital identification signal (DIS) has been too long. Maximum time until response is shown in Figure 5–20. (According to the CCITT standard, the communication procedure is stopped when there is no response from the other party within 35 s, so that the other party releases the line.)

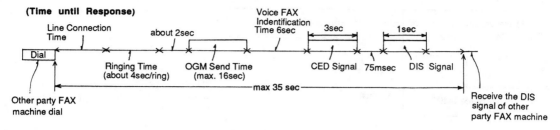

**Figure 5-20**   Time Until Response

*Cause and countermeasure*: As shown in the preceding chart, the total hand-shaking time must be reduced, but because of the long-distance connection and linking of several stations, the line connection time cannot be reduced. Accordingly, the following countermeasures should be tried.

**a.** The automatic reception bell number should be 1 (service mode: code no. 00).

**b.** The OGM recording time should be made as short as possible (8s or less).

**c.** As the count of 35 s is started directly after dialing or directly after the START button has been pushed for models with a START button, the other party should be called manually; if possible, this unit be switched to FAX by (*) button when the OGM is heard, and then the START button should be pushed for fax communication. Another possibility is entry of two pauses at the end of the automatic dial number of the transmission side. In this way, the start time for the count can be delayed by two pauses (about 10 s).

*Note:*   For short OGM recording, the OGM button must be pushed to end the OGM recording.

**2.** *Cause 2*—Erroneous detection occurs because of an echo or echo canceler. The signal from fax 1 reaches fax 2 via the stations 1 and 2, but the reflection signal at station 2 also returns via station 1 (echo) (Figure 5–21). As the distance between stations 1 and 2 is long, the echo returns to fax 1 600 ms (maximum) after transmission, so that there is the possibility that this signal is detected erroneously as the signal from fax 2 and that trouble is caused. In the case of a normal call, there is also the possibility that the echo of one's own voice will make the call difficult to understand. For this reason, each station (1 and 2) attaches echo cancelers (S1 and S2) in case of international lines or long distance lines. For the echo canceler, the level of the transmission signal from fax 1 is compared with the level of the reception signal from the fax 2, and when transmission signal is larger, S1 is closed, whereas S2 is opened when it is smaller. In other words, with transmission from fax 1, S1 is closed and S2 is open, so that the echo does not return to FAX1.

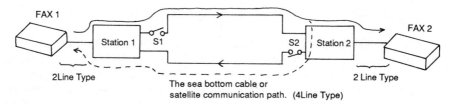

**Figure 5–21** International Circuit with Echo Cancelers

*Cause and countermeasure*: Cause A. When the training signal is transmitted from fax 1 during the communication procedure at the time of transmission from fax 1 to fax 2, there is a delay until the echo canceler operates and S1 is closed, so that a part of the head of the training signal may drop out, normal reception by FAX2 may not be possible, and transmission may not be started.

Countermeasure A. When the international line mode becomes ON in service mode (code no. 03), a dummy signal is attached to the head of the training signal to prevent this problem. As this normally is ON, it is necessary to reconfirm that this has not become OFF. When the international mode is switched OFF, the transmission side will try the training signal three times at each speed (9600BPS, 4800BPS, and 2400BPS), and in case of rejection (NG), it will drop the speed by one rank (fall-back). When the international mode is switched ON, each speed will be tried only twice. In other words, the slower speed with fewer errors are reached more easily. This is done as the line conditions may deteriorate, and the picture may be disturbed more easily during communication in case of international lines or long-distance communication, even when the training has been OK. The default value is ON as preference is given to clearer pictures rather than speed.

Cause B. The echo canceler operation is stopped with a signal of 2100 Hz (i.e., S1 and S2 become ON). Accordingly, when fax 1 has executed automatic reception, a CED signal is output, and if this signal should be 2100 Hz, S1 and S2 will become ON. Then the echo of the DIS signal output afterward may be received and fax 1 may execute erroneous operation, preventing start of communication.

Countermeasure B. In service mode, the CED signal frequency is set to 1100 Hz (code no. 02) or the time setting between the CED signal and the DIS signal is set from 75 ms to 500 ms in service mode (code no. 81). This is done because the echo canceler operation stop mode is canceled with an interval of 250 ms or more.

Cause C. An KS-F80 shall be assumed for fax 1, and a set of a different company shall be assumed for fax 2. In case of transmission from the KX-F80 to fax 2, fax 2 executes automatic reception and transmits a CED signal (2100 Hz), followed by a DIS signal. As the echo cancelers stop as described in cause B, the echo of the DIS signal gives signal returns to fax 2. Conversely, the KX-F80 detects the DIS signal and transmits a DCS signal. In other words, it is possible that the echo of the DIS signal and the DCS signal transmitted from the KX-F80 reach fax

2 one after the other, fax 2 executes erroneous detection, and communication is not started.

Countermeasure C. When international DIS detection setting is made effective in service mode (code no. 82), the KX-F80 does respond to the first DIS signal and returns a DCS signal only for the second DIS signal. In other words, there is an interval of 250 ms between transmission of the first and the second DIS signal, so that the echo canceler operation recovers, and no echo is generated for the second DIS signal.

*Note:* When the other fax does not respond with a DCS signal after DIS signal transmission, the DIS signal is transmitted three times for trial.

The following is a summary of long-distance and international communication operation:

| Symptom | Countermeasure |
| --- | --- |
| Does not receive in automatic mode | 1. The automatic reception ring count should be made 1 (service mode: code no. 00). |
| | 2. The OGM recording time should be made as short as possible (5 or less). |
| | 3. If possible, manual transmission should be made from the transmission side. |
| | 4. If possible, two pauses should be inserted at the end of the automatic dial number of the transmission side. |
| | 5. If possible, the function selector switch should be switched from AUTO/FAX to FAX. |
| Does not transmit | 1. Confirm the international line mode ON (service mode: code no. 03). |
| | 2. International DIS detection setting is made effective (service mode: code no. 82). |
| Does not receive | 1. The time setting between the CED signal and the DIS signal is set to 500 ms (service mode: code no. 81). |
| | 2. The CED frequency is set to 1100 Hz (service mode: code no. 02). |

# UNIT CAN COPY, BUT TRANSMISSION AND RECEPTION IMAGE IS INCORRECT

## Long Distance and International Communication Operation

This depends widely on the transmission and reception capability of the other fax set and line conditions. The countermeasures for this set are shown subsequently.

1. Transmission operation
    a. The transmitting speed is set to 4800BPS (user setting: code no. 08). (Individual correspondence according to the other set is desirable.)

      **b.** The transmitting equalizer is set to 3.6 km (service mode: code no. 09). (Individual correspondence according to the other set is desirable.)

2. Reception operation
      **a.** If 80% or more of the reception is incorrect, set the receiving speed to 4800BPS (service mode: code no. 04).
      **b.** If 80% or more of the reception is incorrect, set the receiving equalizer to 3.6 km (service mode: code no. 05).

## TRANSMISSION IS POSSIBLE EXCEPT AT TIME OF ONE-TOUCH OPERATION

1. *Cause*—This problem occurs because the CNG signal may cause erroneous operation with models of other manufacturers. (The CNG signal is transmitted after dialing only at the time of one-touch transmission.)

    *Countermeasure*: Set CNG output = OFF in service mode (code no. 80), so that the CNG signal will not be output.

# CHAPTER 6

# *Standards and Protocol*

As mentioned previously international standards for facsimile transmission have been established by the CCITT, which is part of the International Telecommunications Union with offices in Geneva, Switzerland. In the United States the Telecommunications Industry Association cooperates with this body to present the U.S. position relative to any new standards or modifications that are being studied for recommendation.

Once a year the CCITT study groups meet and approve recommendations on an individual basis. T-series recommendations address "terminal equipment for telematic services" including facsimile. V-series recommendations address "data communication over the telephone network" including data terminals.

## OVERVIEW OF FACSIMILE AND RELATED MODEM STANDARDS

T.2 to T.5 recommendations cover the facsimile standards of Groups 1 to 4. Groups 1 to 3 are related to the time to transmit an A4 document, ranging from 6 min down to 1 min for Group 3. Actually such documents are generally transmitted much faster than 1 min under Group 3 standards through coding refinements. The details of the standards of Groups 1 to 3 are shown in Table 6–1. The T.4 document references modem standards V.27 ter and V.29 to define modem speed and modulation. T.5 specified Group 4 fax capabilities, which include support for 400-dpi resolution and alternate page formats. T.5 provides for several transmission media including Integrated Services Digital Network (ISDN) the public-switched telephone network,

**TABLE 6–1**  GROUPS 1 TO 3 FACSIMILE STANDARDS

| | Telephone network facsimile | | |
|---|---|---|---|
| Item | T.2 (G1) | T.3 (G2) | T.4 (G.3) |
| Connection control mode | Telephone network signal mode | | |
| Terminal control mode | T.30 tone process | | T.30 binary process |
| Facsimile signal format | Analog | | Digital |
| Modulation mode | AM or FM | AM-PM-VSB | PSK (V.27 ter) or QAM (V.29) |
| Transmission speed | — | — | 300 bps (control signal) 2400, 4800, 7200, 9600 bps (fax signal) |
| Redundancy compression process (coding mode) | Not used | | One dimension: MH mode Two dimension: MR mode (K = 2.4) |
| Resolution | Sub scan: 3.85 l/mm | | Main scan: 8 pel/mm Sub scan: 3.85, 7.71/mm |
| Line synchronization signal | White signal of maximum amplitude equivalent to 5% of line length | | EOL signal |
| One-line transmission time [ms/line] | Constant (333 ms) | Constant (166 ms) | Depends on degree of data reduction Minimum value: 0, 5, 10, 20 Can be recognized in 40 ms |

packet-switched public-data networks, and circuit-switched public-data networks. T.5 adds substantial complexity to simple T.4 fax communications over dial-up lines. Because of media incompatibilities among users, it may never become a mainstream technology.

On a public data network or ISDN, a G4 facsimile can transmit image data at a rate of 48 or 64 kbps as opposed to the highest possible rate of 9,600 bps on the public-switched telephone network. The stepped-up speed translates into a mere several seconds per A4-size document.

The use of a digital network makes it possible for various digital terminal equipment, such as teletex, to talk with each other. Mixed-mode terminals that incorporate functions of various digital equipment already have made their debuts and are expected to use the image-processing and image-printing capabilities of G4 facsimile in sophisticated ways.

The mixed mode is a facsimile-image transmission technique that transmits image data read off documents comprising both text and pictures. Text portions are transmitted using a coded character set (similar to the way text is transmitted by telex using a teletypewriter code), whereas picture portions are transmitted in the form of image data as with an ordinary facsimile.

To provide for communicating with teletex and mixed-mode terminal equipment, standardization efforts were made in the following products classes to G4 standards:

- Class 1—For terminals with facsimile capability only
- Class 2—For complex terminals with receive-only teletex and mixed-mode capabilities
- Class 3—For mixed-mode-equipped complex terminals with receive-transmit teletex and mixed-mode capabilities

The CCITT announced G4 standards in 1984 in the form of recommendations (Table 6–2).

**TABLE 6–2**  SPECIFICATIONS OF G4 FACSIMILES BY CLASS

| Class | 1 | 2 | 3 |
|---|---|---|---|
| Standard resolution (ppi) | 200 | 200 and 300 | 200 and 300 |
| Optional resolution (ppi) | 240, 300 and 400 | 240 and 400 | 240 and 400 |
| Resolution conversion capability | No | Yes | Yes |
| Capability to communicate with telex | No | For reception only | Yes |
| Mixed-mode communication capability | No | For reception only | Yes |
| Page memory for reception | No | Yes | Yes |

T.30 specifies the digital signals and procedures for Group 3. T.30 ECM (error-control mode) defines an enhancement to Group 3 fax that provides a data-link-layer, error-control protocol. V.14 specifies a method to perform character-asynchronous transmissions over synchronous interfaces. The V.XX standards for data modems reference V.14.

## LOW-SPEED MODEM STANDARDS

V.21 and Bell 103 specify 300-bps two-wire full-duplex communications using frequency-shift keying (FSK) modulation schemes. AT&T created the Bell 103 specification during the days of telephone-system monopoly in the United States. The standards differ slightly, but virtually all of today's modems support both standards. Asynchronous modems based on these standards dominate applications worldwide for 300-bps dial-up modems—such as PC modems.

V.22 and Bell 212A specify 1200-bps two-wire full-duplex communications using quadrature-phase-shift keying (QPSK) modulation schemes at 600 Bd. The standards differ slightly, but virtually all of today's modems support both standards. Asynchronous modems based on these standards dominate applications worldwide for 1200-bps dial-up modems.

V.22 bis specifies 2300-bps two-wire full-duplex communications using a QAM quadrature amplitude modulation (QAM) scheme at 600 Bd. Asynchronous modems based on these standards dominate applications worldwide for 2400-bps dial-up modems.

V.23 specifies an asymmetrical communication scheme that implements 1200-bps data transmission in one direction and 75-bps data transmission in a back channel. The FSK-based standard is popular in Europe for applications that require high data rates in only one direction, such as Teletext.

V.24 specifies a serial interface much like RS-232C. V.25 and V.25 bis specify interface protocols for modems similar to the command set Hayes Microcomputer Products employs in its modems.

V.26, V.26 bis, and V.26 ter specify half- and full-duplex leased-line communications at 1200 and 2400 bps. The specifications employ QPSK modulation at 1200 Bd. V.26 ter was the first modem standard to specify echo cancellation.

## HIGH-SPEED MODEM STANDARDS

V.27, V.27 bis, and V.27 ter specify 4800-bps communications requiring two wires for half-duplex applications and four wires for full-duplex applications. The standards specify QAM modulation at 1600 baud. Group 3 fax standard T.4 references V.27 ter as the base requirement for 2-wire half-duplex fax communications.

V.29 specifies 9600-bps communication requiring two wires for half-duplex applications and four wires for full-duplex applications. The standard specifies QAM modulation at 2400 Bd. Group 3 fax standard T.4 references V.29 as an option for fax transmissions faster than 4800-bps V.27 ter. In reality, a high percentage of fax transmissions today rely on V.29, although virtually all machines can fall back to V.27 ter.

V.32 specifies two-wire full-duplex 9600-bps communications using QAM modulation at 2400 Bd and echo cancellation. V.32-based modems offer an upgrade path from V.22 bis for asynchronous dial-up applications. Recently V.32 automode was published as an annex to V.32. The annex defines an automatic fall-back capability to V.22 bis on noisy lines that cannot support 9600-bps communications.

V.33 specifies four-wire full-duplex and two-wire half-duplex communications at 14,400 bps. Most likely, the Group 3 fax study group will modify T.4 to include V.33 14,400-bps communications as an option. Likewise, manufacturers of full-duplex data modems will probably add echo cancellation and take advantage of this specification. V.33 employs TCM (trellis-coded modulation) at 2400 Bd.

## Communications Enhancements

V.42 specifies error-correction techniques that can be implemented in modems independently of transmission speed and modulation scheme. The recommendation includes LAPM and Microcom Networking Protocol (MNP) 2 to 4 methods of error correction.

V.42 bis and MNP 5 specify data compression algorithms that can be implemented in modems independently of transmission speed and modulation scheme. MNP 5 has not been recognized by standards organizations but has become a de facto standard for data compression that offers a 2.1 compression ratio. V.42 bis offers a 4.1 compression ratio and products that implement the standard are starting to emerge.

V.54 specifies loop back and other diagnostic functions for modems.

## FACSIMILE PROTOCOL

The procedures by which two facsimile machines communicate with each other is referred to as protocol or as facsimile call time series. It is divided into five phases as shown in Figure 6–1. These phases may be described as follows:

*Phase A*—Call setting, which can be manual or automatic.

*Phase B*—Premessage procedure, which is a sequence for confirming the status of terminal, transmission routing, and so on, and for terminal control. It implements terminal preparation status, determines and displays terminal constants, confirms synchronization status, and so on, and prepares for the transmission of facsimile messages.

*Phase C*—Procedure for the transmission of facsimile messages.

*Phase D*—Postmessage procedure for confirming that the message is completed and received. In the case of continuous transmission, return is made repeatedly to phase B or phase C.

*Phase E*—Procedure for call retrieval (i.e., circuit disconnection).

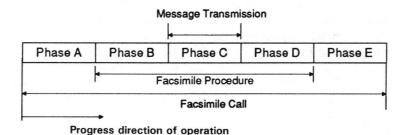

**Figure 6–1** Fax Call-Time Series

As shown in Figure 6–2 transmission time may also be divided into control time, image transmission time, and hold time. Control time is at the start of transmission when functions at the sending and receiving sides are confirmed, transmission mode is established, and transmission and reception are synchronized. Image transmission time is that required for the transmission of the contents of the document or documents (image data). Hold time is that required after the document contents have been sent to confirm that they were received.

**Figure 6–2** Transmission Time

## Phases A and B

Phase A includes call progress tone detection, DTMF dialing, transmission of the calling tone, and reception of the called station identification tone (Figure 6–3). Call progress tones are audible tones sent from switching systems to calling parties to show the status of calls such as dial tone, ring-back tone, and busy tone. They are usually distinguished by their duty cycles instead of their frequencies. After the ring-back tone is detected, the calling station transmits the calling tone (CNG, 1100 Hz) for 0.5 s to declare itself as a facsimile machine. Then it attempts to receive the called station identification tone (CED, 2100 Hz) for 3 s. This sequence will repeat until CED is detected or time has elapsed.

The called station goes off hook after ringing is detected. It will transmit CED to the calling station for a sufficiently long period. Then it will go into phase B by sending the DIS to the calling station. After the CED is detected, the calling station

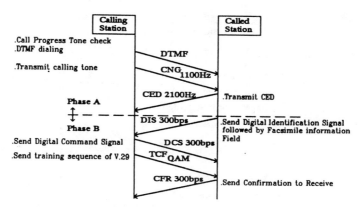

**Figure 6–3** Phases A and B of Call-Time Series

prepares to receive the DIS signal in 300 bps FSK (2400 bps, V.27 ter). The receiving side (the called station) reveals its available facsimile functions or modes to the calling station by means of the DIS command. The transmitting side replies with its selection to the receiving side with the DCS command. Data signals are added to the DIS and DCS signals as shown in Tables 6-3 and 6-4. After the DCS transmission, the calling station will send a training sequence followed by TCF (training check). This sequence is a continuous scrambled "0" for 1.5 s to make sure that the transmission channel can be established at the selected data signaling rate. This training sequence is always required before message transmission to allow circuitry at the receiving side to stabilize. Then confirmation to receive is sent back at 300 bps from the receiving side.

**TABLE 6-3** DIGITAL IDENTIFICATION SIGNAL WITH ADDED DATA SIGNALS

| (Example) | | The added data signals are as follows: | | |
|---|---|---|---|---|
| | Bit no. | Function | Standard setting DIS | Remarks |
| | 1 ~ 8 | Not used (fixed) | 0 | |
| | 9 | Transmission function (T4) | 0 | |
| | 1 0 | Reception function (T4) | 1 | |
| | 1 1 | Modulation mode | × | 11  12 |
| | | | | 0  1  4800 ~ 2400b/s |
| | 1 2 | Data speed | 1 | 1  1  9600 ~ 2400b/s |
| | 13 ~ 14 | Not used (fixed) | 0 | |
| | 1 5 | Sub scan line density 7.7 L/mm | 1 | 0: 3.85 L/mm 1: 3.85, 7.7 L/mm |
| | 1 6 | Two-dimensional coding function | 0 | 0: MH 1: MH, MR |
| | 1 7 | Max. paper width: B4 | 0 | |
| | 1 8 | Max. paper width: A3 | 0 | |
| | 1 9 | Max. paper length: B4 | 0 | |
| | 2 0 | Paper length unlimited | 1 | |
| | 2 1 | 1 Line min. scan time | × | 21  22  23 |
| | 2 2 | | × | 0  1  1  10 ms |
| | | | | 1  1  0  20 ms |
| | 2 3 | | × | 1  0  1  40 ms |
| | 2 4 | Extension field | 1 | |
| | 25 ~ 32 | Not used (fixed) | 0 | |

**TABLE 6-4** DIGITAL COMMAND SIGNAL WITH ADDED DATA SIGNALS

| (Example) | | | The added data signals are as follows: | |
| --- | --- | --- | --- | --- |
| | Bit no. | Function | Standard setting DIS | Remarks |
| | 1 ~ 8 | Not used (fixed) | 0 | |
| | 9 | | 0 | |
| | 1 0 | Reception command (T4) | 1 | |
| | 1 1 | Modulation mode | × | 11  12 |
| | 1 2 | Data speed | × | 0   0   2400b/s  V.27/ter |
| | | | | 0   1   4800b/s  V.27/ter |
| | | | | 1   0   9600b/s  V.29 |
| | | | | 1   1   7200b/s  V.29 |
| | 13 ~ 14 | Not used (fixed) | 0 | |
| | 1 5 | Sub-scan line density 7.7 L/mm | × | 1: 7.7 L/mm 0: 3.85 L/mm |
| | 1 6 | Two-dimensional coding function | 0 | |
| | 1 7 | Max. paper width: B4 | 0 | |
| | 1 8 | Max. paper width: A3 | 0 | |
| | 1 9 | Max. paper length: B4 | 0 | |
| | 2 0 | Paper length unlimited | × | Reception unlimited 1 |
| | 2 1 | 1 line min. scan time | 0 | 22   23 |
| | 2 2 | | × | 0   0   20 ms |
| | | | | 0   1   40 ms |
| | 2 3 | | × | 1   0   10 ms |
| | 2 4 | Extension field | 1 | |
| | 25 ~ 32 | Not used (fixed) | 0 | |

## Phase C

Four different data-signaling rates are available in a Group 3 facsimile machine. They are 2400 bps/V.27 ter, 4800 bps/V.27 ter, 7200 bps/V.29, and 9600 bps/V.29. The image data can be sent at any one of these four rates if the facsimile machines can handle them. The called station reveals its available data transmission speeds to the calling station by means of the DIS command. The transmitting side chooses the data-signaling speed after receiving the DIS command.

The modulation format of the G3 mode is shown in Table 6–1. At the data rates of 2400 bps and 4800 bps, phase modulation is used as shown in Figure 6–4. At 7200 bps and 9600 bps, QAM is used as shown in Figure 6–5. The figures shown are examples of 8-pt phase modulation and 16-pt QAM, respectively.

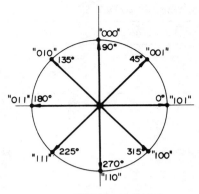

(8 pt PhM : 8 pt = 3 bits)

**Figure 6-4**   Example of 8-pt Phase Modulation

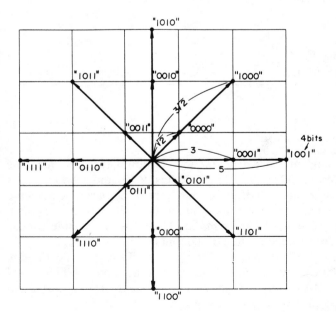

(16pt QAM : 16pt = 4 bits)

**Figure 6-5**   Example of 16-pt Quadrature Amplitude Modulation

**TABLE 6-5** TRAINING AND IMAGE SIGNALS FOLLOWING TRANSMISSION
AND RECEPTION PROCEDURES

| Signal | Identification signal format | Function |
|---|---|---|
| Training 1 | — | Fixed pattern is transmitted to receiving side at speed (2400 to 9600 bps) designated by DCS, and the receiving side optimizes the automatic equalizer, etc., according to this signal. |
| TCF (Training check) | — | Sends 0 continuously for 1.5 s at the same speed as the training signal. |
| CFR (Confirmation to receive) | X0100001 | Notifies sending side that TCF has been properly received. If TCF is not properly received, FTT (failure to train) X0100010 is relayed to sender. Sender then reduces transmission speed by one stage and initiates training once again. |
| Training 2 | — | Used for reconfirmation of receiving side the same as training 1. |
| Image signal | Refer to Phase C | — |
| RTC (Return to control) | — | Sends 12 bit (0 . . . 01 × 6 times to receiver at same speed as image signal and notifies of completion of transmission of first sheet. |
| EOP (End of procedure) | X1110100 | End of one communication. |
| MCF (Message confirmation) | X0110001 | End of one page received. |
| DCN (Disconnect) | X1011111 | Phase E start. |
| MPS (Multipage signal) | X1110010 | Completion of transmission of one page. If ther are still more documents to be sent, they are output instead of EOP. After MCF reception, sender transmits image signal of seconds sheet. |
| PRI-EOP (Procedure interrupt— EOP) | X1111100 | If there is an operator call from the sender, it is output after RTC. |
| PIP (Procedural interrupt positive) | X0110101 | Output in the case of operator call from receiver. |

## Phase D and E

Phase D is the procedure for confirming that the message is completed and received. In the case of continuous transmission, return is made repeatedly phase B or phase C for transmission. Phase E is the procedure for terminating the calls by circuit disconnection.

The functions of phases C to E are covered in detail in Table 6-5.

# CHAPTER 7

# *High-End Plain Paper Machine*

The interest in machines capable of using plain paper rather than thermal paper is high. Most machines available thus far have incorporated laser printers. With such laser printers the received copies are provided on cut sheets of paper rather than paper issuing from a roll as in the case of thermal printers. The cut sheets are fed from cassettes, which can provide different sizes of paper sheets.

The operational details of a large machine (Figure 7–1), such as Ricoh's Rapicom 830D, are described in some detail in U.S. patent no. 4,933,771, issued to the Ricoh Corporation on June 12, 1990. The description as provided in this patent follows.

## GENERAL APPROACH

A facsimile machine generally includes an image sensor for optically reading an original image to be transmitted, a recording unit for recording a received image on a recording medium, and a communication unit for transmitting and receiving an image to and from another facsimile machine at a remote location. As the facsimile machine is disseminated widely, there is a growing demand for an even faster facsimile machine. To make a high-speed facsimile machine, it is necessary to provide not only a high-speed communication unit but also a high-speed image sensor and recorder.

Most facsimile machines currently in use employ a thermal printhead as a recording unit. Typically, the thermal printhead includes a plurality of heat-producing

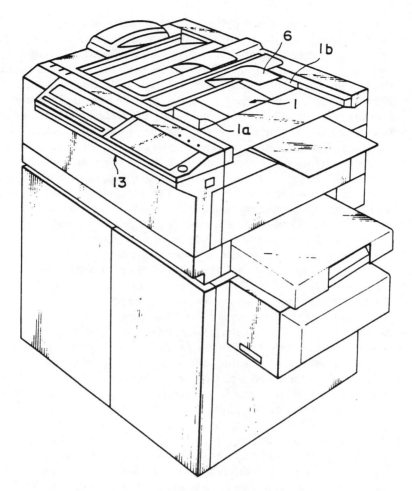

**Figure 7-1** High-End Fax Machine with Laser Printer

elements, such as electrical resistors, which are arranged in a spaced-apart relation-ship at a predetermined pitch along a straight line extending in a direction transverse to the direction of advancement of a recording medium, which is normally a web of heat-sensitive paper stored in the form of a roll. In such a thermal printer–type recording unit, the heat-sensitive paper in the form of a roll is unwound and trans-ported in contact with the thermal printhead, to which an image signal to be re-corded is supplied, and thus dark "burn" points are selectively formed on the heat-sensitive paper to form a printed image thereon.

In such a thermal printer-type recording unit, the heat-sensitive paper is un-rolled, an image is printed on the paper, and the paper is cut to a desired size. The size is usually determined by the size of an original image received from a transmitter. In such a system, when a plurality of original documents different in size are received, cut sheets of printer paper are produced different in size correspondingly. It is often desired, however, that received images are all printed on the same size of cut sheets of paper even if the original documents have a variety of sizes. For this purpose, it has been proposed to provide a facsimile machine having a page-printing function. The most typical example is a facsimile machine including a laser printer as its recording unit. In this case, laser beam modulated by an image signal is deflected by a rotating polygon mirror and the deflected laser beam is scanned across a photosensitive member, thereby forming an electrostatic latent image thereon. Then, the latent image is developed by application of a developer, and thus the developed image is then transferred to a transfer medium. In this case, because an electrophotographic process is used in printing a received image on a recording medium, image information is recorded on a page-by-page basis. In this respect, the laser printer falls into the category of a page printer.

The page printer is fast in operation and allows the use of plain paper as a recording medium, and thus the incorporation of a page printer into a facsimile machine as its recording unit presents an opportunity to provide a high-speed facsimile machine. Other than a laser printer, the page printer also includes an electrostatic printer that uses a multistylus head, to which an image signal is applied, for directly forming an electrostatic latent image on an imaging member, such as photosensitive or dielectric member. A further example of the page printer is a liquid crystal shutter printer that includes an array of liquid crystal shutters disposed between a light source and a photosensitive member, whereby the liquid crystal shutters are selectively operated in accordance with an image signal to form an electrostatic latent image on the photosensitive member.

A facsimile machine having a page printer is preferably provided with two or more cassettes for providing cut sheets of paper different in size. In such a facsimile machine, when an original image out of a predetermined size is received, it is recorded on two or more sheets of paper as divided. For example, however, when a facsimile machine receiving an original image having the A size width and a length beyond the predetermined size is provided with a pair of paper cassettes for B4 and A4 sizes, the larger B4 size paper is first selected so as to minimize the number of recording cycles. In this case, however, if the last remaining portion of the original image is shorter in length than the A4 size, then the A4 size paper will be used to print this portion. This is inconvenient because the same original image is printed on two or more sheets of recording paper different in size (i.e., only the last sheet being different from the other sheets). In addition, if a facsimile machine is provided with a pair of cassettes containing B4- and A4-size cut sheets of recording paper, respectively, and a plurality of original images all in A5 size are being received, each of the A5-size original images is printed on a single cut sheet of B4- or A4-size paper, more than half of which is left unused.

The illustrated facsimile machine generally includes three sections: an image reading section including a image scanner, a recording section including a laser printer, and a control system for controlling the overall operation of the facsimile machine. A control panel is provided at the front side thereby allowing an operator to provide desired instructions to the present facsimile machine. In the illustrated facsimile machine, because use is made of the laser printer, image can be output at high speed using an electrophotographic process.

## READING SECTION

As shown in Figure 7-2, the illustrated facsimile machine includes an original holder (1) for placing thereon a plurality of original documents to be optically read in the form of a stack. The original documents thus stacked on the original holder (1) are fed one by one from the bottommost one by means of a pickup roller 2, which is located at the supply end of the original holder 1. A separating roller (3) is placed

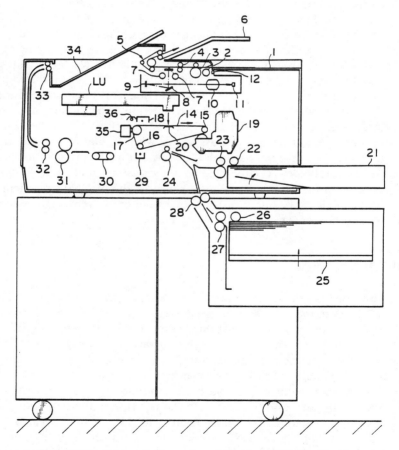

**Figure 7-2** Schematic Illustration of Interior of This Fax Machine

in downstream of the pickup roller 2 with respect to the direction of advancement of the original document, so that it is ensured that only one, or bottommost one, of the stacked original documents is fed into an original document transporting path defined in a housing of the facsimile machine. A transporting roller (4) is placed downstream of the separating roller (3) for transporting the original document separated from the stack by the separating roller (3) through an optical reading section defined at a portion of the original document transporting path. After moving past the reading section, the original document enters an inverting and discharging section (5) so the original document is discharged onto a tray (6) as inverted, or directed upward.

At the reading section defined between the transporting roller (4) and the inverting and discharging section (5), a light source including a pair of lamps (7) is located so that the light emitted from the lamps illuminates the surface of the original document, and the reflected light from the original document is reflected by a pair of reflecting mirrors (8 and 9) and focused onto a line image sensor (11) through a lens (10). Thus, as the original document moves past the image reading section, the image of the original document is optically read line by line.

It is to be noted that, as best shown in Figure 7–1, a pair of adjustable side guides (1a and 1b) is provided at the original holder (1). These side guides are shiftable sideways and thus may be set in position depending on the width of an original document to be read. These side guides (1a and 1b) help to keep the original documents set in position in the widthwise direction when they are stacked on the original holder (1). As shown in Figure 7–2, there is also provided an original document sensor (12) that is operatively associated with the pair of side guides (1a and 1b) for detecting size, or more particularly the width of the original documents stacked on the original holder (1). It should be noted that a signal from the original document sensor (12) indicates not only the width of the original documents placed on the original holder (1), but also the fact whether or not any original document is on the original holder (1).

## RECORDING SECTION

Now, the recording section including a laser printer of the present facsimile machine will be described. As shown in Figure 7–2, the facsimile machine includes a laser unit LU from which a laser beam modulated by an image signal to be recorded is output and directed onto an imaging surface of an imaging member (14), such as a photosensitive member, in the form of an endless belt. In the illustrated embodiment, the imaging belt (14) is extended around three rollers (15 to 17), at least one of which may be driven to rotate, for example, by means of a driver motor, so that the imaging belt (14) may be driven to travel in a direction indicated by the arrow at constant speed. Around the imaging belt (14) are disposed a corona charging unit (18), a developing unit (19), a corona image transfer unit (29), and a cleaning unit (35) in the order mentioned in the traveling direction of the imaging belt (14).

In operation, as the imaging belt (14) is driven to travel at constant speed in the direction indicated by the arrow, the outer or imaging surface becomes uniformly charged to a selected polarity by the corona charging unit (18). The laser beam modulated by an image signal to be recorded is then applied to the imaging belt (14) thus charged uniformly, so that the charge is selectively dissipated in accordance with a light pattern defined by the laser beam, thereby forming an electrostatic latent image on the imaging belt. As the imaging belt further travels, the latent image is developed by the developing unit (19), which typically uses colored pigment, such as toner, and thus there is formed a developed toner image on the imaging belt. It is to be noted that, in the illustrated embodiment, a back plate (20) is provided at an exposure station in contact with the back or inside surface of the imaging belt (14) so as to keep the imaging belt flat as much as possible at least locally at the image exposure station.

Conversely, the present facsimile machine includes a pair of first and second feeding units for feeding a cut sheet of recording medium having a first size and a cut sheet of recording medium having a second size, respectively. In the illustrated embodiment, a cassette (21) is detachably mounted in the facsimile machine, and it stores therein a quantity of cut sheets of recording medium, typically plain paper, having a first predetermined size. The cassette is set in position as partly fitted into the facsimile machine with its supply end located at an entrance to a first recording medium transporting path defined in the facsimile machine leading to the image transfer unit (29). A pickup roller (22) is provided in the facsimile machine so as to be brought into contact with the topmost sheet of the stack of cut sheets of recording medium stored in the cassette (21) when it is set in position. Also provided downstream of the pickup roller is a separating roller (23) for ensuring that only one cut sheet of recording paper is fed into the first recording medium transporting path. Also provided in the present facsimile machine is a registration roller (24), which is located in the first recording medium transporting path and which is intermittently driven to rotate to feed a cut sheet of recording paper in association with the traveling condition of the imaging belt (14). Although not shown specifically in Figure 7–2, it should be understood that a size sensor for detecting the presence and absence, or the size of the cut sheets of recording medium stored in the cassette (21) is provided in the present facsimile machine.

A feeding tray (25) is also provided in the facsimile machine to define a high-volume recording medium supply unit, and the feeding tray is provided to be movable vertically. A great quantity of cut sheets of recording medium having a second predetermined size may be placed on the feeding tray in the form of a stack. It is to be noted that a second recording medium transporting path is defined in the facsimile machine leading from a supply end of the high-volume recording medium supply unit to the image transfer unit (29) through the registration roller (24). Thus, the path between the registration roller and the image transfer unit is shared by the first and second recording medium transporting paths. A pickup roller (26) is disposed at the supply end of the large volume recording medium supply unit, and it is intermittently driven to rotate to feed the topmost sheet of the recording medium stacked on the tray (25). A separating roller (27) is disposed downstream of the pickup roller (26) for ensuring that only one cut sheet of recording medium is fed into the second recording medium transporting path. Also provided in the second recording medium transporting path is an intermediate transporting roller (28). Although not shown specifically in Figure 7-2, it should be understood that a size sensor for detecting the presence and absence, or the size of cut sheets of recording medium stored as stacked on the tray (25) is provided in the present facsimile machine.

With the structure described previously, the pickup rollers (22) and (26) are selectively driven to rotate to supply a cut sheet of recording medium, and, the cut sheet of recording medium thus supplied is transported until its leading edge comes into abutment against the registration roller (24), which normally remains stationary. In association with the traveling motion of the imaging belt (14), the registration roller (24) is driven to rotate so that the cut sheet of recording medium is brought into contact with the imaging belt and moved past the image transfer unit (29), whereby the developed toner image on the imaging belt is transferred to the cut sheet of recording paper. The timing of driving the registration roller in association with the movement of the imaging belt is such that the leading edge of the cut sheet of recording medium transported by the registration roller is aligned with the leading edge of the developer toner image formed on the imaging belt.

After image transfer, the cut sheet of recording medium is separated from the imaging belt (14) and then transported to an image fixing unit (31) by a transporting belt (30). It should be noted that the curvature set by the imaging belt around the roller (16) is so set that the cut sheet of recording medium may be separated from the imaging belt because of its stiffness, which tends to keep the cut sheet of recording medium moving straight toward the transporting belt while the imaging belt is suddenly directed upward toward the roller (17). While the cut sheet of recording medium moves through the image fixing unit (31), the transferred toner image becomes permanently fixed to the cut sheet of recording medium. The completed cut sheet of recording medium is then discharged onto a stacker (34) by means of discharging roller (32 and 33).

Conversely, any remaining toner on the imaging belt (14) after image transfer is removed by the cleaning unit (35) and then collected into a storage tank (not shown). The thus collected toner may be recycled to the developing unit (19) for reuse, if desired. An erasure lamp (36) is also disposed between the cleaning unit (35) and the charging unit (18) for removing any residual charge from the imaging belt (14) by uniform irradiation of light to the imaging belt.

## CONTROL SECTION

Referring now to Figure 7-3, there is shown in block form a control system for controlling the overall operation of the present facsimile machine. As shown, the control system includes a CPU (40), a read-only memory (ROM) (41) for storing a

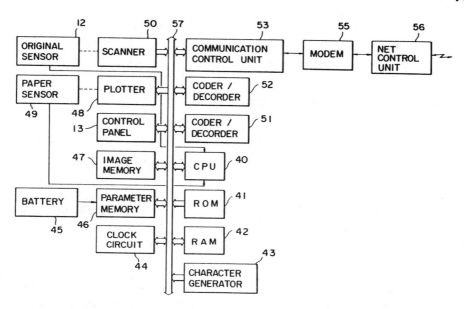

**Figure 7-3**  Block Diagram of Control System of This Fax Machine

predetermined program, and a RAM (42) for storing temporary data and providing a work area. A character generator (43) is also provided in the control system for generating various character and symbol patterns to be displayed at a display section of the control panel (13). The control system further includes a clock circuit (44) for outputting a clock data signal and a parameter memory (46), to which a battery (45) is connected, for storing various data—for example, input from keys provided at the control panel (13). Also provided in the control system is an image memory (47), which temporarily stores noncompressed image data to be supplied to a plotter (48) for printing on a cut sheet of recording medium and compressed image data during transmitting or receiving mode of operation. As shown in Figure 7-4; the image memory (47) is so structured that it includes a predetermined record data area for storing noncompressed data to be recorded corresponding to the maximum size (for example, B4 size) of an image that can be recorded by the plotter (48) and a predetermined compressed data area for storing compressed image data that is to be transmitted to or has been received from another facsimile machine. In one example, the compressed data area has a capacity to store compressed image data of sixty sheets of original documents.

As shown in Figure 7-3, the control system further includes a paper sensor (49) that is partly provided in the cassette (21) and partly provided on the tray (25) for supplying detection signals to the CPU (40). Besides, the original document sensor (12) provided in the original holder (1) for detecting the size of an original document to be read also sends a detection signal to the CPU (40). A pair of coder-

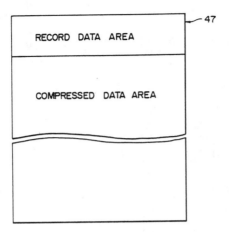

**Figure 7–4** Image Memory Provided in Control System

decoder units (51 and 52) is a₁ₛo provided in the present control system, and each of them provides a converting function between a noncompressed (not encoded or decoded) image data and a compressed (encoded) image data. It is to be noted that each of the coder-decoder units (51 and 52) has a plurality of coding and decoding modes of operation. When an original document is optically read by the scanner (50), there is obtained an image data that is not compressed. The image data thus obtained is encoded according to a predetermined encoding method so that the image data becomes compressed. The image data is transmitted to another facsimile machine in a compressed format. Thus, an image signal received from another facsimile machine is typically compressed or encoded, and thus the received image data is decoded or uncompressed to recover the original image data before being supplied to the plotter (48).

Also provided in the present control system is a communication control unit (53) that takes care of communication of image information with another facsimile machine according to a predetermined facsimile transmission control procedures. The communication control unit (53) is connected to a net control unit (56) through a modem (55) that modulates and demodulates digital data so as to allow to the use of an analog transmission network, such as the public telephone network as a transmission line. The net control unit (56) is provided to allow the present facsimile machine to be connected to the public telephone network. It is to be noted that the net control unit is equipped with an automatic calling and answering function. A bus line (57) is provided to interconnect the previously described elements as shown in Figure 7–3.

In operation, during transmission (storing) mode, an image signal produced from the scanner (50) by optically reading an original document is transferred to the coder-decoder unit (51 or 52) under the control of CPU (40), where the image signal is encoded or compressed. Then, the compressed image data is stored into the compressed data area of the image memory (47) as shown in Figure 7–4. Then, on connection with a destination facsimile machine in accordance with a predetermined procedure, the compressed image data stored in the image memory (47) is transmitted to the destination facsimile machine. In this case, if the encoding method set by the pretransmission procedure differs from the encoding method employed at the time of storing data into the image memory (47), the compressed image data stored in the image memory is again decoded to the original noncompressed image data by the coder-decoder unit (51) and thus the decoded image data is once again encoded by the coder-decoder (52) in accordance with the encoding method set by the pretransmission procedure. The reencoded image data is then transmitted to the destination facsimile machine.

In transmitting compressed image data, transmission identification information is added at the leading edge of a group of data corresponding to a single sheet of original document. In addition, if it is set by an operator, a predetermined statement is added.

Conversely, during receiving mode of operation, all of the received (compressed) image data is at once stored into the compressed data area of the image memory (47). Then, the compressed image data is transferred to the coder-decoder (51 to 52), where the compressed data is decoded to the original uncompressed data in sequence, and the uncompressed data is then stored into the record data area of the image memory (47). As soon as uncompressed image data of the amount corresponding to a single cut sheet of recording medium currently selected for use has been stored into the image memory (47), the uncompressed image data is transferred to the plotter (48) for use in recording on a cut sheet of recording medium. This process is repeated until the receiving mode of operation is completed.

In the case in which a confidential transmission mode has been set, all of the compressed image data as received is stored into the image memory (47). Moreover, if the recording medium runs out in the midst of receiving mode of operation, the image data received thereafter is stored into the image memory (47) as being compressed (proxy transmission). The image data thus stored in the image memory (47) is set in a condition to be transferred to the plotter (48) for recording only when a correct password has been input in the case of the confidential transmission mode or cut sheets of recording medium have been replenished in the case of the proxy transmission mode. Under this condition, when a start key (not shown) provided in the control panel (13) is depressed, the recording operation by the plotter (48) is initiated, so that the image stored in the image memory (47) is first restored to the original uncompressed image data by the coder-decoder (51 or 52) while storing the restored original image data into the record data area of the image memory (47). Each time when the amount of image data stored into the record data area of the image memory (47) reaches a predetermined amount, typically corresponding to the amount of a single page, the image data is transferred from the image memory (47) to the plotter (48).

## DIFFERENT SIZES OF PAPER

Figure 7–5 shows several examples of how cut sheets of recording medium different in size are oriented when set in position. It is to be noted that, in the illustrated case, the maximum size of cut sheets of recording medium that may be set in the plotter (48) is B4. The direction of transportation is indicated by the arrow. As shown, the B4-size and A4-size sheets are transported with their longitudinal directions in parallel with the transporting direction. This mode of transportation may be called "longitudinal" transportation. Conversely, the B5-size and A5-size sheets are transported with their longitudinal directions oriented perpendicular to the transporting direction, and this mode of transportation may be called "transverse" transportation. Because the cut sheets of recording medium are set with particular orientations as indicated in Figure 7–5, original documents of corresponding sizes must be set on the original holder (1) in a corresponding manner. That is, an original document must be transported in a manner having the corresponding size shown in Figure 7–5.

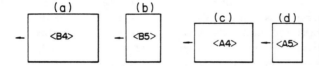

**Figure 7–5**  Several Examples of How Cut Sheets of Recorded Matter Different in Size Are Oriented When Set in Position

Because the B4-size sheet is transported in the longitudinal mode and the B5-size sheet is transported in the transverse mode, there is no difference in the recording width when recording is to be carried out by the plotter (48) using the either the B4-size sheet or the B5-size sheet. Thus, the recording mode using either the B4-size or B5-size sheet has a B-size recording width. Similarly, the recording mode using either the A4-size or A5-size sheet has an A-size recording width. Conversely, the management of data storage in the record data area of the image memory (47) is carried out by the number of lines irrespective of the width of an image.

Typically, in the pretransmission procedure of a facsimile communication, a transmitter normally sends width information of an original document, such as A or B sizes.

## HANDLING OF LONG DOCUMENTS

A process for receiving and recording image data of a relatively long original document in accordance with one embodiment of the present invention is now described with particular reference to Figures 7–3 and 7–6. If the plotter (48) of the present facsimile machine is provided with cut sheets of recording paper whose widths match the width information of original document received during the pretransmission procedure (101), then the receiving mode of operation is initiated. In the first

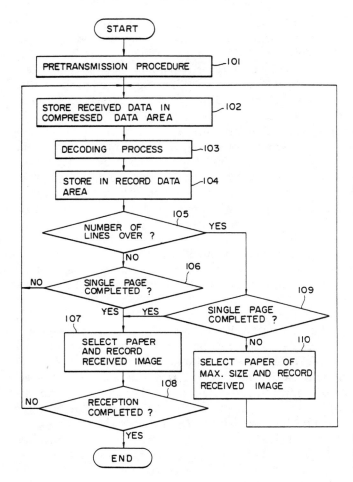

**Figure 7-6** Example of Sequence of Steps Implemented during Receiving Mode

place, under the control of CPU (40), the received image data is at once stored in the compressed data area of the image memory (47) at step 102, and the stored image data is supplied to the coder-decoder (51 or 52) line by line to have it restored to the original image data at step 103. The restored original image data is then sequentially stored into the record data area of the image memory (47) at step 104. In this case, each time when a single line of original image data has been stored, it is checked whether or not the number of lines of the original image data stored exceeds the maximum number of lines of the largest one among those cut sheets that are set in position and have enough width for recording the received image at step 105. If the result at step 105 is negative, then it is determined whether or not image data has been stored into the record data area of the image memory (47) of the amount corresponding to that of a single page at step 106. If the result is negative, then it proceeds back to the step 102.

Conversely, if the result of determination at step 106 is affirmative, then an appropriate cut sheet of recording medium is selected for use depending on the width information of received image and the number of lines of the image data stored in the record data area of the image memory (47), and then the image data stored in the record data area of the image memory (47) is transferred to the plotter (48) in sequence, thereby recording the received image on the selected cut sheet of recording medium at step 107. This process is repeated until the completion of the receiving mode of operation is detected at step 108.

Conversely, if the result of determination at step 105 is affirmative and yet the processing of a single page has not yet been completed (i.e., the result of determination at step 109 is negative, because this indicates the fact that the number of lines of the image data thus processed is more than the number of lines for the largest sized cut sheet among those cut sheets having enough width for recording the received image), the largest cut sheet of recording medium among those currently set in the plotter (48) is selected at this time. Then, the image data now stored in the record data area of the image memory (47) is sequentially transferred to the plotter (48) to effect printing on the selected cut sheet of recording medium at step 110. At the same time, it proceeds back to step 102 to continue the processing of the succeeding received image data.

In this case, however, until the recording of the image data of this relatively long page or sheet of original document has been completed, step 107 is so set that the plotter (48) remains to select the largest cut sheet of recording paper. In other words, for example, supposing that the plotter (48) is provided with B5-size cut sheets of recording medium and A4-size cut sheets of recording medium, if the received image data has a B-size width, then the B5-size cut sheets of recording medium are selected for use; if the received image data has an A-size width, then the A4-size cut sheets of recording medium are selected for use. It is also so structured that, in the case in which both of B4- and A4-size cut sheets of recording medium are set in the plotter (48), the larger B4-size cut sheets of recording medium are selected irrespective of the width of the received image data. Of importance, once a particular size of cut sheets of recording paper has been selected, its selection remains unchanged until recording of all of the image of the single original document has been completed. As a result, it is ensured that the image of a relatively long original document is recorded on a plurality of cut sheets of recording material of the same size as divided at all times.

As the image data stored in the record data area of the image memory (47) is sequentially transferred to the plotter (48) at step 110, there is produced an increasing empty region in the record data area; however, it may be so structured that the succeeding image data is supplied to the empty region thus created. In this case, it is necessary to monitor the boundary between the preceding and succeeding data in the record data area. Conversely, if the result of determination at step 109 is affirmative, then it proceeds to step 107, whereby the image data is recorded as a single page.

In this manner, in accordance with the present invention, if the image data of a long original document has been received, it is recorded on a plurality of cut sheets of recording medium as divided in sequence. The image may be properly received and recorded however long the original document may be. In this case, in accordance with the present invention, it is so structured that the size of cut sheets of recording medium remains unchanged until recording of all of the image data of the same long original document has been completed. Even if the image data of the same original document is recorded on two or more cut sheets of recording paper, it is convenient when the recorded cut sheets are combined one after another because the recorded cut sheets are all of the same size.

Suppose that cut sheets of recording medium having the B5 size are stored in the cassette twenty-one and cut sheets of recording medium having the B4 size are stored as stacked on the tray (25). In this case, both of the cut sheets have the same width with respect to the transporting direction as indicated in Figure 7–5 (a and b). When the image data of a long original document has been received, if the last remaining image data is of the amount less than that of a B5-size cut sheet of recording medium, then it may be recorded on a cut sheet of recording medium of B5 size, if desired, even if the preceding cut sheets of recording medium were all B4 size. Similarly, if the two or more cut sheets of recording medium set in the facsimile machine all have the same A-size width, such as A4 and A5, then the remaining image data may be recorded on a cut sheet of A5 size even if the preceding image data has been recorded on one or more cut sheets of A4 size. Therefore, as long as the width remains unchanged, use may be made of differently sized cut sheets of recording medium when recording image data of a relatively long original document as divided.

Furthermore, it is preferably so structured that a division mark (*) is added at the bottom of the cut sheet of recording medium if there is any succeeding cut sheet of recording medium for recording the remaining image data as divided. In addition, the page number may be inserted at a predetermined location for the second and following pages when recording the image data of a long original document as divided, thereby allowing one to understand how the two or more cut sheets of recording medium should be combined side by side to redefine the original image as a unit.

Referring now to Figure 7–7, there is schematically shown in block form a facsimile machine constructed in accordance with another embodiment of the pres-

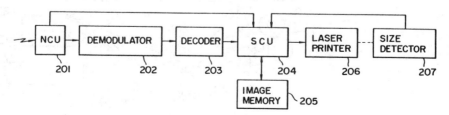

**Figure 7–7**  Overall Block Diagram of This Fax Machine in Receiving Mode

ent invention. As shown, the facsimile machine of this embodiment includes a net control unit (201) that has a function of connecting the present facsimile machine to a transmission line, such as the public telephone network as in the present embodiment. The image data received through the transmission line is modulated and encoded, and then it is demodulated by a demodulator (202) and then decoded by a decoder (203), thereby recovering an original image data without compression. The recovered image data is then supplied to a system control unit (204), which causes the received image data to be temporarily stored in an image memory (205). A laser printer (206) is connected to the system control unit (204). On receipt of a command from the system control unit, the laser printer reads out the image data stored in the image memory and has it recorded on a cut sheet of recording medium. The laser printer is provided with a size detector (207) for detecting the size of cut sheets of recording medium set in the laser printer. The size detection signal generated by the size detector is supplied to the system control unit. In the present embodiment, the system control unit is equipped with a function of controlling the processing of received image data and the recording of the received image data using the laser printer in an asynchronous manner.

## LASER PRINTER OPERATION

Figure 7–8 schematically shows in detail the structure of the laser printer (206) provided in the facsimile machine shown in Figure 7–7. As shown in Figure 7–8, a laser light beam emitted from a beam source (not shown), such as a laser diode, as modulated by an image signal is deflected by a polygon mirror (211), which is driven to rotate in a predetermined direction at constant speed. The deflected laser light beam is passed through a F0 lens (213), whereby the sweeping speed in the scanning direction is made uniform. Then, the laser light beam passes through a cylindrical lens (214) and is reflected by a mirror (215) onto an endless imaging belt (216), which contains a continous photosensitive material. The imaging belt is extended

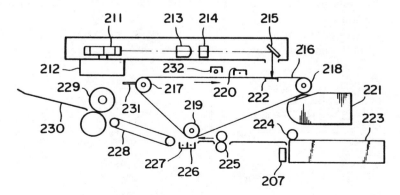

**Figure 7–8**  Schematic Illustration of Overall Structure of Laser Printer

around three rollers (217 to 219), at least one of which is driven to rotate, thereby causing the imaging belt to travel in the direction indicated by the arrow.

As the imaging belt (216) travels, its outer surface is uniformly charged by a corona charging unit (220), and the charged surface is scanned by the laser light beam, whereby the uniform charge is selectively dissipated in accordance with a light image pattern so that an electrostatic latent image is formed on the imaging belt. The latent image is then developed by a developing unit (221) to be converted into a toner image. It is to be noted that a back plate (222) is located to be in contact with the inner surface of the imaging belt at an exposure station so that the imaging belt is maintained substantially flat locally at the exposure station.

A cassette (223) storing therein a quantity of cut sheets of recording medium in the form of a stack is detachably mounted below the developing unit (221). A pickup roller (224) is placed at a supply end of the cassette; and, when the pickup roller is intermittently driven to rotate, the topmost sheet is fed and transported until its leading edge comes into contact with a registration roller (225). The cut sheet of recording medium thus supplied is held stationary for a while. In association with the traveling motion of the imaging belt (216), the registration roller is driven to rotate so that the cut sheet is again caused to advance. As a result, the cut sheet is brought into contact with the imaging belt such that the leading edge of the cut sheet is in registry with the leading edge of the developed toner image on the imaging belt. Then, the cut sheet in contact with the imaging belt moves past a corona image transfer unit (226) so that the toner image on the imaging belt is transferred to the cut sheet. As illustrated, because a separating corona unit (227) is provided adjacent to the image transfer unit, the cut sheet to which the toner image has been transferred is separated from the imaging belt and then guided toward an image fixing unit (229) as riding on a transportation belt (228). While the cut sheet is passing through the image fixing unit, the transferred toner image becomes permanently fixed to the cut sheet, which, in turn, is discharged onto a stacker (230).

A cleaning blade (231) is provided in scrubbing contact with the imaging belt (216) so that any residual toner on the imaging belt is scraped off. Conversely, a charge-removing lamp (232) is also provided, and it applies a uniform illumination to the imaging belt to have any residual charge removed.

## ADJUSTMENT FOR PAPER SIZE

At the front end of the cassette (223), a size indicator is provided that is typically comprised of a magnetic or optical pattern and that indicates the size of the cut sheets of recording paper stored in the cassette. A size detector (207) is provided adjacent to the front end of the cassette for detecting the size indicator. Preferably, the size detector (207) includes a sensor for reading the size indicator and an encoder for a detection signal produced from the sensor, whereby an output signal from the encoder is supplied to the system control unit (204) as a size signal.

It is to be noted that the orientation of cut sheets of recording medium stored in the cassette (223) with respect to the transporting direction is set as illustrated in Figure 7–5. In the illustrated embodiment, it is assumed that the maximum size of cut sheets usable with the laser printer (206) is B4.

Now, the receiving mode of operation of the facsimile machine having the previously described structure will be described with reference to Figures 7–7, 7–9a and 7–9b. At first, when a call is received, the system control unit (204) carries out a predetermined pretransmission control procedure 301, whereby predetermined information is exchanged with a calling or transmitting facsimile machine. On completion of the pretransmission control procedure, counter CNT for keeping track of the page number of image data stored is set to zero at step 302. Then, image data for a single page is received and decoded to the original image data, which, in turn,

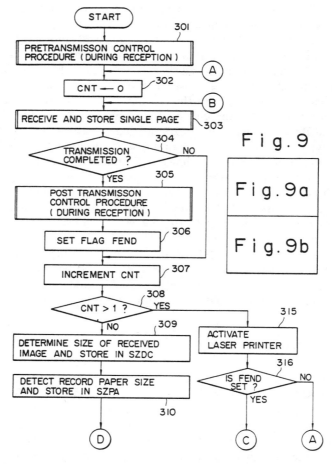

**Figure 7–9 (a)**   First Part of Flow Chart Showing Receiving Mode Operation

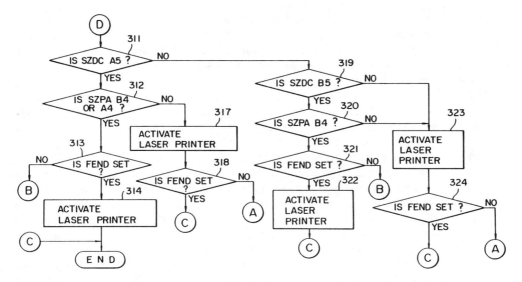

**Figure 7–9 (b)** Second Part of Flow Chart Showing Receiving Mode Operation

is stored into the image memory (205) at step 303. At this juncture, if the transmission has completed (i.e., the result of determination at step 304 being affirmative), then a posttransmission control procedure is implemented at step 305 and then a flag FEND, which indicates the end of transmission, is set at step 306, followed by the step of incrementing the counter CNT at step 307. Conversely, if the transmission has not yet been completed (i.e., the result of determination at step 304 is negative), then it proceeds to step 307 by skipping steps 305 and 306.

Then, it is determined whether or not the count of the counter-CNT is larger than unity at step 308. If the result of this determination at step 308 is negative, then the size of the received image data is determined from the amount of image data so far stored and its result is stored as data SZDC at step 309. In succession, the size of cut sheets of recording medium is detected from an output from the size detector 207, and its result is stored as data SZPA at step 310. If data SZDC indicates A5 size (i.e., the result of determination at step 311 is affirmative), then it is checked whether or not data SZPA indicates either B4 or A4 size at step 312. If the result of determination at step 312 is affirmative, then the condition of flag FEND is examined. If flag FEND has been found to be not set (i.e., the result of determination at step 313 is negative), then it goes back to step 303, thereby starting to receive the image data of the next following page and have it stored in the image memory (205).

Conversely, if the result of determination at step 313 is affirmative, then it indicates the last page of a total number of original documents, which is an odd number. The laser printer (206) is activated to carry out recording of this last page at step 314. If the result of determination at step 308 is affirmative, then the laser printer (206) is activated, whereby two pages of image data stored in the image memory (205) are recorded at step 315. Then, the condition of flag FEND is checked at step 316, and if flag FEND has been found to be set (i.e., the result of determination at step 316 being affirmative), then it goes out of this reception processing routine because it indicates the completion of transmission. Conversely, if flag FEND is not set (i.e., the result of determination at step 316 is negative), then it goes back to step 302 so that the counter-CNT is first cleared to zero, and the image data of the next following page is received and stored.

If the result of determination at step 312 is negative, because it indicates the fact that the size of cut sheets stored in the cassette (223) is either A5 or B5 size, then the laser printer (206) is activated, and a single page of image data is recorded at step 317. Thereafter, the condition of flag FEND is examined at step 318. If flag FEND is set (i.e., the result of determination at step 318 is affirmation), then it goes out of this reception processing routine because it indicates the completion of transmission. Conversely, if flag FEND is not set (i.e., the result of determination at step 318 being negative), then it goes back to step 302.

If the result of determination at step 311 is negative, then it is checked whether or not data SZDC indicates B5 size at step 319. If the result of determination at step 319 turns out to be affirmative, then it is checked whether or not data SZPA indicates B4 size at step 320. In the case in which the result of determination at step 320 is affirmative, then the condition of flag FEND is examined. If flag FEND is not set (i.e., the result of determination at step 321 is negative), then it goes back to step 303, whereby the image data of the next following page is received and stored in the image memory (205). If the result of determination at step 321 is affirmative, then it indicates the last page of a total number of original documents, which is an odd number, so that the laser printer (206) is activated, and the image data of that last page is recorded at step 322.

In the case in which the result of determination at step 319 is negative, and in the case in which the result of determination at step 320 is negative, then step 323 is executed, thereby causing the laser printer (206) to record the received image data. On completion of step 323, the condition of flag FEND is examined at step 324. If flag FEND is set (i.e., the result of determination at step 324 being affirmative), then it goes out of this reception processing routine. Conversely, if flag FEND is not set (i.e., the result of determination at step 324 is negative), then it goes back to step 302.

Accordingly, in the case in which the received image data has A5 size and the cut sheets have either B4 or A5 size, if the image data of an odd-number page is received, then the result of determination at step 308 becomes negative, the result of determination at step 311 becomes affirmative, the result of determination at step 312 becomes affirmative, and the result of determination at step 313 becomes negative, which brings the process back to step 303. As a result, under this condition, the reception of image data of the next following page is carried out; only a single page of received image data being stored in image memory (205), and the count of counter-CNT storing the number of received pages is preserved. Then, when the image of an even-number page is received, the result of determination at step 308 becomes affirmative, so that step 315 is executed, whereby two pages of image data are recorded on a single cut sheet of recording medium. At this time, if the transmission has not yet been completed, the count of counter-CNT is cleared to zero at step 302, and then the image data of the next following page is received.

Now, in the case in which the received image data has a B5 size and the cut sheets of recording medium stored in the cassette (223) has a B4 size, when the image data of an odd-number page is received, the result of determination at step 308 becomes negative, the result of determination at step 311 becomes negative, the result of determination at step 319 becomes negative, and the result of determination at step 320 becomes affirmative, which brings the process back to step 303. As a result, the image data of the next following page is received with a single page of received image data being stored in the image memory (205), and the count of the counter-CNT is preserved. When the image data of an even-number page is received, the result of determination at step 308 becomes affirmative, so that, as previously, two pages of received image data are recorded on a single cut sheet of recording medium. If the transmission has not yet been completed, then, after clearing the count of counter-CNT to zero, the image data of the next following page is received.

In the case in which the received image data has neither a B5 nor a A5 size, each time when the image data of each page has been received, the result of determination at step 308 becomes negative, the result of determination at step 311 becomes negative, and the result of determination at step 319 becomes negative, so that a single page of received image data is recorded on a single cut sheet of recording medium by the laser printer (206). When the transmission is completed, the count of the counter-CNT is cleared to zero, and then the image data of the next following page is received. In this reception processing, the condition of flag FEND is checked at steps 313, 316, 318, 321, and 324. If set, the reception processing is terminated.

In the previously described reception processing, no description has been given as to the case of a combination of a size of received image data, which cannot be recorded as it is, and a size of a cut sheet of recording medium. In such a case, however, a process similar to the conventional one may be carried out. For example, if the received image data has an A4 size and a cut sheet of recording medium has a B5 size, then the received image data may be recorded on the cut sheet as reduced in size appropriately.

If the image data received from a transmitting facsimile machine is such that an original document of either B5 or A5 size has been read with its longitudinal direction in parallel with the transporting direction, then the received image data may be appropriately adjusted in orientation in conformity with the orientation of cut sheets of recording medium of these sizes at the system control unit (204) before being supplied to the laser printer (206).

It should be noted that the previously described embodiments used the laser printer as the page printer. Any other type of printer, such as an electrostatic printer or liquid-crystal shutter printer, may also be used in place of the laser printer, however.

# CHAPTER 8

# *Fax and the Computer*

A wide variety of boards to permit facsimile operation with PCs is available. In addition to the board a program of software is required. A description of such a board and program, as available from Panasonic, is given subsequently.

Most fax boards have microprocessor control and memory capacity to enable them to operate in the background, so that the computer can perform other functions without interruption. There are advantages to be gained by combining a PC and a fax machine at the same site, however. Ricoh has explored such advantages and proposed means for facilitating them in their U.S. patent no. 4,964,154, issued to Ricoh Corporation on October 16, 1990.

The communication adapter device used in this system not only contains the elements of a fax board, but also provides for linkage between a fax machine and a PC at the same site.

## PANASONIC FAX BOARDS

- *Model no. FX-BM88*—Designed for use with the Panasonic Business Partners Series Computers with a holder for the standard LED indicator on the front of the Business Partner computer.

  The new LED indicator includes a fax button (to start the fax program without typing any commands at the DOS prompt) and "send" and "receive"

LEDs (which monitor fax communications while not in the fax application program).

- *Model no. FX-BM89*—Intended for use with IBM compatible PCs other than the Panasonic Business Partner, which includes magnetic-type LEDs indicator with "send" and "receive" LEDs (which monitor the FAX communications while using another application program)

---

CAUTION

The indicator assy (FM-BM89 only) has a magnetic base that can damage data on floppy disks. To prevent data loss, do not place the magnetic indicator assy on or near floppy disks.

---

**1.** *Hardware*—Fax board consists of main board, modem board and speaker assy. The LEDs indicator assy is separate. The main board houses the CPU, BIOS ROM, DRAM, Synchronous Data Link Control (SDLC), tone generator, and other parts. The modem board is a synchronous serial 9600-bps modem designed for fax operation. The fax button (FX-BM88 only) is part of the LEDs indicator assy. It is used to start the fax program. LEDs and speaker indicate to the user when they are receiving or sending a fax message.

**2.** *Fax program*—The fax program is compatible with all G3 facsimile machines.

The program does the following:

1. Background send-receive operation
2. Auto-dial, group-dial functions
3. Retransmission on error
4. Graphics editing
5. Phone book utility
6. Journal
7. Capacity of 9600-bps with auto-fall-back
8. Polling of data received and sent

It is compatible with popular software and hardware.

A block diagram of the fax board is shown in Figure 8–1, and a layout of a PC installation working with a facsimile machine at another location is shown in Figure 8–2.

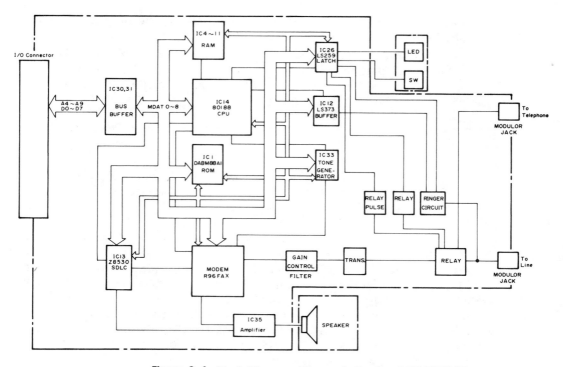

**Figure 8-1**  Block Diagram of Panasonic Fax Board FX-BM88/89

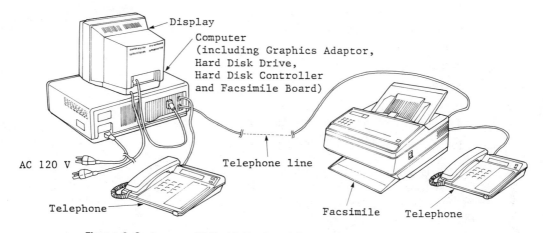

**Figure 8-2**  Layout of PC with Fax Board Communicating with Remote Fax Machine

## Role of Digital Interface

In the recent years, a facsimile device provided with a digital interface portion conforming to the normal standard such as RS-232C, GP-1B, and so on has been already used practically. Facsimile devices can be connected with various sorts of computers such as PCs through such an interface portion.

In such a way, by connecting the facsimile device and the computer with each other, it can be possible to perform various processings, such as control of the facsimile device by the computer at the time of transmitting and receiving of messages, management of the facsimile communication state including such items as the past records of correspondence, correspondence fees, and so on. The device also allows taking in of the image information received by the facsimile device into the computer, or transferring of the image information made by the computer by use of the facsimile device to the other facsimile device.

In recent years, the ordinary facsimile device has been already widely popularized together with the personal computer. If the ordinary facsimile device is not provided with the digital interface portion as mentioned earlier, however, even though both the PC and the ordinary facsimile device are installed on the same place it was impossible to perform a communication between the computer and the facsimile device.

Conversely, in the recent years, an additionally provided board and its software specially used for performing facsimile communication by use of the PC have been already put on the market. When the additionally provided board and the software are set to the PC and the operation of the PC is started, the PC can transmit the image information to the opposite party and receive the image information therefrom.

On this occasion, because the PC functions on the condition equal to that of a stand-alone facsimile device, exchanging of the image information or the like between the PC and the ordinary facsimile device, both of which have already been installed on the same place, does not occur.

Further, in general, the PC is often used for various purposes at the same time. When the PC receives the image information from the other facsimile device, the PC is practicing other processing in many cases. Usually, the PC does not have a processing ability for performing the facsimile communication and the other processing at the same time as a multiple job. Therefore, in the case of receiving the signal (image information) as mentioned earlier, the image information cannot be received, if the processing under execution is not interrupted for a while. This is an inconvenience of the prior art device.

## COMPUTER WITH LOCAL AND REMOTE FAX MACHINES

As mentioned heretofore, conventionally, the computer could not freely make a mutual correspondence of the image information between the computer and the ordinary facsimile device installed at the same place as that of the computer, or between the computer and the other facsimile device connected with the public telephone circuit network. The same could not administrate the correspondence state of the ordinary facsimile device. The communication adapter device comprises the following:

1. Public telephone circuit
2. First transmission means for connecting the circuit terminal of the local facsimile device and the digital signal interface terminal with each other, supplying electrical power to the circuit terminal of the local facsimile device to create an electrical condition equivalent to that of the public telephone circuit, and conversely transmitting the image information between the remote facsimile device and the computer
3. Second-transmission means for mutually transmitting the image information between the local facsimile device and the computer
4. Third-transmission means for mutually transmitting the image information between the remote facsimile device and the local facsimile device

In such communication device, one of the previously mentioned three sorts of transmission means is selected, and the selected means performs transmission of the image information, respectively. Conversely, the information based on the communication between the remote-side and local-side facsimile devices is transferred to the aforementioned computer. Further, when the message is received from the remote-side facsimile device, the computer or the local-side facsimile device executes facsimile correspondence on the basis of the state of the computer or the local-side facsimile device. This arrangement is characterized by the fact that the execution of facsimile correspondence is changed over to the computer or to the local-side facsimile device. An embodiment of the present invention is described in detail in accordance with the accompanying illustrations.

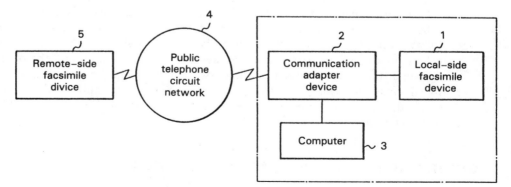

**Figure 8–3**  System Using Communication Adapter Device with Computer and Both Local and Remote Fax Machines

Figure 8–3 is an outlined system construction block diagram showing a facsimile communication system in relation to an embodiment according to the present invention. In Figure 8–3, a local-side facsimile device (1) is a facsimile device based on the ordinary G3 specification employed conventionally. Its circuit terminals are connected with a communications adapter (2). A computer (3) and telephone circuits guided from the public telephone circuit network (4) are connected with the communication adapter device (2).

A remote-side facsimile device (5) is connected with the public telephone circuit network (4). The remote-side facsimile device (5) is also a facsimile device based on the ordinary G3 specification employed conventionally.

## COMMUNICATIONS ADAPTER CIRCUIT

Figure 8–4 is a detailed circuit diagram showing the circuit construction of the communication adapter (2). In Figure 8–4, an interface portion (21) of the telephone circuit is employed for connecting the circuits and transmitting-receiving signals from one device to the other. The telephone circuits are connected with its terminals T1 and T2.

An interface portion (22) of the facsimile device is employed for transmitting the signals to the local-side facsimile device (1) and receiving the signal therefrom. The circuit-connecting terminals of the local side facsimile device (1) are connected with its terminals T3 and T4. A digital interface portion (23) is employed for transmitting the signals to the computer (3) and receiving the signals therefrom. The interface (23) is a standard RS-232C type digital interface, and the same is connected with the computer (3) through a connector (CN).

The transmission control portion (24) is a microcomputer system. When a correspondence by facsimile is performed between the respective devices, the transmission control portion practices, as occasion demands, control of transmission with the remote facsimile device, transporting of the image information to be transmitted to and received from a predetermined device, observation of the correspondence state between the facsimile devices, and control of the various portions of the facsimile device.

The correspondence portion (25) of the computer (3) is employed for use in transmitting various facsimile signals to the remote facsimile device and receiving the same therefrom. A local facsimile monitoring portion (26) is employed for monitoring the operational condition of the local facsimile device (1).

A change-over circuit (27) is employed for changing over the transmission path of the signal in accordance with the operational condition of the communication adapter device (2). An analog switch (28) is employed for changing over the transmission signal to be transmitted to one of the opposite facsimile devices. An analog switch (29) is employed for changing over the transmission signal to be transmitted to either one of a correspondence portion (25) of the facsimile device and a monitoring portion (26) of the local facsimile device.

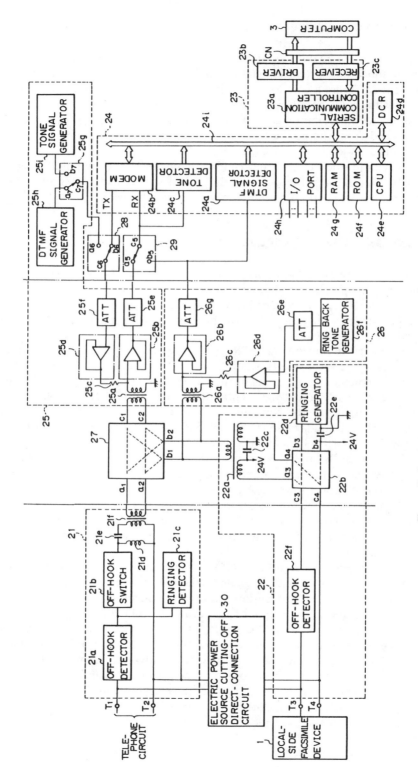

**Figure 8-4** Block Diagram of Communication Adapter Circuit

An electric power source cutting-off direct connection circuit (30) is a relay circuit for directly connecting the telephone circuit with the local-side facsimile device (1) when supplying of electric power is stopped—for instance, at the time of power stoppage and so on.

In the interface portion (21) of the telephone circuit, both of the terminals T1 and T2 are connected with an I/O line of the direct-connection circuit (30). Furthermore, the terminal T1 is connected with one end of an off-hook detector (21a) and another end thereof is connected with an off-hook switch (21b) and a ringing detector (21c). The off-hook switch (21a) is employed for judging whether the (telephone) circuit is physically connected with the opponent device by use of the electric current flowing through the line of network at the time of connecting the circuit with the opponent device.

The other end of the off-hook switch (21b) is connected with a direct current passing coil (21d) and a direct current cutting-off capacitor (21e), and the other end of the capacitor (21e) is connected with one end of the primary winding (21f-1) transformer (21f). The respective other ends of those windings (21f-1, 21d, and 21f) are connected with terminal T2.

The secondary winding of the transformer (21f) is connected with the terminals a1 and a2 of a change-over circuit (27). The terminals b1 and b2 of the change-over circuit (27) are, respectively, connected both with one of windings of a transformer (22a) in an interface portion (22) of the facsimile device and with one of windings (primary winding) of a transformer (26a) in a local facsimile monitoring portion (26).

The transformer 22a has two other windings, one end of which are respectively connected with terminals a3 and a4 of a changeover circuit 22b. The other end of one of the two windings is earthed and the other end of the other winding is earthed via a bypass capacitor 22c. DC voltage of 24 V is applied thereto.

The terminal b3 of the change-over circuit 2ib is connected with the terminal b4 thereof through a ringing generator (22d) and a bypass capacitor (22e). A junction point of the ringing generator 22d and the bypass capacitor (22e) is also earthed, and DC voltage of 24 V is applied to the line of the terminal b4.

The terminal c3 of the change-over circuit 22b is connected with the terminal T3, and the terminal c4 thereof is connected with the terminal T4. Further, the terminals T3 and T4 are connected with the other I/O lines of the electric power source cutting off direct connection circuit (30). An off-hook detector (22f) detects the state of circuit connection of the local-side facsimile device (1) by detecting DC current of the lines.

The terminals c1 and c2 of the change-over circuit (27) are, respectively, connected with one of the windings of a transformer (25a) in a correspondence portion (25). One end of the other winding of the transformer (25a) is directly earthed, whereas the other end thereof is directly connected with one input terminal of a voltage follower amplifier (25b). The same end is connected via a resistor (25c) with another voltage follower amplifier (25d).

The output terminal of the voltage follower amplifier (25b) is connected through an attenuator (25e) with the contact point (a5) of an analog switch (29). The other input terminal of the voltage follower amplifier (25d) is connected through another attenuator (25f) with the common terminal c6 of an analog switch (28).

The contact point (ab) of the analog switch (28) is connected with the common terminal c7 of an analog switch (25g). Further, the contact point (a7) of the analog switch (25g) is connected with a DTMF signal generator (25h). The contact point (b7) thereof is connected with a facsimile tone signal generator (25i).

In the local facsimile monitoring portion (26), one end of the other winding of the transformer (26a) is earthed. Further, the other end thereof is directly connected with the input terminal of a voltage follower amplifier (26b), which is connected with the output terminal of another voltage follower amplifier (26d) through a resistor (26c). A ring-back tone generator (26f) is connected with the input terminal of the voltage follower amplifier (26d) through an attenuator (26e). The output terminal of the voltage follower amplifier 26b is connected with the contact point (b5) of the analog switch (29) and a DTMF signal-detecting circuit (24a) of a transmission-control portion (24) both through another attenuator (26g). The common terminal c5 of the analog switch (29) is connected with the signal receiving terminal (RX) of a modem (24b) in the transmission control portion (24) and a facsimile tone detecting circuit (24c). The signal transmitting terminal (TX) is connected with the contact point (b6) of an analog switch (28).

In the transmission control portion (24), data compression and reconstruction (DCR) (24d) is employed for converting the data-compressed image information received from the facsimile device back to the image information constructed with the original pixel (picture element) unit. A CPU (24e) is employed for performing various control actions in accordance with the control program stored in a ROM (24f), and a RAM (24g) is employed for temporarily storing the image information to be transmitted and various sorts of data. Further, an I/O port (24h) in Figure 8–4 is connected with various detection circuits, various signal-generating circuits, and various change-over circuits arranged in the circuits described heretofore; this port is employed for inputting and controlling the detection signals. The respective portions in the transmission control portion (24) is mutually connected by means of a signal bus (24i).

The signal bus (24i) is connected with a serial communication controller (23a) in a digital interface portion (23). The serial communication controller (23a) is employed for performing a serial communication with the computer (3) in conformity to RS-232C. Both a driver (23b) (RS-232C type) and a receiver (23c) (RS-232C TYPE) are connected with the computer (3) by a CN.

In the circuits described heretofore, the change-over circuit (27) performs change-over connection in three states: a connection state a-c of connecting terminals a1 and a2, respectively, with terminals c1 and c2; another connection state a-b of connecting terminals a1 and a2 with terminals b1 and b2; and still another state b-c of connecting terminals b1 and b2 with terminals c1 and c2.

The change-over circuit (22b) performs change-over connection in two states;

a connection state a-c of connecting terminals a3 and a4 with terminals c3 and c4; and another state c-b of connecting terminals c3 and c4 with terminals b3 and b4.

The transformer (22a) side (primary) winding of the transformer 26a is set at a very high impedance. The transformer (21f) is made in consideration of the state so as not to disturb its impedance matching. For instance, in general the transformers (21f) and (22a) respectively, have an I/O impedance ratio of 1:1 matching 600 $\Omega$. However, the suitable impedance value of the mentioned, (primary) winding is 10 k$\Omega$ or more.

The attenuators (25e) and (26g), respectively, have an automatic gain control function for the received signal and a filtering function of removing unnecessary frequency bandwidth. The attenuators (25f) and (26e) are, respectively, set at each proper transmission signal level.

A ring-back tone generator (26f) outputs a calling-out sound of the telephone network produced by AM modulating with 16 Hz the tone signal of 400 Hz. In the construction as mentioned heretofore, the facsimile communication system performs correspondence and administration as follows:

1. Facsimile correspondence between remote-side facsimile device (5) and the computer (3)

2. Facsimile correspondence between the remote-side facsimile device (5) and the local-side facsimile device (1)

3. Facsimile correspondence between the local-side facsimile device (1) and the computer (3)

4. Monitoring of facsimile device correspondence executed between the remote-side facsimile device (5) and the local-side facsimile device (1), by use of the computer (3).

A predetermined software is set in the computer (3) for performing the correspondence and administration as mentioned earlier.

Now, in the case of making use of the facsimile communication system, when a telephone call from the facsimile device (5) arrives at the local station, whether the local-side facsimile device (1) responds thereto or the computer (3) responds thereto is previously set at the computer (3).

## Communications from Remote Facsimile to Computer

Assuming that the computer (3) is set such that the same responds thereto now, the operation of the signal arrival in the case of transmitting telephone call from the remote-side facsimile device (5) is described hereinafter.

Figure 8-5 is an explanatory view showing a procedure of transmitting and receiving the respective signals between the respective devices on that occasion. Namely, referring back to Figure 8-4 the direct-connection circuit (30) is opened usually. When the remote-side facsimile device (5) transmits a telephone call to the

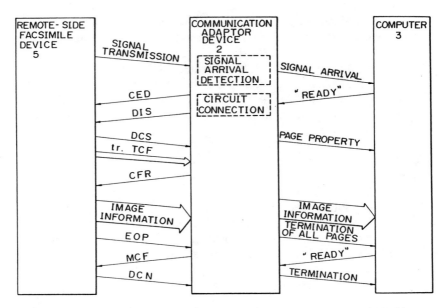

**Figure 8–5**    Transmission and Reception to Computer from Remote Fax Machine

local station, the telephone call arrival is detected by a ringing detector (21c) of the communication adapter (2). The transmission control portion (24) detects the telephone call arrival to the computer (3) through the serial communication controller (23a) and the driver (23b) of the digital interface portion (23).

The aforementioned telephone call arrival is noticed to the computer (3) in a state of being idle. In case that facsimile communication is enabled, the computer (3) returns a response showing "READY" to the transmission control portion (24) through the receiver (23c) and the serial communication controller (23a).

When the transmission control portion (24) confirms the aforementioned state of "READY," the same closes the off-hook switch (21b) to connect the circuit with each other and starts the predetermined transmission control procedure in conformity to the article T.30 of the standard rule established by CCITT. Namely, the change-over circuit (27) is turned to the connection state a-c, the analog switch (28) to a6 side, and the analog switch (25g) to the contact point b7 side, respectively. The facsimile tone signal generator (25i) outputs the called station identification (CED) signal.

The CED signal that is output therefrom is transmitted to the remote-side facsimile device (5) via the telephone circuit, through the attenuator (25f), the voltage follower amplifier (25d), the resistor (25c), the transformer (25a), the change-over circuit (27), and the telephone circuit interface portion (21), in that order.

Next, the transmission control portion (24) changes over the analog switch (28) to the contact point b6 side and the analog switch (29) to the a5 side. The

MODEM (24b) outputs the DIS signal and transmits it to the remote-side facsimile device (5) in a similar way.

Conversely, the digital command signal (DCS) signal, the phase–adjusting–training signal and the training check (TCF) signal are returned back to the transmission control portion (24) from the remote-side facsimile device (5). Those signals are received by a modem (24b) through a telephone circuit interface portion (21), a change-over circuit (27), a transformer (25a), a voltage follower-amplifier (25b), an attenuator (25e), and an analog switch (29). The transmission portion (24) succeeds in executing the modem training; the transmission control portion (24) sends out the CFR signal. During the period of executing the previously mentioned transmission control procedure, the DCS signal causes the remote-side facsimile device (5) to receive various page property information to be received thereafter, such as page size of image information, line density, coding mode, and so on. Such page property information is transmitted to the computer (3).

Next, the remote-side facsimile device (5) transmits data-compressed image information. Such image information is received by the modem (24b) and directly transmitted to the computer (3) through the digital interface portion (23). At the same time, the DCR (24d) converts again the image information back to the original image information constructed with the former picture element unit. Further, existence or nonexistence of data error is checked on a line-per-line basis in the received data.

When the remote-side facsimile device (5) finishes transmission of the image information, it sends out the end of procedure (EOP) signal. The transmission control portion (24) receives the EOP signal and provides notification to the computer (3) that the portion (24) receives all the pages of the image information. Furthermore, when the portion receives the information normally, it sends out the message confirmation (MCF) signal to the remote-side facsimile device (5). Conversely, the remote-side facsimile device (5) sends out the disconnect (DCN) signal and cuts off the circuit. The off-hook switch (21b) is thereby opened and cuts off the circuit.

The computer (3) stores the transmitted image information into the memory device or the like. When it is noticed that all pages are received, the computer (3) returns back the response showing "READY" to the transmission control portion (24) at the time of receiving the information normally. When the portion (24) receives the response thereof from the computer (3), that portion notifies the termination of signal receiving process to the computer (3) and completes the signal arrival process.

Conversely, when the transmission control portion (24) receives image information and detects a data error in this information, it identifies the pages of the received image information that contain data errors and transmits this information to the computer (3). Also, after receiving all of the image information, the portion (24) notifies the remote facsimile device (5) of the data error of the received signal with a predetermined procedure.

In such a way, a telephone call is emitted from the remote-side facsimile device (5), which executes transmission of the image information to the computer (3).

## COMMUNICATION FROM COMPUTER TO REMOTE FAX MACHINE

Next, Figure 8–6 is an explanatory view showing a respective signals transmitting a telephone call to the remote-side facsimile device (5) from the computer (3). On that occasion, a telephone call transmitting request is noticed to the communication adapter device (2) side from the computer through the digital interface portion (23), by means of the program of the computer or the manipulation performed by an operator.

The transmission control portion (24) performs a "READY" response when it is in a state of being idle. The computer (3) transmits the information of a destination telephone number to the transmission control portion (24) after confirming the state of "READY."

The transmission control portion (24) judges the transmission of the telephone call to the public telephone circuit network (4) when the information of the destination telephone number is transmitted. Then, the same closes the off-hook switch (21b) and thereby connects the circuits with each other. Furthermore, the same changes over the change-over circuit (27) to the connection state a-c. At this time, it is checked that the off-hook detector (21a) physically connects the circuits with each other. When it cannot be checked, the operation is stopped.

When the circuits are correctly connected, the transmission control portion (24) next sends out a dial signal. In case the telephone circuit is now that of a dial-pulse type, portion (24) sends out a predetermined dial-pulse signal onto the circuit

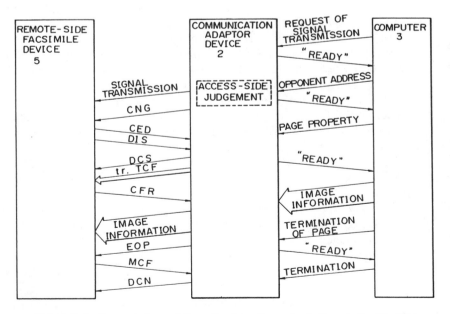

**Figure 8–6**　Transmission and Reception from Computer to Remote Fax Machine

by the action of opening-closing control of the off-hook switch (21b). In the case of employing the circuit of PB type, the analog switch (28) is turned to a6 side, and the analog switch (25g) is turned to a7 side. Further, DTMF signal generator (25h) sends out a predetermined DTMF signal. Thereby, the remote-side facsimile device is called out.

During this time, communication adapter (2) sends the "READY" response to computer (3), and a page property information of the image information to be transmitted next is transmitted to the communication adapter (2). The page property information, in the same way as mentioned before, includes the page size of the image information, line density, coding mode, and so on. This information further includes data to be sent to the DCS signal, which is sent with the transmission control procedure executed next.

After a constant period elapsed until the remote-side facsimile device (5) receives a telephone call and performs circuit connection, the analog switch (25g) is changed over to the contact point b7 side, and a calling tone (CNG) signal is sent out from the facsimile tone signal generator (25i). Thereafter, the analog switch (28) is turned to the contact point a6 side, and the analog switch (29) is turned to the contact point a5 side. When the remote-side facsimile device (5) receives a telephone call, it confirms the CNG signal, and sends out the CED signal and the DIS signal.

At the communication adapter device (2) side, the aforementioned CED signal is detected by the facsimile tone detecting circuit (24c), and the DIS signal is received by the modem (24b). Next, the modem (24b) sends out the phase–adjusting-training signal tr for a high-speed modem and the TCF signal. Thereby, the remote-side facsimile device (5) executes MODEM training. When the device (5) succeeds in executing modem training, the remote-side facsimile device sends out the CFR signal.

When the communication adapter device (2) sends out the response "READY" to the computer (3) through the digital interface portion (23), the computer (3) sends back to the device (2) the image information consisting of compressed data to be transmitted. The communication adapter device (2) transmits the sent-back image information to the remote-side facsimile device (5) from the modem (24b) of the device. Further, when the termination of the page sent out from the computer (3) is noticed to the communication adapter device (2), the device sends out the EOP signal to the remote-side facsimile device (5).

When the remote-side facsimile device (5) receives the image information normally, it sends back the MCF signal. When the communication adapter device (2) receives the MCF signal, it transmits the response "READY" to the computer (3). Responding to it, the computer (3) notices the termination of the image information to the communication adapter device (2) when the image information terminates. Here, the communication adapter device (2) sends out the DCN signal to the remote-side facsimile device (5) and cuts off the circuit thereof. At this time, the remote-side facsimile device (5) receives the DCN signal and also cuts off the circuit thereof. In such a way, the communication between the both terminates.

Moreover, in case that the RTN signal showing a signal receiving error is returned from the remote-side facsimile device (5) instead of the MCF signal after transmitting image information, the modem training is executed again in accordance with a predetermined transmission control procedure. Thereafter, the image information is transmitted again.

In such a way, a telephone call is generated and transmitted from the computer (3) to the remote-side facsimile device (5). Thereafter, the image information is transmitted by means of the predetermined facsimile communication.

## COMMUNICATION FROM COMPUTER TO LOCAL FAX MACHINE

Next, Figure 8–7 is an explanatory view showing the transmitting-receiving procedure in the case of transmitting the image information from the computer (3) to the local-side facsimile device (1). On this occasion, a telephone call issuing demand is noticed to the communication adapter device (2) side from the computer (3) through the digital interface portion (23) by use of the program of the computer or by operator's manipulation.

Conversely, in a state of being idle, the transmission control portion (24) performs a response "READY." The computer (3) transmits the destination (address) information showing the local-side facsimile device (1) to the transmission control portion (24) after confirming the state of "READY."

The transmission control portion (24) discriminates the opponent to be ac-

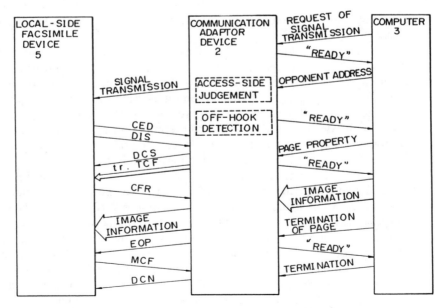

**Figure 8–7**   Transmission and Reception from Computer to Local Fax Machine

cessed in accordance with the destination (address) information. Now, because the local-side facsimile device (1) is shown, the change-over circuit (22b) is turned to a connecting state b-c and the ringing generator (22d) outputs the telephone call signal. The bypass capacitor (22e) has a capacitance of low impedance in comparison with the calling-out signal of AC. Further, because DC voltage is applied to the one end of the bypass capacitor (22e), the previously mentioned calling-out signal is superposed with the DC voltage, and the signal thus superposed is sent out to the local-side facsimile device (1) through the bypass capacitor (22e).

When the previously mentioned DC voltage is applied to the local-side facsimile device (1) and the latter received a calling-out signal, the local-side facsimile device (1) operates in the same way as the case of being connected with the ordinary telephone circuit and executes a predetermined signal receiving operation by connecting the circuits therewith.

When the local-side facsimile device (1) receives calling-out signal, the off-hook detector (22f) detects the state of signal receiving. The detector stops the operation of the ringing generator (22d), and the change-over circuit (22b) converts the state of connection a-c, the analog switch (29) to the contact point b5 side, and the analog switch (28) to the contact point b6 side, respectively.

Thereafter, the local-side facsimile device (1) sends out the CED signal and the DIS signal. After that time, the aforementioned change-over circuits (switches) transmit and receive various sorts of procedure signals and send out the image information transmitted from the computer (3) to the local-side facsimile device (1). Because this procedure is the same as that of Figure 8–6, however, the explanation thereof is omitted here.

Next, the case the transmitting the image information to the computer (3) from the local-side facsimile device (1) is described. On this occasion, a specified telephone number not existing in the ordinary telephone numbers is previously settled to designate the computer (3) from the local-side facsimile device (1). The operator sets the specified telephone number to the local-side facsimile device (1) as a destination (address) telephone number and performs a predetermined transmission manipulation. Thereby, the operation of the local-side facsimile device (1) is started, and the device sends out a predetermined dial signal.

In the communication adapter (2), usually the change-over circuit (22b) is set to the connection a-c, the analog switch 29 is turned to the contact point b5 side, and the device is kept in a state of waiting.

Now, in case the local-side facsimile device (1) is the one of dial-pulse signal system type, the previously mentioned specified telephone number received by use of the dial pulse is detected by the off-hook detector (22f). Conversely, in case the local-side facsimile device (1) is the one of DTMF signal system type, the previously mentioned specified telephone number received by use of the DTMF signal is detected by the DTMF signal detection circuit (24a).

When the transmission control portion (24) discriminates the detected number as a calling-out signal to the computer (3), the portion notices to the computer that the telephone call arrives at the computer from the local-side facsimile device (1).

Further, when the portion confirms the state "READY" of the computer, the same executes a predetermined transmission control procedure between the transmission control portion (24) and the local-side facsimile device (1) as is the case of executing the procedure between the portion (24) and the remote-side facsimile device (5) as shown in Figure 8–5. In such a way, transmission-reception of the image information is executed between the local-side facsimile device (1) and the computer (3).

Next, the case of transmitting the image information in such a manner that the local-side facsimile device (1) gives a telephone call to the remote-side facsimile device (5) is described hereinafter. On this occasion, in the local-side facsimile device, the operator sets a destination (address) telephone number and performs a predetermined transmission manipulation.

In such a manner, the operation of the local-side facsimile device (1) is started, and thereafter a dial signal is sent out. The dial signal, as mentioned earlier, is detected by the off-hook detector (22f) or the DTMF signal detection circuit (24a). Next, in case the detected telephone number is not the aforementioned specified number, the transmission control portion (24) discriminates the calling-out to the public telephone circuit network (4) side, which closes the off-hook switch (21b) to connect the telephone circuits with each other.

Further, as is illustrated in Figure 8–6, the dial signal showing the previously mentioned detected dial signal is sent out to the public telephone circuit network (4) by use of the off-hook switch (21b) and the DTMF signal generator (25h). After the aforementioned dial signal is detected, the change-over circuit (22b) is changed over to the connection state a-c, and the ring-back tone generator (26f) is caused to operate. Thereby, a calling-out sound showing that the destination (address) is called out is transmitted to the local-side facsimile device (1) side. Such procedure of operation is done for the purpose of noticing to the operator that the communication adapter device (2) is performing a calling out operation to the public communication circuit when the telephone call is manually sent out from telephone.

Next, the change-over circuit (27) is changed over to the connection state a-b. A signal transmission path for connecting the local-side facsimile device (1), and the telephone circuit side with each other is formed by the aforementioned changing-over operation. In consequence, when the remote-side facsimile device (5) as a destination (address) responds thereto, an image information is transmitted by use of a predetermined facsimile communication.

In case a telephone call arrives at the communication adaptor device (2), assuming that the local-side facsimile device (1) is set so as to respond thereto, the action of receiving the telephone call transmitted from the remote-side facsimile device (5) is explained hereinafter. When the telephone call from the telephone circuit is detected by the ringing detector (21c), the transmission control portion (24) converts the change-over circuit (22b) to the connection state b-c and causes the ringing generator (22d) to operate to call out the local-side facsimile device (1).

Thereafter, when the off-hook detector (22f) detects circuit connection executed by the local-side facsimile device (1), the change-over circuit (27) is changed over to the connection state a-b. The change-over circuit (22b) is converted to the connection state a-c, respectively, and then the circuit connection is executed by closing the off-hook switch 21b.

In such a way, a signal transmission path for connecting the local-side facsimile device (1) and the telephone circuit side with each other is formed; the image information is received by the local-side facsimile device by means of a predetermined facsimile communication.

## ADMINISTRATION OF COMMUNICATION STATE

Next, the administration of the communication state executed by the computer (3) at the time of performing the facsimile communication between the remote-side facsimile device (5) and the local-side facsimile device (1) is described hereinafter.

Figure 8–8 is an explanatory view for explaining the administration of the communication state. In Figure 8–8, during the period of executing the previously mentioned facsimile communication (correspondence), the analog switch (29) is changed over to the contact point b5 side. Further, various sorts of procedure signal transmitted between the local-side facsimile device (1) and the remote-side facsimile device (5) are received by the modem (24b).

The transmission control portion (24) distinguishes the contents of the correspondence on the basis of the detection time of the various received procedure signals and other information related thereto. Also, depending on this information, the transmission control portion (24) logs times of outgoing and incoming telephone calls, corresponding time, corresponding page numbers, and the correspondence

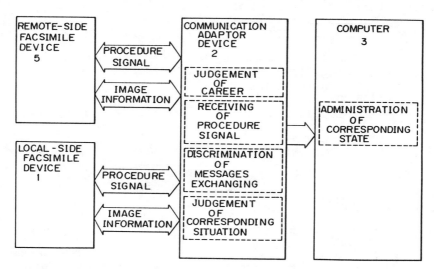

**Figure 8–8**  Operation of Administering State of Correspondence Executed by Computer

result. In addition, when the local-side facsimile device (1) sends out a telephone call the off-hook detector (22f) detects the dial signal and determines the telephone number of the destination (address).

The transmission control portion (24) temporarily stores various sorts of information obtained in such a way into the RAM (24g) as the correspondence information. The transmission control portion transfers the information to the computer (3).

Furthermore, even on the occasion that the telephone at the local-side facsimile device (1) gives a telephone call to the public telephone circuit network (4) side, the transmission control portion (24) judges the correspondence career such as calling-out time, receiving time, and corresponding period; temporarily stores those data herein in a same way; and transfers the same data to the computer (3) side.

On the basis of the previously mentioned correspondence information, the computer (3) administers the correspondence state of the local-side facsimile device (1). This includes the career of the facsimile correspondence, the communication fees per one case and a constant period, and so on.

## Selection of Computer or Local Fax to Communicate

When a telephone call is previously transmitted at the communication adapter device (2), whether the transmitted telephone call is transferred to the local-side facsimile device (1) or the computer (3) side is set at the communication adapter device.

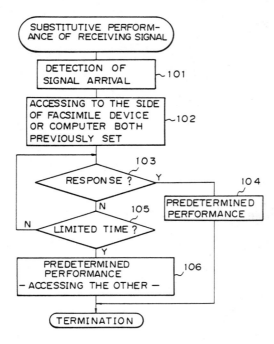

**Figure 8-9** Substitutive Signal Receiving Operation Executed between Computer and Local Fax Machine at Time of Signal Arrival

On some occasions, however, the device set therefore cannot receive the transmitted telephone call because of executing other processing or being out of order (broken down, out of paper, or the like).

On that occasion, as shown in Figures 8-8 and 8-9, when the arrival of telephone call is detected (processing 101), a predetermined access is executed at first, for the side of the device being already set among the local-side facsimile device (1) or the computer (3). For instance, a calling-out signal is sent out for the local-side facsimile device (1), whereas an arrival of telephone call is noticed to the computer (3) (processing 102). Further, when the accessed device responds to the telephone call (processing 103Y), the communication adapter device (2) executes the aforementioned predetermined operation of receiving the signal (telephone call) arrival and the image information (processing 104).

Furthermore, presence or absence of its response is detected during a predetermined constant period (from processing 103N to 105, and from processing 105N to 103). In case no response for such notification occurs after a constant period elapses (processing 105Y), the accessing to the device being already set is stopped. Next time, both of the aforementioned predetermined operations of transmitting signal (telephone call) arrival and receiving the image information are forced to be executed for the other device not yet set among the local-side facsimile device (1) or the computer (3) (processing 106).

## Bypassing of Communication Adapter

Next, when the power source for the communication adapter device (2) is broken down or the communication adapter is out of order, the operator sets the device so as to turn on the power failure direct connection circuit (30). The telephone circuit side is directly connected with the local-side facsimile device (1) side by means of the lines so that a correspondence can be done in the conventional way without intervention of the communication adapter device (i.e., a fail-safe mode).

In case the computer (3) transmits a signal (telephone call), the destination (address) is set in the computer (Figure 8-7). The manipulation of signal transmission to the telephone circuit can be also done from the local-side facsimile device (1), however.

Figure 8-10 is an explanatory view for showing the procedure of transmitting and receiving the respective signals on this occasion. Namely, on this occasion, the computer (3) is previously set to the manually transmitting mode. When such a setting is done, the manually transmitting mode is noticed to the communication adapter device (2) from the computer.

On this occasion, the operator performs a dial manipulation to the destination (address) by use of the telephone of the local-side facsimile device (1) side. When the communication adapter device (2) inputs therein (receives) the dial signal from the local-side facsimile device, the same notices the state of "READY" to the computer (3). Conversely, the same performs connection to the telephone circuit network (4) side and sends out a dial signal of the same telephone number.

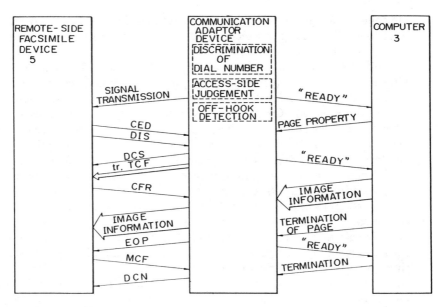

**Figure 8–10**   Transmission and Reception between Respective Devices at Time of Transmission of Image Information to Remote Fax Machine from Computer by Practicing Telephone-Call-Creating Manipulation

Next, the communication adapter device (2) receives information of the page property information from the computer (3). Further, after the signal (telephone call) from the remote-side facsimile device (5) arrives at the computer, the image information is transmitted from the computer in a same way as mentioned earlier.

According to the embodiment of the present invention, the communication adapter device (2) is installed in the system of the embodiment and connected with the telephone circuit, the ordinary local-side facsimile device (1), and the computer (3). Further, in the communication adapter device, each signal-transmitting path between two of the three respective devices is formed, respectively. Furthermore, the communication adapter device executes the transmission control procedure with the opponent facsimile device as occasion demands.

In this way, transmitting and receiving various sorts of information can be freely done between the computer and one of the facsimile devices by use of the ordinary facsimile device(s), even though a specialized facsimile device provided with a digital interface portion as is in the conventional way is not used.

Consequently, for instance, it may be possible that a communication state is set between the PC (3) and the local-side facsimile device (1). The PC can freely employ the plotter installed in the facsimile device in place of the graphic printer not shown, and the scanner is also installed in the same facsimile device as an image scanner.

Further, the procedure signal transmitted between the local-side facsimile device (1) and the remote-side facsimile device (5) is read out by the communication adapter device (2). The contents of correspondence can be discriminated and transferred to the computer (3) side as a correspondence information. In such a way, the administration of the facsimile correspondence state executed by the computer can be done very easily.

The signal-receiving treatment of the image information can be done either by the local-side facsimile device (1) or by the computer (3). Therefore, when the signal (telephone call) arrives at either the local-side facsimile device (1) or the computer (3), even though one of the two devices cannot receive the signal, the other one can receive the signal. Namely, the system can exhibit a function of mutual substitutive signal-receiving so that the signal-receiving treatment can be done with certainty.

In the aforementioned embodiment, the signal arrives at either one of the both devices from the remote-side facsimile device (5), the changing-over setting of whether the image information should be received by the local-side facsimile device (1) or by the computer (3) is performed by the computer. Such changing-over setting can be done in such a manner that a specified telephone number is dialed by use of the telephone of the local-side facsimile device side, however, and the communication adaptor device (2) detects and discriminates the specified telephone number. Otherwise, it may also be possible that, with respect to the previously mentioned changing-over setting, impossibility of the signal arrival because of breakdown or execution of the other processing procedure is automatically judged by the computer (3) or the communication adapter device (2) to set automatically the one device that is capable of causing the signal to arrive.

Furthermore, it may be also possible that not only the cutting off of the power source for the communication adapter device (2) but its internal breakdown shall be self-diagnosed; thereby, the power failure direct-connection circuit (30) shall be operated even if the system goes out of order. Further, although a microcomputer is included in the communication adapter device (2), control of the respective portions can also be done by the computer (3). In the embodiment of the present invention, the facsimile device of the G3-specification type, the present invention can also be applied to the facsimile device of the other-specification type in a similar way.

As is apparent from the foregoing description, according to the present invention, because a communication adapter is installed at the facsimile station, the telephone circuit, the local-side facsimile device, and the computer are connected; respective signal-transmitting paths are formed in the correspondence adapter between the destination addresses. Those are between the remote-side facsimile device and the computer, between the remote-side facsimile device and the local-side facsimile device, and between the local-side facsimile device and the computer. It may be possible that an ordinary facsimile device can be employed instead of the conventional special facsimile device provided with the digital interface portion; thereby, the transmission of the image information can be done freely. Furthermore, because the information based on the correspondence executed between the remote-side facsimile device and the local-side facsimile device is transferred to the previously mentioned computer, the administration of the correspondence state executed by the computer apparently turns out to be increasingly easy. When the signal arrives at the facsimile station, the substitutive signal receiving can be done mutually on the basis of the state between the computer and the local-side facsimile device. As a result, the treatment of signal processing can be performed with a high degree of certainty.

# CHAPTER 9
## *Data Compression*

Although efforts for G3 standards began in 1974, six years past before they were issued by the CCITT. A major delay was due to much disagreement between what is referred to as the Western camp (US and Europe) and the Japanese camp. The former was satisfied with MH one-dimensional coding, whereas the Japanese sought a two-dimensional coding method, called READ. When agreement was reached in 1980, the MH method was adopted as the C3 standard coding method, and the MR was chosen as an option.

The MH code was developed to compress the commonest lines (all white) to the shortest codes. Because this code is used to encode-decode one scanned line at a time, it is referred to as one-dimensional coding. To incorporate other developments in compression technology, today's G3 fax machines have more than one option from which to choose a coding scheme. The first of these is MR, which is an optional compression scheme allowed by CCITT. Another name for MR is two-dimensional coding. Simply put, MR compresses two scanned lines at a time, initially scanning two lines, then comparing the first line with the second line, and transmitting only the changes between them. Obviously, this compression method if faster than the MH one. CCITT allows manufacturers to create portions of their protocol, enabling further reduced transmission and reception times. For example, Ricoh Company developed a system to enhance the speed of MH and MR, called estimated fill bit control (EFC). EFC reduces the number of bits required for transmission. Both MR and EFC will only work with those receivers that are capable of reconstructing these codes. Compression technology has developed sufficiently to produce a throughput time of under 15 s per page. Most fax machines maintain a downward compatibility to communicate with other manufacturers' G1 to G3 machines. The G3 machines also have the ability to determine and select the most compatible compression scheme when transmitting to another machine.

At the end of 1977, Study Group XIV of CCITT agreed that G3 equipment should use a one-dimensional RL coding scheme and a MH code. A one-dimensional code was chosen as a suitable compromise between obtaining a high-compression efficiency while minimizing the susceptibility to transmission errors and keeping the implementation costs to a low level. Its freedom from patent restrictions was also an important consideration. In 1979, an optional two-dimensional coding scheme, in the form of an extension to the one-dimensional coding scheme, was added to the recommendation T.4 for G3 apparatus. The two-dimensional scheme allows a greater compression efficiency to be obtained for many documents, particularly when they are scanned at twice normal vertical resolution. The additional factors considered when choosing this code were compatibility with the one-dimensional code and possible future extensions to other codes.

## CRITERIA FOR SELECTING A ONE-DIMENSIONAL G3 CODE

The main purpose of a G3 standard was to allow typical A4 documents to be transmitted digitally over telephone networks in an average time of 1 min. The digital image representing a document is obtained by scanning it and quantizing each sample or pel into one of two logical levels, representing black and white. At a normal G3 scanning density of 3.85 lines/mm (about 1188 lines on an A4 page) with each line divided into 1728 pels, the amount of data generated would require, in the absence of source coding, a transmission time of just over 7 min at a transmission rate of 4800 b/s. Because of the strong statistical dependencies between pels, however, the transmission times for most documents can be considerably reduced with a suitable source coding method.

The relative importance of actors such as compression efficiency, error susceptibility, and complexity of implementation depend on each facsimile application. A high-compression efficiency is particularly important for high-volume usage. In other applications, the need is for reliable equipment providing acceptable copies over national or international telephone networks at reasonable terminal costs. In addition, the mechanical limitation of some equipment must be considered, and machines with a wide range of facilities must be able to interwork with more basic equipment.

Based on these criteria, a one-dimensional RL coding scheme using a MH code was chosen as a basic G3 standard. RL codes have been widely employed in data-reduction systems and are easy to implement. In most cases, MH codes offer high-compression efficiencies, and the use of a "modified" code simplifies implementation. Damage caused by errors is kept to acceptable levels by using a single-line coding scheme and by transmitting a robust line synchronization codeword. Other codes were investigated but were found to be equally susceptible to errors and generally performed less efficiently.

## ELEMENTS OF THE G3 RECOMMENDATIONS

The specifications needed to provide for interworking of G3 facsimile equipment over the general switched telephone network are given in CCITT recommendations T.4 and T.30. Recommendation T.4 contains standards concerning the following parameters: document size, resolution, scanning rate, source coding methods, and modulation method. Associated with these are several options that enable facsimilate equipment to communicate in alternative modes (e.g., a higher vertical resolution is provided so that higher-quality copies can be obtained). Two facsimile machines may communicate using any of the options by mutual agreement; otherwise they must use the appropriate recommended standard.

Recommendation T.30 specifies the digital signals and procedures used by G3 apparatus for call setup, premessage procedures for identifying and selecting the required facilities, message transmission, postmessage procedure, and call release. The following subsections summarize the parameters defined in T.4.

1. Parameters of Document Size and Resolution

a. Facsimile machines should be able to accept A4-size documents. As an option, documents up to A3 in size may be transmitted with the same resolution.

b. The normal vertical resolution is 3.85 lines/mm. A high vertical resolution of 7.7 lines/mm is available as an option.

c. Each scan line on an A4 document is divided into 1728 black and white pels. The number of pels may be optionally increased to about 2600 to allow documents up to A3 size to be transmitted at the same resolution.

d. The scanning line length on an A4 document is 215 mm. Other line lengths may be used provided that the vertical resolution is adjusted to maintain the correct picture proportions.

The normal vertical resolution is chosen to be the same as that used in G1 and G2. A higher resolution is included to allow higher-quality copies to be obtained. A horizontal resolution that is nearly twice that of the normal vertical resolution is required to ensure that staircase effects on vertical black and white edges owing to the sampling and quantizing processes do not impair legibility.

2. Minimum Scan Line Times and Message Format. These are specified so that transmitters and receivers can keep in step on a line-by-line basis and to allow for mechanical limitations of some machines. Also, some receivers operate at normal resolution by printing each scan line twice at high resolution. The recommended

standard minimum scan line times (MSLT) is 20 ms (equipment to a minimum of 96 coded b at a transmission rate of 4800 b/s); there are options of 10 ms (48 b), 5 ms (24 b), and 0 ms (i.e., no restriction). Any machine offering an option must be able to operate at all longer MSLTs down to 20 ms. The recommendation also includes a 40-ms option. The coding procedure includes a method of adding varying length strings of "fill" bits to those coded lines containing fewer than the required number of bits. Fill bits are easily recognized by the receiver and are discarded.

Figure 9–1 shows the format of the data for several coded lines. The end of document transmission is indicated by six consecutive EOL codewords, which form the return to control (RTC) signal.

**3.** Modulation and Demodulation Methods. When operating on the general switched telephone network, it is recommended that G3 equipment should use data rates of 4800 b/s and 2400 b/s, and the modulation, scrambler, equalization, and timing signals defined in CCITT recommendation V.27 ter. When higher speeds of operation are possible, however, it has been agreed that G3 equipment may operate optionally at 9600 b/s, and 7200 b/s using the modulation, scrambler, equalization, and timing signals defined in CCITT recommendation V.29. Some PTT administrations pointed out, however, that it might not be possible to guarantee the service at a data signaling rate higher than 2400 b/s.

## ONE-DIMENSIONAL CODING

This code was first suggested by the Plessey Company in 1976. Later a revised version of the code was proposed jointly by a number of British and American companies under the auspices of the British Facsimile Industries Compatibility Committee (BFICC) and the Electronic Industries Association (EIA). It is this version of the code that was eventually accepted by SGXIV of the CCITT. The extended code table described in section C-2 is due to a proposal made by the British Post Office.

**1.** *Coding scheme*—Each scan line is regarded as a sequence of alternating black and white lines. All lines are assumed to begin with a white run to ensure that the receiver maintains color synchronization; if the first actual run on a line is black, then a white run of zero length is transmitted at the beginning of the line.

Separate code tables used to represent the black and white runs are given in Table 9–1. Each code table can represent a RL value up to the maximum length of

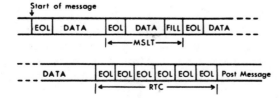

**Figure 9–1**  Group 3 Message Format
© *1980 IEEE [7]; reprinted with permission.*

**TABLE 9-1** MODIFIED HUFFMAN CODE

| | Terminating codewords | |
|---|---|---|
| Run length | White runs | Black runs |
| 0 | 00110101 | 0000110111 |
| 1 | 000111 | 010 |
| 2 | 0111 | 11 |
| 3 | 1000 | 10 |
| 4 | 1011 | 011 |
| 5 | 1100 | 0011 |
| 6 | 1110 | 0010 |
| 7 | 1111 | 00011 |
| 8 | 10011 | 000101 |
| 9 | 10100 | 000100 |
| 10 | 00111 | 0000100 |
| 11 | 01000 | 0000101 |
| 12 | 001000 | 0000111 |
| 13 | 000011 | 00000100 |
| 14 | 110100 | 00000111 |
| 15 | 110101 | 000011000 |
| 16 | 101010 | 0000010111 |
| 17 | 101011 | 0000011000 |
| 18 | 0100111 | 0000001000 |
| 19 | 0001100 | 00001100111 |
| 20 | 0001000 | 00001101000 |
| 21 | 0010111 | 00001101100 |
| 22 | 0000011 | 00000110111 |
| 23 | 0000100 | 00000101000 |
| 24 | 0101000 | 00000010111 |
| 25 | 0101011 | 00000011000 |
| 26 | 0010011 | 000011001010 |
| 27 | 0100100 | 000011001011 |
| 28 | 0011000 | 000011001100 |
| 29 | 00000010 | 000011001101 |
| 30 | 00000011 | 000001101000 |
| 31 | 00011010 | 000001101001 |
| 32 | 00011011 | 000001101010 |
| 33 | 00010010 | 000001101011 |
| 34 | 00010011 | 000011010010 |
| 35 | 00010100 | 000011010011 |
| 36 | 00010101 | 000011010100 |
| 37 | 00010110 | 000011010101 |
| 38 | 00010111 | 000011010110 |
| 39 | 00101000 | 000011010111 |
| 40 | 00101001 | 000001101100 |
| 41 | 00101010 | 000001101101 |
| 42 | 00101011 | 000011011010 |
| 43 | 00101100 | 000011011011 |
| 44 | 00101101 | 000001010100 |
| 45 | 00000100 | 000001010101 |
| 46 | 00000101 | 000001010110 |
| 47 | 00001010 | 000001010111 |

*(continued)*

**TABLE 9-1**  Continued

| Run length | White runs | Black runs |
|---:|:---:|:---:|
| 48 | 00001011 | 000001100100 |
| 49 | 01010010 | 000001100101 |
| 50 | 01010011 | 000001010010 |
| 51 | 01010100 | 000001010011 |
| 52 | 01010101 | 000000100100 |
| 53 | 00100100 | 000000110111 |
| 54 | 00100101 | 000000111000 |
| 55 | 01011000 | 000000100111 |
| 56 | 01011001 | 000000101000 |
| 57 | 01011010 | 000001011000 |
| 58 | 01011011 | 000001011001 |
| 59 | 01001010 | 000000101011 |
| 60 | 01001011 | 000000101100 |
| 61 | 00110010 | 000001011010 |
| 62 | 00110011 | 000001100110 |
| 63 | 00110100 | 000001100111 |
| Makeup codewords | | |
| 64 | 11011 | 0000001111 |
| 128 | 10010 | 000011001000 |
| 192 | 010111 | 000011001001 |
| 256 | 0110111 | 000001011011 |
| 320 | 00110110 | 000000110011 |
| 384 | 00110111 | 000000110100 |
| 448 | 01100100 | 000000110101 |
| 512 | 01100101 | 0000001101100 |
| 576 | 01101000 | 0000001101101 |
| 640 | 01100111 | 0000001001010 |
| 704 | 011001100 | 0000001001011 |
| 768 | 011001101 | 0000001001100 |
| 832 | 011010010 | 0000001001101 |
| 896 | 011010011 | 0000001110010 |
| 960 | 011010100 | 0000001110011 |
| 1024 | 011010101 | 0000001110100 |
| 1088 | 011010110 | 0000001110101 |
| 1152 | 011010111 | 0000001110110 |
| 1216 | 011011000 | 0000001110111 |
| 1280 | 011011001 | 0000001010010 |
| 1344 | 011011010 | 0000001010011 |
| 1408 | 011011011 | 0000001010100 |
| 1472 | 010011000 | 0000001010101 |
| 1536 | 010011001 | 0000001011010 |
| 1600 | 010011010 | 0000001011011 |
| 1664 | 011000 | 0000001100100 |
| 1728 | 010011011 | 0000001100101 |
| EOL | 000000000001 | 000000000001 |

one scan line (1728 pels) and contains two types of codewords: terminating code-words (TC) and makeup codewords (MUC).

Runs between 0 and 63 pels are transmitted using a single terminating codeword. Runs between 64 and 1728 are transmitted by a MUC followed by a TC. The MUC represents a RL value of 64 × N (where N is an integer between 1 and 27), which is equal to, or shorter than, the value of the run to be transmitted. The following TC specifies the difference between the MUC and the actual value of the run to be transmitted.

The coding of each scan line continues until all runs on the line (i.e., a total of 1728 pels) have been transmitted. Each coded line is followed by the EOL codeword. The EOL codeword is a unique sequence that cannot occur within a valid line of coded data. It can be detected irrespective of the way in which the decoder breaks up the coded line into codewords. Thus, if a transmission error corrupts some of the coded scan line data, then the error cannot prevent the EOL from being detected.

If the number of coded bits in a line is fewer than a certain agreed minimum, then "fill" bits consisting of varying length strings of "0's" are inserted between the line of coded data and the EOL codeword.

**2.** *Extended code tables*—The G3 standard provides an optional extension to the coding scheme allowing machines to transmit larger paper widths up to A3 in size, which require nearly 2600 pels/line. This option is provided by two extended code tables formed by adding 13 extra MUC listed in Table 9–2 to each of the basic code tables given in Table 9–1. The construction of the extra codewords is described in section C-3. The use of the extended code table is signaled in the recommendation T.30 control procedures.

**TABLE 9–2**   EXTENDED MODIFIED HUFFMAN CODE

| Run length (black or white) | Makeup codeword |
|---|---|
| 1792 | 00000001000 |
| 1856 | 00000001100 |
| 1920 | 00000001101 |
| 1984 | 000000010010 |
| 2048 | 000000010011 |
| 2112 | 000000010100 |
| 2176 | 000000010101 |
| 2240 | 000000010110 |
| 2304 | 000000010111 |
| 2368 | 000000011100 |
| 2432 | 000000011101 |
| 2496 | 000000011110 |
| 2560 | 000000011111 |

© *1980 IEEE [7]; reprinted with permission.*

**3.** *Construction of MH code tables*—The properties of the EOL codeword can be further understood by considering the construction of the MH code tables. Each code table was initially designed according to Huffman's procedure and to contain the codeword 0000000 (7 × 0), which was designated to signal the end of a scan line. Redundant bits were then added to the codeword 7 × 0 to form the codeword 10 × 0 + 1. By examining Table 9–1, it can be seen that no codeword ends in a sequence of more than three 0's or begins with a sequence of 0's larger than six and therefore 10 × 0 + 1 forms a unique sequence that cannot be produced by a concatenation of codewords. The final 1 of the EOL is included to indicate the start of the next coded line, because fill bits may extend the sequence beyond 10 × 0.

The extended black and white code tables were formed using the codeword 7 × 0 as the prefix for the thirteen extra MUC. The 7 × 0 codeword originally designated to signal the end of a scan line now needs to be increased to 8 × 0. Redundant bits are then added to this codeword to form the EOL codeword 11 × 0 + 1, which is unique using either the basic or extended code tables. This process can be carried out without altering any of the other codewords in Table 9–1. The same thirteen extra codewords can be added to each code table without a loss in efficiency because long runs occur very infrequently.

**4.** *Error concealment techniques*—Unless the number of decoded pels between two successive EOL codewords is equal to 1728, then it can be assumed that an error has occurred in a transmitted line. In this case one of the following error concealment processes may be adopted:

**a.** Replace the damaged line by an all white line.

**b.** Repeat the previous line.

**c.** Print the damaged line.

**d.** Use a line-to-line processing or correlation technique to reconstruct as much of the line as possible.

The RLs decoded after resynchronization are displaced from their correct positions on the scan line. If the displacement is more than about 4 pels, then the picture information on the damaged line will become disassociated from that on adjacent lines. Because this effect is very noticeable and causes a disturbing streak across a page, it is usually preferable to use method a. or b. rather than to print the damaged line. For small displacements; however, method c. may provide a simple means of minimizing the loss of information owing to an error.

Correlation method d. takes advantage of the fact that the recovery period is often short and attempts to retain as much as possible of the correctly decoded data on a damaged line. This is achieved by attempting to locate the damaged RLs. One method is to measure the correlation between groups of pels on the damaged line with corresponding groups on the adjacent lines above and below. When the correlation is good, generally at the beginning and end of the damaged scan line, the scan line data is used to reconstruct the line. The part of the scan line that is assumed to be damaged is then replaced by a corresponding part of the previous line.

# TWO-DIMENSIONAL CODING

The MR code is a line-by-line scheme in which the position of each changing element on the coding line is coded with respect to either the position of a corresponding changing element on the reference line, which lies immediately above the coding line, or with respect to the preceding changing element on the coding line. After the coding line has been coded, it becomes the reference line for the next coding line. To prevent the vertical propagation of damage caused by transmission errors, no more than $K-1$ successive lines are two-dimensionally coded and the next line is one-dimensionally coded. Usually $K$ is set equal to 2 at normal resolution and set equal to 4 at high resolution. Before describing the coding procedure, it is necessary to define the changing pels and the three coding modes used in the coding procedure.

**1.** Definition of changing picture elements—A changing picture element is one whose "color" (black or white) is different from that of the previous element along the same line.

The coding algorithm makes use of five changing elements situated on the coding and reference lines. These are defined below with examples given in Figure 9–2.

> $a_0$—The reference or starting changing element on the coding line. Its position is defined by the previous coding mode as described in section D-3. At the start of the coding line, $a_0$ is set on an imaginary white changing element situated just before the first actual element on the coding line.
>
> $a_1$—The next changing element to the right of $a_0$ on the coding line. This has the opposite color to $a_0$ and is the next changing element to be coded.
>
> $a_2$—The next changing element to the right of $a_1$ on the coding line.
>
> $b_1$—The next changing element on the reference line to the right of $a_0$ and having the same color as $a_1$.
>
> $b_2$—The next changing element on the reference line to the right of $b_1$.

If any of the coding elements $a_1$, $a_2$, $b_1$, $b_2$ are not detected at any time during the coding of the line, they are set on an imaginary element positioned just after the last actual element on the respective scan line.

**2.** Definition of coding modes—The coding procedures use three coding modes, which are defined subsequently and illustrated by the examples given in Figure 9–2.

> **a.** *Pass mode coding*—This is identified when the position of $b_2$ lies to the left of $a_1$. The purpose of the pass mode is to identify white or black runs on the

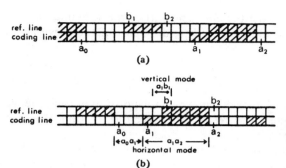

**Figure 9-2** (a) Pass Mode in Two-Dimensional Coding; (b) Horizontal Mode in Two-Dimensional Coding © *1980 IEEE [7]; reprinted with permission.*

reference line that are not adjacent to corresponding white or black runs on the coding line. The pass mode is represented by a signal codeword in the two-dimensional code table (Table 9–3).

**b.** *Vertical mode coding*—When this mode is identified, the position of $a_1$ is coded relative to the position of $b_1$. The relative distance $a_1b_1$ can take on one of seven values $V(0)$, $V_R(1)$, $V_R(2)$, $V_R(3)$, $V_L(1)$, $V_L(2)$, and $V_L(3)$, each of which is represented by a separate codeword. The subscripts $_R$ and $_L$ indicate that $a_1$ is to the right or left, respectively, of $b_1$, and the number in parentheses indicates the value of the distance $a_1b_1$.

**c.** *Horizontal mode coding*—If vertical mode coding cannot be used to code the position of $a_1$, then its position must be coded by horizontal mode coding. That is, the run lengths $a_0a_1$ and $a_1a_2$ are coded using the codewords

**TABLE 9-3** TWO-DIMENSIONAL CODE

| Mode | Elements to be coded | | Notation | Codeword |
|---|---|---|---|---|
| Pass | $b_1$, $b_2$ | | P | 0001 |
| Horizontal | $a_0a_1$, $a_1a_2$ | | H | $001 + M(a_0a_1) + M(a_1a_2)$ |
| | $a_1$ just under $b_1$ | $a_1b_1 = 0$ | V(0) | 1 |
| | | $a_1b_1 = 1$ | $V_R(1)$ | 011 |
| | $a_1$ to the right of $b_1$ | $a_1b_1 = 2$ | $V_R(2)$ | 000011 |
| Vertical | | $a_1b_1 = 3$ | $V_R(3)$ | 0000011 |
| | | $a_1b_1 = 1$ | $V_L(1)$ | 010 |
| | $a_1$ to the left of $b_1$ | $a_1b_1 = 2$ | $V_L(2)$ | 000010 |
| | | $a_1b_1 = 3$ | $V_L(3)$ | 0000010 |
| Two-dimensional extensions | | | | 0000001XXX |
| One-dimensional extensions | | | | 000000001XXX |
| End-of-line codeword (EOL) | | | | 000000000001 |
| One-dimensional coding of next line | | | | EOL + 1 |
| Two-dimensional coding of next line | | | | EOL + 0 |

$M(a_0a_1)$ and $M(a_1a_2)$ are codewords taken from the MH code tables given in Tables 9–1 and 9–2. The bit assignment for the XXX bits is 111 for uncompressed mode.

© *1980 IEEE [7]; reprinted with permission.*

$H + M(a_a a_1) + M(a_1 a_2)$. H is the flag codeword "001" taken from the two-dimensional code table (Table 9-3), and $M(a_0 a_1)$ and $M(a_1 a_2)$ are codewords taken from the appropriate code tables to represent the colors and values of the run lengths $a_0 a_1$ and $a_1 a_2$.

**3.** *Coding procedure*—Having determined the next set of changing elements $a_1$, $a_2$, $b_1$, and $b_2$, the coding procedure identifies the next coding mode, selects the appropriate codeword from Table 9-3 and then resets the reference element $a_0$ as defined subsequently. The coding procedure is formally defined by the flow diagram shown in Figure 9-3 and basically consists of two steps.

**a.** *Step 1*—

    **i.** If $b_2$ is detected before $a_1$ then a pass mode has been identified and the

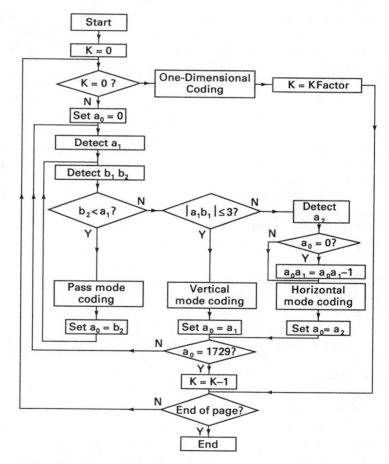

**Figure 9-3** Flow Diagram for Two-Dimensional Code © *1980 IEEE [7]; reprinted with permission.*

codeword "0001" is issued. The reference element $a_0$ is set on the element below $b_2$ in preparation for the next coding.

    **ii.** If a pass mode is not detected, proceed to step 2.

  **b.** *Step 2*—Determine the number of elements that separate $a_1$ and $b_1$.

    **i.** If $a_1b_2 \leq 3$ then code the relative distance $a_1b_2$ by vertical mode coding. Set $a_0$ on the position of $a_1$ in preparation for the next coding.

    **ii.** If $a_1b_2 \geq 3$ then code the positions of $a_1$ and $a_2$ by horizontal mode coding—that is, transmit the codewords $H + M(a_0a_1) + M(a_1a_2)$. After the coding, $a_2$ is regarded as the new position of the reference element $a_0$.

It is possible to vary the preceding procedure without affecting the compatibility between coder and decoder, but further studies into the use of these variations are required. For example, it is possible to restrict the use of the pass mode to a single pass made to prevent long sequences of pass modes, which might give inefficient coding. Also, if $a_1b_1 \leq 3$, each $a_1$ may be coded by both vertical and horizontal mode coding and the most efficient coding mode chosen as in the original READ code. Preliminary tests have not indicated that these particular variations lead to increased compression factors, however.

    **4.** *Coding First and Last Elements on Line*—If horizontal mode coding is used to code the first element on the coding line, then the value of $a_0a_1$ is replaced by $a_0a_1 - 1$ to ensure that the correct RL value is transmitted. Therefore, if the first element on a line is black, then the first codeword $M(a_0a_1)$ will be that which represents a white run of zero length.

    The coding of the line continues until the imaginary changing element situated just after the last actual element on the coding line has been coded. Thus, exactly 1728 elements are coded on each line, and the receiver can check that each line has been correctly decoded.

    **5.** *Code table*—The two-dimensional code table is given in Table 9–3 and is also drawn in the form of a code tree in Figure 9–4. The code tree is constructed so that it contains the codeword "0000000," which is then extended to form the EOL codeword $11 \times 0 + 1$. The remaining codewords are then added to the code tree according to the relative frequencies of the required coding elements. These frequencies were obtained by computer simulation tests on the CCITT documents. Finally the two-dimensional extension codeword (section D1) is assigned to the shortest remaining codeword. This construction method ensures that the same unique EOL codeword is used whether a line is coded by the one- or two-dimensional coding procedure.

    **6.** *EOL codeword, tag bits, fill bits, and return to control*—Each EOL codeword is followed by a single tag bit, a 1 or a 0, which indicates that the next line is one or two dimensionally coded, respectively. "Fill" bits consisting of vari-

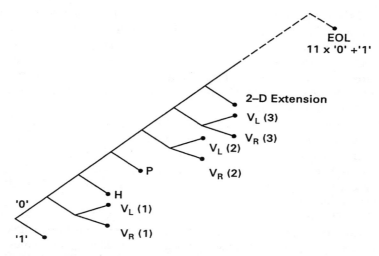

**Figure 9-4** Code Tree For Modified READ Code © *1980 IEEE [7]; reprinted with permission.*

able length strings of 0's are inserted, when required, at the end of a coded line and before the EOL and tag bit. The RTC signal consists of six consecutive EOL codewords, each of which is followed by a 1 tag bit.

7. K factor—As stated earlier, it is recommended that, after a one dimensionally coded line, not more than K–1 successive lines are two-dimensionally coded, where K is equal to 2 for documents scanned at normal resolution, and 4 for those scanned at higher resolution. More scan lines than suggested by the value of K can be one-dimensionally coded without affecting compatibility if this proves useful in terms of either compression or error susceptibility.

## REPRODUCTION OF GRAY SCALE OR HALFTONES

Facsimile manufacturers typically employ sophisticated circuitry at the transmitter to determine the color (black or white) of a pel. This system is ideally suited for transmitting typed documents and sketches, which comprise most facsimile traffic, because this information has fundamentally only two levels of brightness. This system is not well suited, however, to the transmission of imagery having a continuous range of gray scale values, such as photographs and x-rays. By introducing a minor modification into the basically bilevel facsimile system, dither coding delivers an output image that conveys gray-scale information.

Dithering is an image processing technique that creates a two-level picture, which gives the illusion of a multilevel picture by appropriately arranging the spatial density of the two levels (usually black and white) on the picture.

Dithering techniques consist of comparing a multilevel image with a position-dependent threshold and setting pels to white when the input signal exceeds the threshold and setting other pels to black. The matrix of threshold values, called the dither matrix, is repeated over the entire picture to provide the threshold pattern for the whole image.

In dither coding, the threshold is purposely varied (or "dithered") in amplitude from pel to pel, as shown in Figure 9–5. If the threshold is dithered uniformly over the dynamic range, the average value of the output image over several neighboring pixels will approximate the input gray value. The eye will tend to perform an averaging function on the dither pattern, and the observer will perceive the input gray value.

The rapid transmission time of a page (typically 30 s) for G3 facsimile is a key reason for its unprecedented market acceptance. This time reduction is in turn based on data compression technology, which reduces the redundancy inherent in typical transmitted pages. Unfortunately, the dithering process reduces this redundancy and, by introducing more black-white transitions, will lengthen the transmission time for a page.

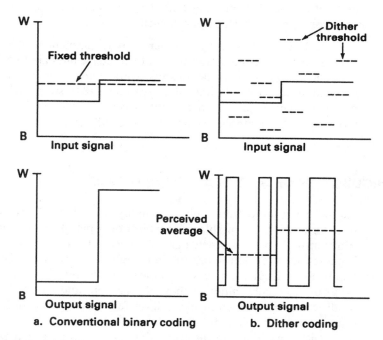

**Figure 9–5**  Conventional Binary Coding versus Dither Coding © *1989 IEEE [2]; reprinted with permission.*

## DITHER CODING TECHNIQUES

### Random Dither

The random dither technique differs from the other concepts because the dither pattern is not synchronized to the pel structure. This compression technique employs a pseudorandom number generator to vary the 8-b gray level of each input pel before it is compared to a fixed threshold to determine its binary color (black or white). Spurious artifacts such as moire beat patterns are largely avoided because the technique is spatially independent. The algorithm is fairly simple, employing a congruence method to generate pseudorandom numbers.

### Clumped Dither

The clumped dither compression technique is an electronic approximation of the photomechanical screening process (3). It employs a matrix of fixed threshold, shown in Figure 9–6, which are arranged in such a way that a "dot" grows outward from the center as successively darker gray levels are encountered in low-contrast regions of the image. The numbers in the matrix represent threshold values out of 256 possible brightness levels. The 8-b gray level of each input pel is compared with its corresponding threshold as the image is scanned and processed.

### Distributed Dither

The distributed dither compression technique employs an ordered matrix of thresholds in which the threshold values are distributed pseudorandomly throughout the

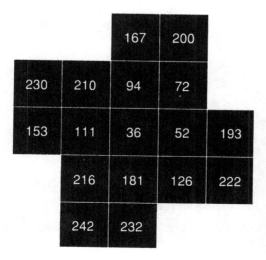

**Figure 9–6** Clumped Dither Threshold Matrix © *1989 IEEE [2]; reprinted with permission.*

matrix. Figure 9–7 illustrates one example of a pattern of threshold values for a distributed dither algorithm having a 4 × 4 matrix.

This technique was considered for the analysis but was not selected for computer simulation. The compression it achieves, and the complexity of its algorithm are comparable with those of the random dither technique; the output image quality, however, is subject to spurious distortions, edge effects, and beta patterns. Because the distributed and random dither compression techniques are similar in all but output image quality, the random dither technique was selected for analysis over the distributed dither. The way in which the modes of fine-normal-superfine and halftone (gray scale) transmission are handled in the Panasonic KX-F220 machine is described subsequently.

The read circuit is composed of eight blocks (1 to 8), and different blocks are used at the time of normal fine-normal transmission and at the time of halftone transmission. Switching is executed by the multiplexer IC36. This reading method has the following special features. The output scatter of the image sensor is corrected by the ROM (IC34) in which the data has been stored in advance. A high-quality reading image is obtained by correcting these data (shading). In other words, even when white paper of the same density is read, the output (VIDEO signal) of an image sensor shows differences mainly because of scatter of the LED light volume. Here, a ROM for compensation of the scatter corresponding to each individual image sensor is equipped. Accordingly, when the image sensor is exchanged, the ROM (IC34) is also exchanged.

## Reading path at the time of fine-normal-superfine transmission

The output (VIDEO signal) from the close-contact image sensor (Figure 9–8) is amplified 1.2 times by the buffer amplifier (1). At this time, the output of this amplifier when the close-contact image sensor has read black is adjusted to DV 0V by VR13. This amplified VIDEO output enters at pin (4) of IC40 of the comparator (8). This output also enters the peak hold circuit (2) and the integrating circuit (3), the thresh-

| 0 | 8 | 2 | 10 |
| 12 | 4 | 14 | 6 |
| 3 | 11 | 1 | 9 |
| 15 | 7 | 13 | 5 |

**Figure 9–7** 4 × 4 Distributed Dither Threshold Matrix © *1989 IEEE [2]; reprinted with permission.*

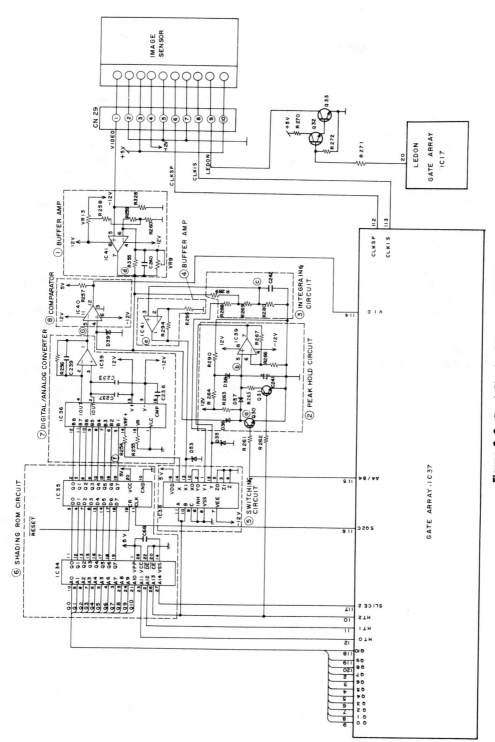

**Figure 9-8** Read Circuit of Panasonic KX-F220

old level is formed in the circuits (4 to 7), and it is entered at pin (5) of IC40 of the comparator (8). Here, it is compared with the previously mentioned output from (1), the discrimination is made between white and black. In other words, when the VIDEO signal is larger than the threshold level, the output of the comparator (8) is white (high level = 5 V), and when it is smaller, the output is black (low level = 0 V), and this is given as input to the gate array IC37 pin (114) VID for processing. The principle of the threshold generation circuit is explained subsequently.

The peak of the signal entered into the peak hold circuit (2) is held by C241, and the brightest level of the normal underground is output to pin (7) of IC39. Here Q31 is in ON condition. In other words, large changes of the underground level discharge C241 via R265. The peak hold output of IC39 pin (7) enters R268 of the integrating circuit (3) via the pins (15 and 1) of IC38 of the switching circuit (5).

On the one hand, this signal charges C242 via R269, whereas on the other, C242 is charged and discharged via R289 according to the VIDEO signal at point (d) so that the point (c) follows the VIDEO signal. The relation between this charging and discharging is adjusted so that a temporary threshold level is generated as shown in Figure 9–9.

This output passes through the pins (13 to 14) if IC38 of the switching circuit (5) and enters pin (14) of IC36 of the D/A converter circuit (7). With Vf as the input at this point (f), output Vg of pin (1) of IC39 is compensated as shown subsequently by the input to B1 to B8 of IC36.

Selection of the compensation area of this ROM and selection of the compensation data for each dot in this area is done by the gate array IC37, Q0 to Q10, HT0, HT1, FT2, and SLICE2; the output is latched once by IC35; and it is given as input to the D/A converter IC36.

The output of pin (115) of the gate array IC37 becomes low level only during reading of about 10 cm at the center of a line of an A4 document, and Q30 becomes

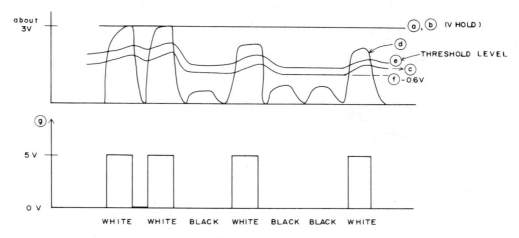

**Figure 9–9**  Generation of Threshold Level

| B1 | B2 | B3 | B4 | B5 | B6 | B7 | B8 | 16 Binary | 10 Binary | |
|----|----|----|----|----|----|----|----|-----------|-----------|--|
| 1 | 1 | | 1 | 1 | 1 | 1 | 1 | FF | 255 | $Vg = \dfrac{255}{255} Vf = Vf$ |
| 1 | 1 | 1 | 1 | 1 | 1 | 1 | 0 | FE | 254 | $Vg = \dfrac{254}{255} Vf$ |
| 0 | 0 | 0 | 0 | 0 | 0 | 0 | 0 | 00 | 0 | $Vg = \dfrac{0}{255} Vf = 0$ |

OFF; in other words, peak hold is executed, and the underground of the document is read. This is done because when peak hold is executed for the entire area of an A4 document, the white of the roller will be read as the background level when a document smaller than A4 or a document with colored background is inserted, so that the threshold level will be set too high, and the entire colored document will be read as black.

## Reading path at the time of halftone transmission

At the time of halftone transmission, the signal does not pass through the integrating circuit (3) and the buffer amplifier (4) in the threshold generation circuit for fine, normal, and superfine, and the output of the peak hold circuit enters the pin (14) of the D/A converter IC36 via the pins (15 to 2 to 12 to 14) of IC38 of the switching circuit (5). As Q31 of the peak hold circuit always is OFF, the peak value of the level of the underground is held at all times.

## Halftone principle

The dither method is used for expression of halftones. With the dither method, the threshold level is changed for each dot according to the dither pattern (Figure 9–10), and binary output is obtained. Concretely speaking, looking at a 4 × 4 dot pixel block in the document, the 16 pixels in this block are expressed as quasi-halftones by means of the density of the black pixels (number of black pixels) according to the density of the document. As the realization method, halftones in sixteen steps can be realized by changing the threshold level for black-white discrimination for each dot of the 4 × 4 dots.

As shown in Figure 9–10, weighting is executed for each dot, calculation is

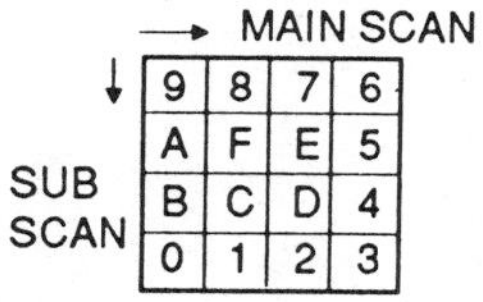

**Figure 9–10** Dither Pattern Used in Panasonic KX-F220

executed regarding the white level, and the threshold level is decided. The calculation method is shown subsequently.

$$Vs = Vw \times \alpha/16$$

Vs:    Threshold level

Vw:    White level

$\alpha$:    Weight

This weighting pattern is called the dither pattern.

# CHAPTER 10
## *Scanners*

Scanners consist of the sensor, which converts the document into electrical signals; the means for lighting the document; whatever optics is employed; and other parts to form the complete scanner assembly.

As mentioned in chapter 1 it was a natural for facsimile equipment designers to look at CCDs as logical sensors for use in document scanners. They were finding much favor in video cameras and camcorders in the late 1970s and early 1980s. In facsimile equipment the scanning was greatly simplified over that in television equipment, where both horizontal and vertical electronic scanning were required. In facsimile, with the flat-bed scanner approach it was only necessary to move the document past a linear CCD array as shown in Figure 10–1. The electronic performance was excellent, but the need for an optical system to match the size of the scanned data to the somewhat smaller CCD presented the principal disadvantage. Unless the light path was folded by the use of mirrors, the optical system could run almost the full length of the facsimile machine as shown in Figure 10–2. Thus, the size of the machine could be limited by the CCDs optical requirements.

Nevertheless, CCD scanners have been used in many facsimile machines owing to some extent because of their lower cost than contact-type scanners. As seen later in this chapter, much effort has been expended to reduce the cost of contact-type scanners and to improve their performance.

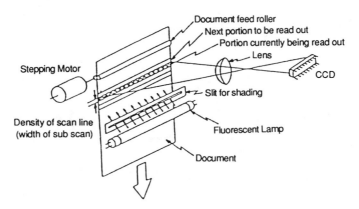

**Figure 10-1**  Composition of Image Reader Section Using CCD Scanner in Panasonic KX-F120 Fax Machine

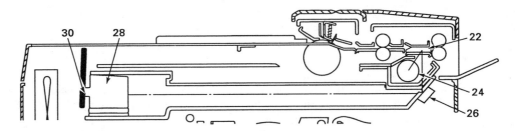

**Figure 10-2**  Long Optical Path in Some Early Digital Fax Machines Using CCD Scanners (22, Target Glass; 24, Light Source; 26, Mirror; 28, Lens Unit; 30, CCD)

## CCD SCANNER DESIGN AND OPERATION

In a CCD scanner design used in some Panasonic machines, three mirrors are used to save space by having the light reflected five times. A description of the circuit operation of this scanner is given subsequently. A circuit diagram of the CCD board as related to the main board is shown in Figure 10-3. The image signal timing chart is shown in Figure 10-4.

### Circuit Operation

CCD and read section

The CCD control signals are generated by IC8, pass through IC33, and form signals 01TTL, 02TTL, 0RTTL, and 0SPTTL. The timing chart of each signal is shown in the image signal timing chart diagram. 0SPTTL is a start pulse against CCD and

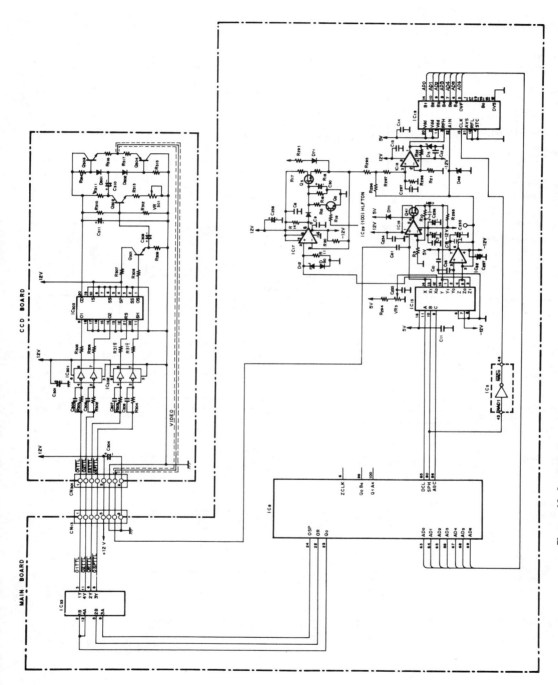

**Figure 10-3** CCD Scanner Board Associated with Main Board in Panasonic KX-F120

207

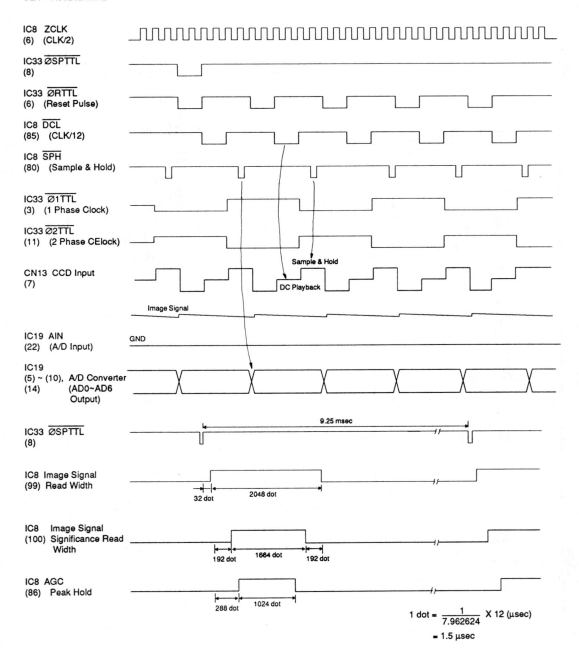

**Figure 10-4**   Image Signal Timing Chart of CCD Scanner Shown in Figure 10-1

is generated once every 9.25 ms. 01TTL and 02TTL are CCD clock pulses and $f = 1/24 \times 7.962624$ MHz. 0RTTL is the CCD reset pulse and $f = 1/12 \times 7.962624$ MHz. Moreover, CCD image signal output is made synchronous with 0RTTL, then output. The aforementioned signals (01TTL, 02TTL, 0RTT1, 0SPTTL) are input to CCD along the route IC33 to connector CN13 (main board) to connector CN301 (CCD board) to IC301, IC302 (driver IC) to IC303 (CCD). Image signal output of CCD is transmitted along the following route.

$$IC303\ (1) - > Q301 - > Q302,\ VR301 - > Q303,\ Q304 - > connector\ CN301$$
$$(7) - >\ connector\ CN13\ (7) - > C61 - > IC16 - > Q41 - > IC15\ (1)\ - > IC15\ (2)$$
$$- > IC32 - > IC19\ (22)$$

IC15 is an analog switch that performs the following operations:

$\overline{\text{DCL}}$   Low level $- >$ X(14) - XO (12) ON
       High level $- >$ X(14) - X1 (13) ON

$\overline{\text{SPH}}$   Low level $- >$ Y(15) - YO (2) ON
       High level $- >$ Y(15) - Y1 (1) ON

AGC   Low level $- >$ Z(4) - Z0 (5) ON
       High level $- >$ Z(4) - Z1 (3) ON

When DCL is at low level, direct current reproduction of image signal occurs. When SPH is at low level, the image signal is charged in C16, sampled, and held.

When AGC is at high level, the peak-hold circuit is connected. The timing of DCL, SPH, and AGC as mentioned earlier is shown in the image signal timing chart.

IC19 is a 7-b A/D converter. It delivers digital outputs 5 to 10 and 14 through analog input of image signal AIN (22) and RFH (3). The readout width of the CCD is 2048 dots (B4 size), but the effective width used for copy and forwarding is 1664 dots (A4 size). Here 1 dot $= 12 \times 1/7\ .962624\ \{\mu s\} = 1.5\ \mu s$; and 8 dot = 1mm. IC8 (99) is the monitor terminal of CCD image signal readout width (2048 dots). IC8 (100) is the monitor terminal of effective readout width (1664 dots).

## CONTACT-TYPE IMAGE SENSORS

By the time that the G3 standard recommendations had been made, it was apparent that an image sensor that required a much shorter light path than that needed for small photodiode arrays and CCDs was very desirable. Such a sensor had to have the same width as that of the document, which was being scanned. A sensor, called a planar-type reader was proposed. As shown in Figure 10–5, it consisted of an insulating substrate(1), a photoconductive layer (2) deposited on the substrate, and

**Figure 10-5** Planar-Type Reader Element

a pair of electrodes (3 and 4) mounted on the photoconductive layer. Each one of these devices corresponded to just one bit of sensed signal, so a large number of them had to be arranged in an array as long as the width of the document. The speed of response of this arrangement was limited, because it was impossible to bring the electrodes 3 and 4 closer together than about 10 $\mu$m. At this speed, the time required to scan one line on an 8 1/2" x 11" sheet is 20 milliseconds with a resolution of 8 elements/mm. Such a limited reading speed was too low to meet the requirements of a facsimile machine. Another problem that hampered this device for facsimile application was the use of chalcogenide glass for the photoconductive element. It was unstable and could not be controlled uniformly in its manufacture.

To solve these problems and provide a workable contact-type sensor for facsimile machines, a team of Japanese engineers invented in 1981 what they called an "Elongate Thin-Film Reader." T. Hamano, H. Ito, M. Takenouchi, T. Ozawa, M. Fuse, and T. Nakamura filed a U.S. patent application for this device in December, 1981. The patent, no. 4,419,696, was granted about two years later and was assigned to the Fuji Xerox Company, Tokyo, Japan. The objects of this invention were to provide the following advantages:

1. To provide a manuscript reader incorporating photosensitive elements of amorphous silicon capable of high-speed reading operation along an elongated zone (the width of a document);
2. To provide a novel reader having a faster response to light, comprising photosensitive elements that are of relatively uniform sensitivities, operably stable for an increased period of time, and easy to fabricate.

The inventors concluded that these objectives could be achieved by providing an elongate thin-film reader comprising an insulating substrate, a plurality of metal electrodes each for one bit of sensed signal, a layer of amorphous silicon deposited flatwise on the plurality of metal electrodes, and a transparent electrode deposited flatwise on the amorphous silicon layer in opposite relation to the plurality of metal electrodes. The amorphous silicon was preferably i-type or p-type. To achieve accurate binary conversion of the analog output voltages from the sensors, it was stated that individually adjustable threshold voltages could be provided.

This invention was one of the first approaches to the use of amorphous silicon in a contact-type sensor. In 1982, T. Ozawa, M. Takenouchi and others presented a paper entitled "Design and Evaluation of A4 Amorphous Silicon Hybrid Image Sensor." Because the preceding invention presented the basic approach to present-day contact image sensors, further details follow.

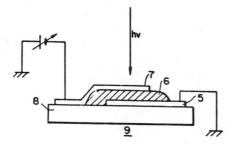

**Figure 10-6** Cross-Sectional View of Reader Device in Elongated Thin-Film Reader (U.S. Patent No. 4,419,696)

As shown in Figure 10-6, a reader device (9) according to this invention consisted of an insulating substrate (8), a lower metal electrode (5) deposited on the insulating substrate (8), a layer of amorphous silicon (6) deposited on the lower metal electrode (5), and an upper transparent electrode (7) deposited on the layer of amorphous silicon. The insulating substrate (8) could be made of any material that has a relatively high mechanical strength and is a good insulator, such as ceramic, glass, or plastics. The insulating substrate may be used as it is, or may be glazed for improved smoothness, or may be provided with a deposited substance that would enable stronger adhesion to the lower metal electrode or would improve the electrical characteristics of the lower metal electrode.

The lower metal electrode (5) was composed of a plurality of electrode members corresponding to the bits required for reading information. The lower electrode members were preferably arranged in a row as shown in Figure 10-7a with lead wires attached thereto at a desired side of the row of electrode members. As illustrated in Figures 10-7b to 10-7d, the lower electrode members may be in a plurality of rows with lead wires (not shown) arranged in a manner similar to the pattern shown in Figure 10-7a.

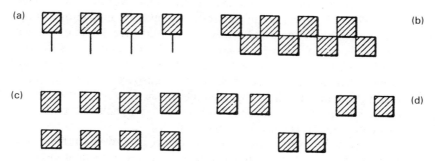

**Figure 10-7** (a) Electrodes in Single Row with Leads on One Side of Array; (b) Electrodes in Two Rows with Electrode Positions Alternating between Two Rows; (c) Electrode Pattern Composed of Two Rows with Electrodes in Two Rows Arranged Side by Side; (d) Electrode Pattern Composed of Two Rows with Electrodes in Each Row Arranged in Pairs with Pair Position Alternating between Rows along Array

As shown in Figure 10–8, the lower electrode members 5-1 to 5-5 may be square or of other desired shapes. Photosensitive regions are defined by areas in which the lower electrode members and the transparent electrode are superimposed with the amorphous silicon layer interposed between. The lower metal electrode (5) may be made of various materials such as Cr-Au (in two layers), Ni, Al, Cr, Pt, Pd, Mo, or Ti.

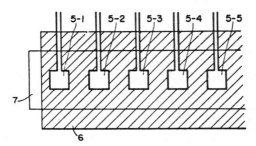

**Figure 10–8**  Reader Device of This Invention as Seen from Upper Transparent Electrode

The layer of amorphous silicon can be deposited uniformly by plasma CVD, sputtering, or vapor deposition, and is preferably not doped. If it is to be doped, it can be made i-type by doping with a small amount of hydrogen, or p-type by doping with boron or elements in Group III of the Periodic Table. The amorphous silicon layer thus formed is uniform and should have a thickness which ranges from 0.5 $\mu$m to 5 $\mu$m. The amorphous silicon layer is preferably of a single coating covering all of the lower metal electrode members, which serve as photosensitive elements. The layer of amorphous silicon formed should have a volume resistivity of $10^{10}$ $\Omega$ cm or higher, and preferably $10^{12}$ $\Omega$ cm or higher.

The upper transparent electrode (7) is preferably comprised of a film of ITO ($In_2O_3 + SnO_2$) with a suitable ratio between the amounts of these elements. The layer of ITO is preferably of a thickness ranging from 500 to 2000 A and covers the layer of amorphous silicon at least in the areas over the lower metal electrode members. Thus, the lower metal electrode, the layer of amorphous silicon, and the upper transparent electrode jointly form a photosensitive device or a group of photosensitive devices of a sandwiched construction. The amorphous silicon layer should be so deposited as to avoid direct contact between the lead wires connected to the lower metal electrode members and the upper transparent electrode. The positions of the metal electrode and the transparent electrode may be reversed from that in the illustrated structure. The relationship between bit signals and photoelectric outputs for this construction is shown in Figure 10–9.

Operation of the photosensitive device according to this invention is described with reference to Figure 10–10, which shows an equivalent circuit. The photosensitive elements (9) shown in Figure 10–6 are equivalent to parallel-connected circuits of capacitors 10 (10-1, . . . , 10-n) and diodes 11 (11-1, . . . , 11-n). The capacitors (10) have a capacitance created by the lower metal electrode (5), the layer of amorphous silicon (6), and the upper transparent electrode (7), the capacitance including capacitances between the lead wires. The diodes 11 (11-1, . . . , 11-n) are constituted

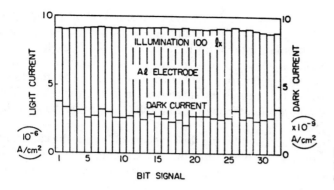

**Figure 10-9** Graph of Relationship between Bit Signals and Photoelectric Outputs in Device of This Invention

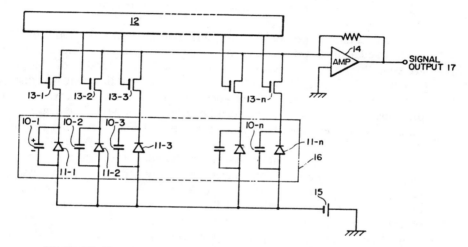

**Figure 10-10** Equivalent Circuit Diagram of Photosensitive Devices According to This Invention

by the layer of amorphous silicon. Each of the read devices composed of the capacitors (10), and the diodes (11) correspond to one bit in one line, and the read devices are provided for the extent of one line. A manuscript or an object to be read can thus be read by scanning the line of read devices.

As switching devices (13-1 to 13-n), such as CMOS, are successively energized by a shift register (12), the read devices (10 and 11) are sequentially grounded through an operational amplifier (14). The terminals of the read devices (10 and 11) remote from the operational amplifier (14) are connected to a biasing power supply (15) through the upper transparent electrode.

At the time of starting scanner operation, the read devices (10 and 11) are free of electric charges. All of the switches (13-1 to 13-n) are then turned on, allowing currents to flow from the amplifier (14) through these switches to charge the capacitors (10-1 to 10-n), but these currents are not considered to be read signals. Under this condition, the upper side of each capacitor will be substantially at ground potential while the lower side is negative. On the scanning entering a line to be read, and provided a portion of the manuscript that positionally corresponds to the capacitor 10-1 is white, the corresponding layer of amorphous silicon is rendered conductive, thereby permitting a current to flow from the higher potential side of the capacitor to the biasing power supply (15) to thereby discharge the capacitor (10-1). The drop in potential will be communicated through the switch (13-1) to be detected by the operational amplifier (14).

When the switch (13-2) is energized by the shift register (12) with the capacitor (10-2) corresponding in position to a black portion of the manuscript, the amorphous silicon remains nonconductive, and the capacitor (10-2) remains charged with electric charges supplied during a previous cycle of operation. Thus no current signal is fed to the operational amplifier (14). The line is successively scanned in this manner, and so are subsequent lines.

On scanning one line with the shift register (12), all photosensitive elements are charged again in preparation for reading a next line. The photosensitive elements are kept illuminated by a source of light, which would tend to discharge the capacitors that correspond to white image portions of the line that has just been read. The amount of discharge owing to being illuminated with light while staying on the previous line that has been read can be reduced to a negligible degree, however, by simultaneously reading all elements at the end of a line scan just before shifting to the next line.

Although U.S. patent no. 4,419,696, laid down the basics for contact scanners employing amorphous silicon, there were many aspects of such devices that were subject to further inventions to improve their performance and reduce the cost of manufacturing them. In this regard, it was a fertile field for inventors, and many patents have been applied for a substantial number have been granted. Although contact-type sensors made possible the production of more compact facsimile machines, their cost has been about 1.5 times that of sensor systems using CCDs. In addition, there has been the matters of reliability, stability, good contrast, good signal-to-noise ratio, and ease of manufacture and adjustment.

Although there are literally dozens of patents in the contact-sensor field, some of them are more representative than others. The details of two such patents follow.

## CONTACT AND DIRECT CONTACT SCANNERS

A common feature of contact scanners used in facsimile machines is that they cover the width of the original document. Differences in the assembly of their components are found in the placement of the photosensitive elements relative to the document being scanned; in the materials used in the sensors and in certain parts of the assembly; and the number of chips assembled to provide the full scanning width. They are described in one category simply as contact scanners or close contact scanners. In another category they are classed as direct contact scanners. In the first category the photosensitive elements are separated from the original document by a rod lens array, while in the second category the photosensitive elements are separated from the original document by only a thin protector glass sheet or a thin transparent film.

The cross-sectional view of a close contact scanner incorporating a rod lens array is shown in Figure 10-11. Light from an LED array (1) illuminates the document (2), and reflected light passes through the rod lens array (3), forming an image in the photosensitive area (4). When a rod lens array is used, the original document is separated from the sensor elements by the conjugate length of the lens array. This separation results in a thickness of 20 to 30 mm for such a sensor assembly, which limits the physical size to which it can be reduced. Of course, this size is much less than that of a CCD system, but designers would like to see it reduced further. Consequently, there is much interest in direct contact scanners where the thickness can be further reduced by at least 10:1. The adjustment of the rod lens array in production is also eliminated. A U.S. patent application for a direct contact scanner was applied for by Hiroaki Kakinuma, Yukio Kasuya, Masaaki Sakamoto, Tsukasa Watanabe and Mikio Mouri of the Oki Electric Industry Co., Ltd. of Tokyo, Japan, on May 20, 1988, and was granted as U.S. patent no. 4,887,166, on December 12, 1989. According to the Oki inventors, the direct contact scanner shown in Figure 10–12 has a problem in that friction arises between the paper document (5) and the transparent dielectric protective film (7). The film becomes charged, and its electric field causes malfunction of the photosensitive elements. This electrical charge is induced by the friction between film and the paper owing to the high resistivity of the film ($>10^{15}$ ohm-cm). An object of their invention was to eliminate this problem, to prevent malfunction of the photosensitive elements, and to provide a highly reliable direct contact image scanner. Other objectives were to provide good contrast, good S:N ratio, and high reliability.

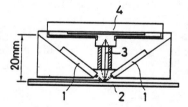

**Figure 10–11** Cross-Sectional View of Typical Contact-Type Image Sensor

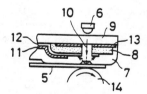

**Figure 10–12** Cross-Sectional View of Direct Contact-Type Image Sensor

A direct-contact–type image scanner according to this invention comprises an array of photosensor elements for receiving light reflected from a document and a protective layer located above the photosensitive array for protecting it when contact is made with the document. The characteristic feature of the invention resides in the means for discharging the electric charges generated by the friction of the protective layer.

## Improvement of Direct Contact Scanner

Figure 10–13a is a cross-sectional view of a direct-contact–type image sensor illustrating an embodiment of this invention. In this drawing the numeral 21 denotes a transparent dielectric substrate such as glass; 22 is a common electrode made of an opaque metal that also acts as a light shield. The common electrode (22) may be formed by evaporation or sputtering, followed by photolithography and etching for patterning: 23 is a layer of photoelectric-converting semiconductor such as amorphous silicon. The amorphous silicon layer (23) can be formed by a method such as plasma-assisted chemical vapor deposition (P-CVD), photo-CVD, electron cyclotron resonance-CVD (ECR-CVD), or reactive sputtering through a mask.

Individual electrodes (24) are made of a transparent conductive film such as an indium-tin oxide (ITO) film. The intersecting portions of these common (lower) and individual (upper) electrodes (22) and (24) function as photosensor elements. The individual electrodes may be formed by evaporation or sputtering, followed by photolithography and etching.

Light-admitting windows (28) are opened through the common electrode (22), the photoelectric-converting semiconductor layer (23), and the individual electrodes (24). The light-admitting windows (28) can be formed by removal of the common electrode (22), the photosensitive layer (23), and the individual electrodes (24) from designated regions. This may be implemented by photolithography and etching.

The numeral 25 denotes a high-resistivity dielectric film such as a $SiN_x$ (nitride) film, and 26 denotes a transparent protective film with a relatively low resistivity $\leq 10^{14}$ ohm-cm. The high-resistivity dielectric film (25) may be formed by evaporation or sputtering through a mask. The low-resistivity dielectric film (26) may also be formed by evaporation or sputtering through another mask having openings a little larger than the mask used for the formation of the film (25).

In a modification, the same mask may be used for the formation of the films (25 and 26). In this case, the resulting film (26) has a thickness reduced toward its edges, as shown in Figure 10–13b. Such a film (26) has been found to provide satisfactory electrical connection with the common electrode (22). This method of using

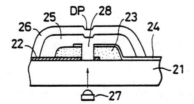

**Figure 10–13 (a)**  Cross-Sectional View of Direct Contact-Type Image Sensor Illustrating Invention of U.S. Patent No. 4,887,166

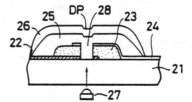

**Figure 10–13 (b)**  Cross-Sectional View of Modification of Image Sensor in Figure 10–13a

the same mask for the two films (25 and 26) is advantageous in that the cost of the production is reduced.

If a material with such a relatively low resistivity of $10^{14}$ ohm-cm or less is used, even if the surface of the transparent protective film becomes charged due to friction with a sliding document the surface charge is discharged into the interior of the film, with a certain time constant $\rho$. This $\tau$ can be expressed in terms of the dielectric constant $\epsilon$ and the resistivity $\rho$ of the film as follows:

$$\tau = \epsilon_0 \cdot \epsilon \cdot \rho$$

($\epsilon_0$: dielectric constant of the vacuum)

The constants $\epsilon$ and $\rho$ are properties of the film that are unrelated to its thickness or leakage path. If, for example the classic values for $SiN_x$ of $\epsilon = 4$, $\rho = 1 \times 10^{15}$ ohm-cm are substituted into the preceding equation, then $\tau = 623$ ss, so even if a single-document page causes only a minute charge, is so long that as document pages are repeatedly scanned the charge will accumulate. This can be prevented by reducing the time (on the order of one second) between documents; then the charge will not accumulate.

Setting $\tau = 5$ seconds and $\epsilon = 4$, for example, and solving for $\rho$ yields $\rho = 1.4 \times 10^{13}$ ohm-cm.

It follows that, in this case, charge will not accumulate if a material used is with a $\rho$ or smaller than this value. It has been confirmed through experiments, that, for rapid discharge, the value of $\rho$ should not exceed $3 \times 10^{13}$ ohm-cm.

As the material of this transparent protective film it is possible to use amorphous silicon carbide (a-SiC) produced by plasma-assisted CVD or sputtering, amorphous carbon (a-C), a $Ta_2O_5$ or Si-rich amorphous silicon nitride (a-$SiN_x$), amorphous silicon oxide (a-$SiO_x$), or AlSiN, AlSiON, SiON, $Al_2O_3$, $TiO_2$, $ZrO_2$, BN, AlNMgO, or a material such as a-$SiN_x$ or a-$SiO_x$ doped with phosphorous (P) or boron (B) to reduce the value of $\rho$. To allow charge to escape, this transparent protective film (26) is coupled to the common electrode (22), which is grounded. The numeral 27 denotes a LED array.

Figure 10-14 is a cross-sectional view of a direct-contact-type image sensor illustrating another embodiment of this invention, in which the transparent protective film (35) is made solely of a material with a value of $10^{14}$ ohm-cm. In this case, the value of $\rho$ of the transparent protective film (35) must be greater than the value of $\rho$ of the photoelectric-converting semiconductor (33) to prevent leakage of charge into the photoelectric-converting semiconductor (33). If the photoelectric-converting semiconductor (33) is made of hydrogenated amorphous silicon (a-Si:H), for example, it is necessary for the value of $\rho$ to be at least $10^{11}$ ohm-cm. The numeral 31 denotes a transparent dielectric substrate such as glass, 32 is an opaque common electrode, 34

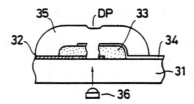

**Figure 10-14** Cross-Sectional View of Direct Contact-Type Image Sensor Illustrating Another Embodiment of This Invention

denotes individual electrodes made of a transparent conductive film, and 36 is an LED array.

As described in detail earlier, the preceding embodiment uses a material with a comparatively small resistivity for the transparent protective film and couples this film to the common electrode, so charge generated by friction between the transparent protective film and the document paper does not accumulate on the surface of the transparent protective film. Malfunctioning of the photosensor elements is thereby prevented, making it possible to obtain a direct-contact–type image sensor possessing high stability and durability.

Figure 10–15 is a plan view showing the schematic structure of a contact-type image sensor according to another embodiment of this invention. Only part of the contact-type image sensor is shown is this plan view. Figure 10–16 is a cross-sectional view showing a schematic cross section of the contact-type image sensor in Figure 10–15 along the line VI–VI.

The numerals identical to those in Figure 10–13a indicate similar components or parts. The substrate (21) is provided with a transparent protective layer (42), which can be a film of a high-resistivity dielectric substance such as $SiN_x$ formed by a suitable method such as sputtering. The resistivity of the layer (42) may be $10^{15}$ ohm-cm or higher. Thus, the protective layer (42) itself is not with the resistivity of $10^{14}$ ohm-cm or less. According to this embodiment, however, a conductive layer (41) is provided on the protective layer (42). The purpose of this conductive layer (41) is to allow electrical charge that accumulates on the protective layer (42) to

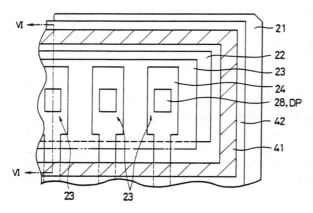

**Figure 10-15** Plan View Showing Schematic Structure of Another Embodiment of This Invention

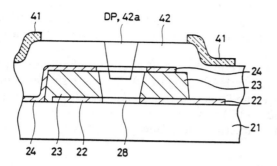

**Figure 10–16** Schematic Cross-Sectional View of Contact-Type Image Sensor Shown in Figure 10–15 along Line VI-VI

escape from the protective layer (42) to the outside. In this embodiment, the conductive layer (41) has the form of a window frame located on the protective layer (42) outside the region corresponding to the region in which the photosensor elements are formed (see Figure 10–15). Because the purpose of the conductive layer (41) is to allow the escape of electric charge that accumulates in the protective layer (42), it is necessary for the conductive layer to be grounded in some way. Various methods of grounding can be considered; in this embodiment the conductive layer (41) is grounded by connecting it to the common electrode (22) of the photosensor elements. This permits an effective grounding without changing the fabrication process of the contact image sensor and is preferable in that it can prevent a variety of undesired effects resulting from the accumulation of electrical charge.

The material of the conductive layer (41) must satisfy the requirement of possessing electric conductivity, and when the conductive layer is located so that it makes direct contact with the document, as in this embodiment, the conductive layer should preferably possess a flat surface and excellent resistance to wear. Thin films of, for example, Cr (chrome) and Ta (tantalum) are among the materials having these properties. A conductive layer comprising this type of thin metal film can be created by well-known, established techniques of film deposition and photoetching.

For example, the conductive layer (41) can be disposed in the interior of the protective layer (42). Specifically, the first part of the protective layer (42) can be formed, then the conductive layer, then a protective layer can be formed again overlying the conductive layer. In this case, because the conductive layer does not make direct contact with the document, it does not need to be made of a wear-resistant material. In this case, too, the conductive layer should preferably be grounded by connection to the common electrode of the photosensor elements.

In the embodiment described herein, the conductive layer had the plane configuration of a window frame, but this shape can be altered to any other shape that efficiently removes electrical charge, as required by design considerations. It is of course also possible for the conductive layer to be a transparent electrode covering the photosensor area.

Because a contact-type image sensor according to the preceding embodiment has a conductive layer disposed on the surface or in the interior of the dielectric protective layer that tends to accumulate static charge, as described earlier, if the conductive layer is suitably grounded, electrical charge generated by friction arising from contact between the document and the protective layer will not accumulate in the protective layer.

Figure 10–17 is a cross-sectional view of another embodiment of this invention. The numerals identical to those in Figure 10–13 denote similar components or parts. According to this embodiment, a transparent conductive film (46) of, for example, indium-tin oxide (ITO) is formed on the high-resistivity protective film (42) by a method such as sputtering and connected to the common electrode (22).

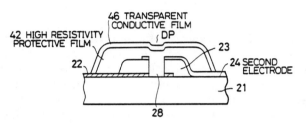

**Figure 10–17** Cross-Sectional View of Another Embodiment of This Invention

The individual electrode layer (24) and the high-resistivity protective film (42) are formed on the photosensor layer (23), and the transparent conductive film (46) is formed by a method such as sputtering.

The document is pressed in contact with the transparent conductive film (46), so friction between the document and this transparent conductive film generates carriers. The carriers generated in this way are conducted through the transparent conductive film to the first electrode layer (22) and are thus removed from the contact image sensor.

Figure 10–18 is a cross-sectional view of a further embodiment of this invention. The contact-type image sensor shown in Figure 10–18 has an additional protective film (47) formed on the transparent conductive film (46). The purposes of this conductive film are to protect the transparent protective film and to facilitate the escape of carriers generated by friction with the document to the transparent protective film (42). This is achieved by use of the protective film having a lower resistivity than the high-resistivity protective film.

In the contact-type image sensor shown in Figure 10–18, although the transparent conductive film (46) is formed between the high-resistivity protective film (42) and the protective film (47), carriers generated in the protective film by friction

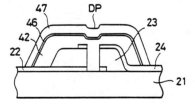

**Figure 10–18** Cross-Sectional View of Another Embodiment of This Invention

with the document can still be removed through the transparent conductive layer as in the contact-type images sensor shown in Figure 10–17.

In the embodiments of Figures 10–17 and 10–18, a transparent conductive film is formed on the surface or in the interior of a high-resistivity protective film, and this transparent conductive film is connected to the electrode of the photosensor layer, so carriers generated in the contact-type image sensor by friction with the document are conducted through the transparent conductive film to the photosensor electrode and thus removed.

In the various embodiments described, depressions (DP) are present on the surface of the protective layer (26, 35, 42, or 47), or of the conductive film (46) covering the protective film (42). The depressions are formed because of formation of the light-admitting windows—that is, local removal of the common electrode (22), the photoreceptor layer (23), and the individual electrode layer (24). The shape of the DP conforms to the shape of the cross section of the light-admitting windows (28), as is best seen from the combination of Figures 10–15 and 10–16.

## LINEAR SENSORS CONSISTING OF TWO OR MORE CHIPS

Since 1983 onward a number of Japanese patents, covering the use of more than one chip as linear solid-state image sensors for facsimile applications, were issued. Generally, two chips were arranged linearly to cover the width of the document being scanned. There seemed to be little question that it was easier to manufacture two photosensitive chips only half as long as the width of the document than one chip as long as the width of the document. In addition to a better yield, more uniform quality could be maintained. There are problems in joining the two chips so that uniform scanning can be maintained at their junction, however.

In 1989 at the Annual Convention of the Society for Information Display, Seiko Epson Engineers described a linear contact sensor consisting of two chips composed of a-Si/a-SiC photodiodes and poly-Si TFT drivers on a quartz glass substrate. They reported that a high yield of chips was obtained leading to a lower cost sensor as narrow as 1 mm. On February 6, 1990, Masumitsu Ino, Mitsuhiro Kohata, Masanori Itagaki, Takehito Nagata, and Hiroyuki Tanaka of the Ricoh Company, Ltd., and the Ricoh Research Institute of General Electronics Co., Ltd., applied for a patent on a linear solid-state image sensor consisting of two chips of a-SiH photodiodes with TFT drivers on the same substrate. Patent no. 4,977,304 was granted on December 11, 1990.

### Improvement of Method for Joining Two Chips in Linear Sensor

Figure 10–19 indicates a basic configuration of a linear solid-state image sensor. A linear solid-state image sensor (10) has a substrate (34) of quartz or some other material that is optically transparent. On this substrate (34) are formed an element

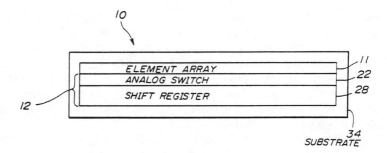

**Figure 10-19**   Arrangement of Element Array, Analog Switch, and Shift Register on Substrate

array (11) in which photoresponsive elements are disposed linearly, and a drive circuit (12) formed from a thin-film transistor (TFT) provided so as to correspond with each of the photoresponsive elements of the element array (11). The drive circuit (12) has a structure with an analog switch (22) and a shift register (28).

The linear solid-state image sensor (10) scans a wide area at once. Accordingly, it is desirable that the linear solid-state image sensor (10) is as long as possible.

From the viewpoint of manufacturing technology, however, it is difficult to form the element array (11) in a uniform state on the long substrate (34). Accordingly, in considering the manufacturing yield and the dimensional rating of the currently existing manufacturing apparatus, when a long linear solid-state image sensor (10) is manufactured, it is the best process to connect a plural number of short image sensors to create the linear solid-state image sensor (10)

Figure 10–20 indicates a conventional solid-state image sensor in which two image sensors are connected. A first image sensor (hereinafter known as the first chip 34-1) and a second image sensor (hereinafter known as the second chip 34-2)

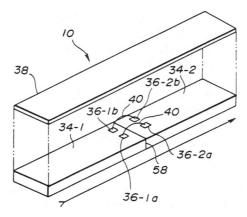

**Figure 10-20**   Configuration of Conventional Two-Chip Sensor

are connected at their end surfaces and in the direction of their length. The first chip 34-1 and second chip 34-2 have a structure whereby an element array (11) and drive circuit (12) are formed on the substrate (34), as indicated in Figure 10-1. The surface of the first chip 34-1 and the second chip 34-2 in the vicinity of the connection portion (58) of the first chip 34-1 and second chip 34-2, has pads 36-1a, 36-1b, 36-2a, and 36-2b formed on it. These pads 36-1a, 36-1b, 36-2a, and 36-2b are connected by wires 40 that are bonded.

These wires (40) are the data transfer wires, the power wires and the control signal wires connecting the first chip 34-1 and second chip 34-2.

In addition, when the linear solid-state image sensor (10) is applied to the image processing apparatus 100 such as indicated in Figure 10-21, a solid-state image sensor (10) of the completely contact type is used. A protector glass (38) provided on the first chip 34-1 and the second chip 34-2 protects the image sensor from dust and static electricity that is generated by the original (102) as it runs between the contact roller (104) and the paper guide (106) of the image processing apparatus (100). In the sensor of the completely contact type, image forming optical system elements are not used and the original (102) is slided on the element array (11), and the image information is directly read by the element array (11). In a conventional solid-state image sensor as indicated in Figure 10-20, however, the wire (40) can be damaged by the protector (38).

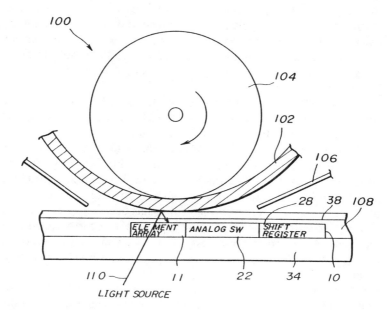

**Figure 10-21** Application of Image Sensor Making Direct Contact with Document

## Summary of Invention

Accordingly, it is a general object of the present invention to provide a novel and useful linear solid-state image sensor in which the problems described earlier are eliminated. A further object of the present invention is to provide a linear solid-state image sensor that is compact, has excellent device characteristics, and few manufacturing processes.

The preceding objects of this invention can be achieved by a linear solid-state image sensor comprised of two chips on a long substrate. Each chip consists of the following:

1. A plural number of photoresponsive elements formed in a line on the substrate along the direction of the length thereof;
2. An analog switch, formed on the substrate, driving the photoresponsive elements;
3. A shift register, formed on the substrate, to make the analog switch circuit successively effective.

The second chip is mechanically connected to the first chip so that a shift direction of its shift register is in agreement with a shift direction of the shift register of the first chip. External wiring connects a first stage of the shift register circuit of the first chip and a final stage of the shift register circuit of the second chip. Input wiring formed on the substrate of the second chip leads signal input from the terminal at the end opposite a connection portion with the first chip to a first stage of the shift register circuit of the second chip. Other objects and characteristics of the present invention will become apparent from the following description and the appended drawings.

The following is a description of an embodiment of the solid-state image sensor according to this invention. Figure 10–22 shows the circuit configuration of a solid-state sensor (10). As has already been described, a linear solid-state image sensor has a drive circuit (12) and an element array (11) formed on a substrate (34).

The element array (11) has a plural number of photoresponsive elements, which are photocells (14) arranged in a line. These photocells (14) are formed with a metal-semi-insulator-semi-insulator (MSS) structure and the photocells (14) have a photodiode D (which receives light that has been reflected from an original and for which the status for the conductivity changes in accordance with the amount of light received), and a connection capacitance C. One of the electrodes of each of the photocells (14) is connected to read output wiring (16). The read output wiring is connected to a read circuit (18). The read circuit converts the current that is input via the read output wiring, into corresponding voltages, and these voltages are integrated. Then, the read circuit forms the image signals in accordance with the integrated values.

The other electrodes of the photocells (14) are connected to a source drain circuit of transistors (22a) that configures a plural number of corresponding analog

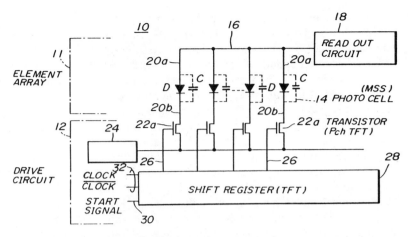

**Figure 10–22**  Circuit Arrangement of Linear Solid-State Image Sensor

switches. The transistors are P-channel TFT in the present embodiment. The other ends of the source drain channels of each of the transistors are connected to a power source (24). The control electrodes (26) of the transistors are also connected to a shift register circuit (28) that also comprises TFT. The shift register circuit has a data input terminal (30) and clock terminals (32). When data are input as start signals from the data input terminal (30), shift register circuits (28) successively shift that data in synchronization with the clock from clock terminals (32).

Each of the transistors (22a) in the analog switch (22) are successively driven by data (start signals) that are successively shifted inside shift register circuit (28). This shift register circuit (28) and analog switch (22) form a TFT drive circuit (12).

Figure 10–23 indicates the conceptual structure of a linear solid-state image sensor (10) of the completely contact type and according to the present invention.

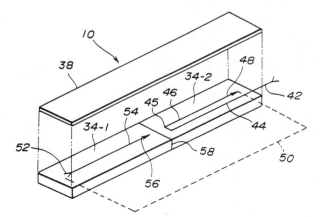

**Figure 10–23**  Conceptual Structure of Linear Solid-State Image Sensor

In the same manner as in Figure 10–20, this linear solid-state image sensor (10) has a first chip 34-1 and a second chip 34-2. The wires (40) that cross over the connection portion (58) of the first chip 34-1 and second chip 34-2 are removed, however. Data transfer is independently performed for both first chip 34-1 and second chip 34-2.

The first chip 34-1 and second chip 34-2 are mechanically connected. These are connected by adhesive, for example. The direction of the shift of the data of the shift register circuit (28) in the first chip 34-1 is in the direction from the opposite end of the connection portion (58) to the connection portion (indicated by arrow, 54). The direction of the shift of the data of the shift register circuit (28) in the second chip 34-2 is in the direction from the connection portion to the opposite end thereof (indicated by arrow, 46). The opposite end portion of connection portion (58) in the second chip 34-2 is provided with an input terminal (42). The surface of the second chip 34-2 has a data input wiring (44) formed in the direction along the length of the second chip 34-2. One end of this data input wiring is electrically connected to the input terminal (42). External data (start data) from an input terminal is supplied to an initial stage (45) of the shift register circuit (28) via the data input wiring (44). The data input to the initial stage of the shift register circuit (28) is successively shifted through each of the stages (arrow, 46). The data that has reached the final stage of the shift register circuit is output to an external connection line (50).

This external connection line (50) is indicated by a dotted line in Figure 10–23 and is a connection line provided external to first chip 34-1 and second chip 34-2. The external connection line (50), for example, is formed by the printed pattern on the printed circuit board. The other end of the external connection line (50) is connected to an input terminal (52) of a shift register circuit (28) in the first chip 34-1. The data supplied to this input terminal (52) from the external connection line (50) is successively shifted in the direction of the arrow (54), from the initial stage of the shift register circuit (28). Data that has reached the final stage is discharged externally from an output terminal (56).

Because of the wiring connections indicated in Figure 10–23, the data from the input terminal (42) of the first chip 34-1, is successively shifted inside the shift register circuit (28) of the first and the second chips 34-1 and 34-2, and is output from the output terminal (56) of the second chip 34-2. The status of this shift operation is indicated in the timing chart in Figure 10–24. In the timing chart in Figure 10–24, the signals to each portion of the chip have reference numbers appended to each of the portions so as to correspond to the timing that occurs.

In the process where the shift operation described earlier is repeated, timing

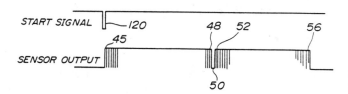

**Figure 10–24**  Status of Signals at
Each Portion of Image Sensor

control is performed so that the signals output from the element array (11) of the second chip 34-2 are output after the signals output from the element array (11) of the first chip 34-1. Whereby, the element arrays (11) on the first chip 34-1 and second chip 34-2 function as a single long element array (11).

The first chip 34-1 and the second chip 34-2 are mechanically connected. The wiring electrically connecting the first chip 34-1 and the second chip 34-2 is not formed in the central portion of the image sensor with a connection portion (58) for each chip, however.

The electrical wiring is connected to the external connection line (50) in the outer terminal portion of the first chip 34-1 and the second chip 34-2. Figure 10–21 shows the configuration when the linear solid-state image sensor (10) described earlier is configured as a completely contact type of sensor. An adhesion layer (108) formed on a substrate (34) (including first chip 34-1 and second chip 34-2) adheres a protector glass (38) to a substrate (34). Light (110) from a light source is reflected by the surface of an original (102) transported while in contact with the surface of the protector glass (38). Then, in the status where that reflected light is directly input to the element array (11), each of the photocells (14) of the element array is successively driven to scan of the original. This linear solid-state image sensor (10) is not adversely influenced by the electrical wiring when the original is pressed against it because there is no electrical wiring in the central portion even for the completely contact type.

The analog switch (22) and the shift register circuit (28) are formed on the substrate of the linear solid-state image sensor (10). This analog switch (22) and shift register (28) form a structure whereby TFTs are situated. The electrical characteristics of TFTs positioned in the vicinity of the substrate (34) are deteriorated. Figure 10–25 indicates the status for this deterioration of characteristics. In Figure 10–25 the ○ mark represents the characteristics before cutoff, the ● mark represents the characteristics of a TFT after cutoff, and the □ mark represents the characteristics of a TFT 100 $\mu$m remote from the cutoff surface. In addition, it is difficult for the photocells (14) forming the element array (11) formed on the substrate (34) to receive the influence of the cutoff surface of the substrate as is the case for TFTs. Figure 10–26 indicates the electrical characteristics of the photocells (14) when there an illumination of 100 lx is irradiated. In Figure 10–26 the ○ mark represents the electrical characteristics of the a photocell 1 before cutoff, the ● mark represents the characteristics of a TFT after cutoff, and the □ mark represents the characteristics of a TFT 100 $\mu$m remote from the cutoff surface.

Because of the characteristics of the TFT described earlier, the shift register circuit (28) and the analog switch (22) configured with the TFT is configured at a predetermined distances L1 and L2 from the cutoff surface (60) of the substrate (34), as indicated in Figure 10–27. From the characteristics given in Figure 10–25, these predetermined distances L1 and L2 can be each less than approximately 100 $\mu$m, for example. When a TFT is formed remote from the cutoff surface (60) in this manner, there is no deterioration of the characteristics. Accordingly, misoperation during data transfer and delays in the data transfer speed can be prevented. In addi-

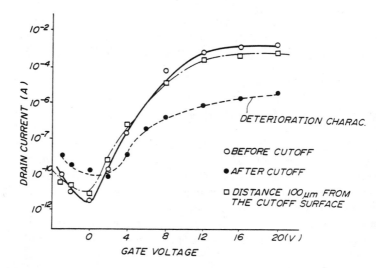

**Figure 10-25**  Characteristics of TFT in Vicinity of Cutoff Portion of Chip

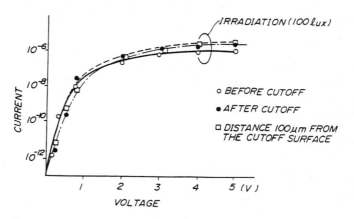

**Figure 10-26**  Electrical Characteristics of Photocells When Illumination of 100 lx Is Irradiated

tion, the characteristics of the photocells (14) that are not susceptible to the influence of the cutoff surface enable the element array (11) configured from the photocells (14) to be formed in the vicinity of the cutoff surface of the substrate (34). This is to say that the interval between the final stage photocell of the first chip 34-1 and the initial stage photocell of the second chip 34-2 can be made smaller. Accordingly, the fallout of the image owing to the position with respect to the connection portion (58) between the first chip 34-1 and the second chip 34-2 can be held to a minimum.

Figure 10-28 indicates the sectional structure of a photocell (14). A $Si_3N_4$ pro-

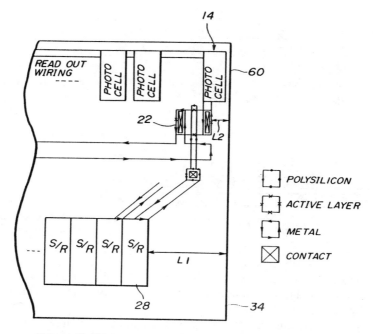

**Figure 10-27**   Elements in Vicinity of Cutoff Portion of Chip

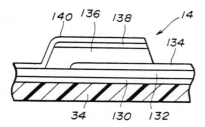

**Figure 10-28**   Sectional Structure of Photocell

tector layer (130) is formed on a quart substrate (34). A SiO$_2$ insulating layer (132) is formed on the Si$_3$N$_4$ protector layer. On top of the insulating layer are laminated a Cr metal electrode (134), an amorphous silicon film a-SiH (136), which is the active layer, and an a-SiOH film (138) and on the SiOH film (138) is formed a transparent electrode (ITO) (140), as indicated in Figure 10-28.

The planar structure of the TFT is indicated in Figure 10-29, and the sectional structure is indicated in Figure 10-30. On the substrate (34) are formed a polysilicon p+ dispersion layer (142) and the polysilicon n+ dispersion layer (144). A polysilicon active layer (146) is formed in the p+ dispersion layer and n+ dispersion layer. On top of these active layers are laminated either a gate oxide film (148), and gate electrode (150) formed of phosphorous or boron doped polysilicon. These active

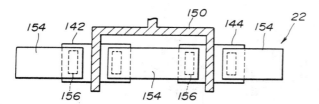

**Figure 10-29**  Planar Structure of CMOS Inverter

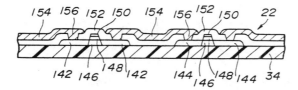

**Figure 10-30**  Sectional Structure of CMOS Inverter

areas are covered by a protector film (152) of PSG or SiO$_2$. The dispersion layers (142) and (144) are connected to a metal electrode (154) formed of aluminum or the like by a contact (156).

Each of the transistors (22a) of the analog switch (22) are connected to a power source (24), as indicated in Figure 10-22. Each of the transistors (22a) and the power source are connected by wiring formed by a conductive wire the same as the metal electrode (154). The conductor metal that is actually used as the wiring material is aluminum with a specific resistance of 0.0006 Ω cm. The resistance of this wiring causes a drop in the voltage, and the amount of this drop in the voltage is dependent on the length of the wiring from the power source (24). This voltage drop causes the voltage supplied to the transistor (22a) configuring the analog switch (22) to change in accordance with the distance from the power source (24) and is not desirable because it is not possible to have the same output from the analog switch (22).

With respect to this, in the present embodiment, the shape of the TFT is changed to correspond to the distribution of the wiring resistance. Accordingly, the output current of the analog switch (22) becomes a value within a predetermined allowable range, not depending on the position. More specifically, as indicated in Figure 10-31, the width of a channel W1 of a TFT (22a) close to the power source (24) is less than the width of a channel W2 of a TFT (22b) remote from the power source (24). That is say, as indicated in Figure 10-32, that the channel width of the TFT is changed depending on the distance from the power source (24) namely bit position of the element array (11). Accordingly, as indicated in Figure 10-33, the output current from the analog switch (22) becomes uniform.

In this manner, the output current from the analog switch (22) is made stable and so the read time of the element arrays (11) becomes uniform. Therefore, the circuit configuration of the read circuit (18) to which the signals from the element array (11) are input becomes simple, and the number of processes required for the

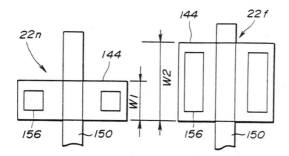

**Figure 10–31** Channel Status of Analog Switch in Position Remote from Power Source and Channel Status of Analog Switch in Position in Vicinity Power Source

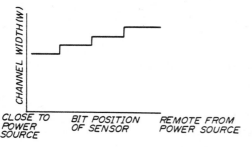

**Figure 10–32** Change of Channel Width of Thin-Film Transistor Depending on Distance from Power Source

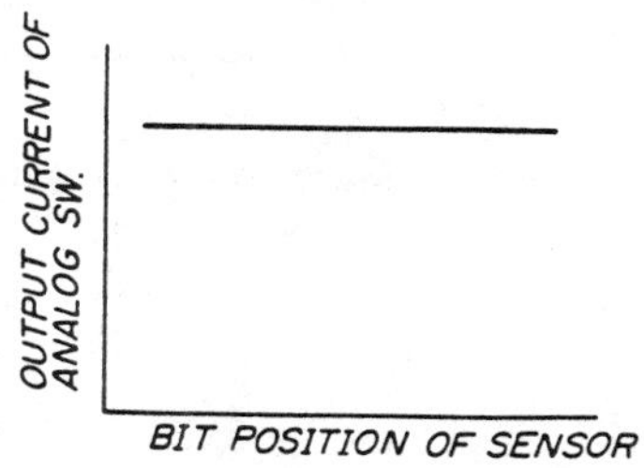

**Figure 10–33** Output Current from Analog Switch Becomes Uniform

fine adjustment of each of the elements in the process of manufacture becomes fewer.

Another embodiment of this invention is covered briefly by referring to Figures 10–34 to 10–36. Figure 10–34 indicates the overall circuit configuration. In Figure 10–34 parts that are similar to parts indicated in Figure 10–22 are indicated with the same numbers. The first chip 34-1 second chip 34-2 are provided with data input stabilization circuit (70) at the input stage of their shift register circuit (28), and with data output circuits (72) at the output stage of their shift register circuits (28). The data input stabilization circuit (70) is a circuit to prevent the waveforms of the input signal to the shift register rounding because of the resistance and the capacitance in the external connection line (50), and the data input terminal wire (44). The data output circuit is a circuit to shape the waveform of output data from the shift register to compensate the timing lag of the output data and to transfer the appropriate data. Either of the data input stabilization circuit (70) or the data output circuit may be provided to each of the chips 34-1 and 34-2. In addition, both of the circuits (70 and 72) may be provided to both or each of the chips first chip 34-1 and second chip 34-2. Alternatively, both can be provided in the second chip 34-2, in particular.

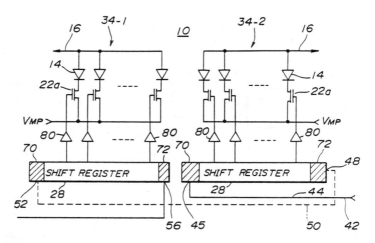

**Figure 10–34**  Overall Circuit Configuration of Image Sensor in Another Version of This Invention

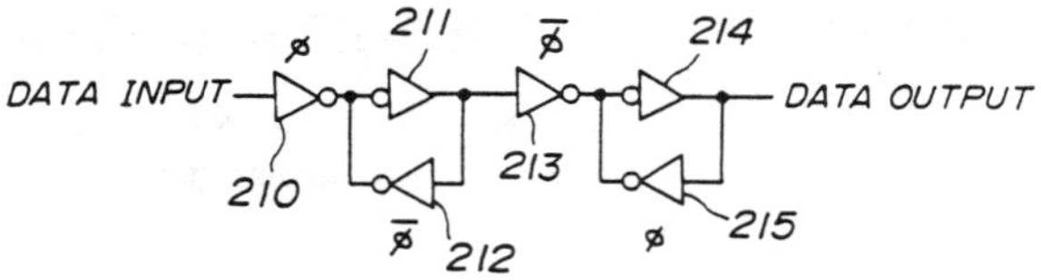

**Figure 10–35**  Logic Circuit of Static Shift Register

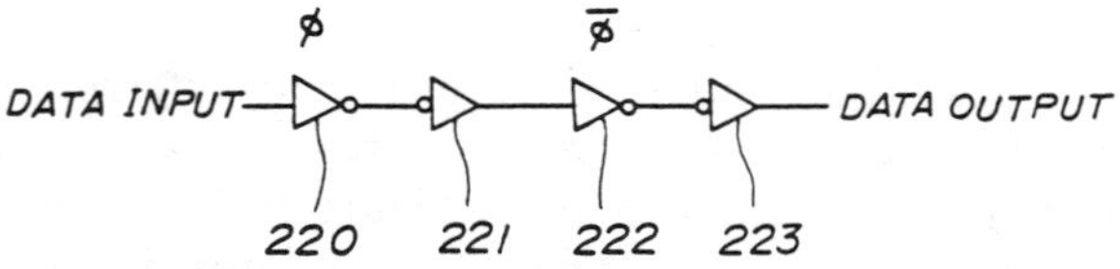

**Figure 10–36**  Logic Circuit of Dynamic Shift Register

When data is input to the shift register circuit (28), for example, the capacitance and resistance in the long wiring (44) causes the input timing to be late, and the rise and fall of the signal waveform in particular to become rounded. This rounding of the signal can cause the signal's input to the initial stage of the shift register circuit (28) to be wrongly identified as data. In addition, this signal rounding can result in the shift register no longer being possible to perform synchronized operation with the clock signal for control. Normally, the shift register circuit (28) is configured of a logic circuit such as that indicated in Figures 10–33 or 10–36. Figure 10–35 indicates an example of the configuration of a static shift register.

## CONTACT-TYPE IMAGE SENSOR IN CURRENT MODELS

Several of the Panasonic machines currently available use contact-type image sensors. The internal construction of this image sensor is shown in Figure 10–37. A block diagram of this sensor is shown in Figure 10–38 and the timing chart is shown in Figure 10–39.

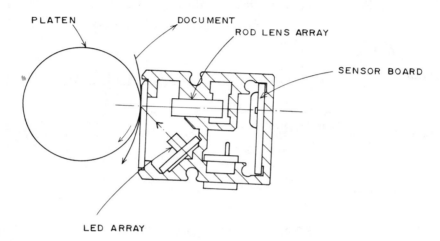

**Figure 10–37**  Contact-Type Image Sensor in Panasonic KX-F220 Fax Machine

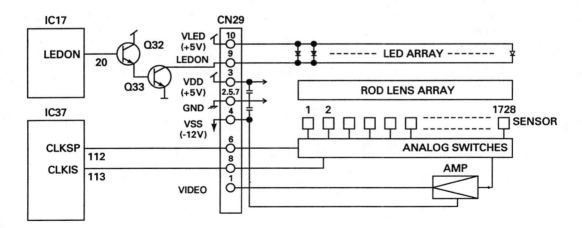

**Figure 10–38**  Block Diagram of Image Sensor in Panasonic KX-F220

## Circuit operation

When the COPY button (or the START button) is pushed, the gate array IC17 pin (20) becomes high level, Q32 and Q33 becomes ON, CN29 pin (9) (LEDON) becomes low level, current flows through the LED array, and a light source is generated (Next, the reading start pulse is output from the gate array IC37 pin (112) and synchronized with the trailing edge of the clock output afterward by the gate array IC37 pin (113); a video signal (VIDEO) corresponding to one line of pixels (1 to 1728) is output sequentially via the internal array at CN29 pin (1).

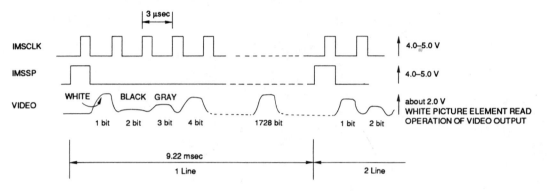

**Figure 10–39** Timing Chart of Image Sensor in Panasonic KX-F80

Here, the video signal is the signal with the reflection light from the pixels converted to voltage. When the original is completely white (Figure 10–39), the video signal has a peak value of 2 V, whereas the peak value becomes O V for a completely black original.

# CHAPTER 11
# *Printers*

It is sometimes mentioned that at least six different methods of recording or printing have been used in facsimile equipment. These are thermal, electrostatic, plain paper, thermal transfer, electrophotographic and ink-jet. By far the thermal recording method and the laser printer have dominated the market, however. In low-end and midrange machines, thermal printing is used in most models and laser printers are used in high-end models. Of course, the other methods are used in a few instances and thermal-transfer and ink-jet printing are likely to play greater roles when color facsimile becomes more viable. In this chapter more space is devoted to thermal transfer printers and ink-jet printers than might appear to be justified. This has been done, however, because these two types are generally not covered in any detail beyond a paragraph or two.

## THERMAL PRINTERS

Thermal printing works on the principle of heating a special chemically treated paper, which is sensitive to a certain threshold of temperature. Beyond that threshold, the white paper darkens at the point of heat contact. A device known as a thermal head provides the source of heat. The thermal head contains an array of heating elements that are configured in a row corresponding to one main scan line across the width of the copy paper. There are 1728 heating elements in an $8\frac{1}{2}''$ print head and 2048 heating elements in a 10.1″ print head.

By 1981, Toshiba had developed a high-speed direct drive printing head for use with A4 ($8\frac{1}{2}'' \times 11''$) documents in facsimile equipment. It included 1728 heating resistor elements and was driven by 54 LSIs. The heating elements, as shown in the block diagram of Figure 11-1, were arranged in a straight line of 216 mm in length with 8 dots/mm resolution. All heating elements were driven by individual output drivers of LSIs, whereas each LSI's I/O terminals for the shift registers and the enable shifters were cascaded regarding each other. The other control signal terminals were bussed together.

The operating timing diagram for the head is illustrated in Figure 11-2. The E-IN and E-CLOCK control enabled the shifter to perform time sequential operation of individual LSI chips. When the output Q of the enable shifter was 1, the

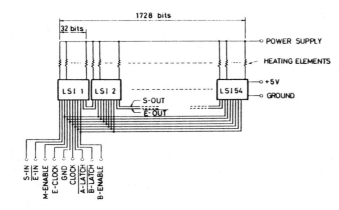

**Figure 11-1** Block Diagram of Thermal Print Head by Toshiba (ca. 1981) © *1982 IEEE [21]; reprinted with permission.*

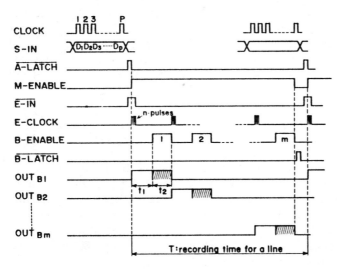

**Figure 11-2** Timing Diagram of Thermal Print Head of Figure 11-1 © *1982 IEEE [21]; reprinted with permission.*

output buffers became active. The E-CLOCK consisted of m bundles of n pulses, whose period was so short (about 1 $\mu$s) that n LSI chips appeared to be driven simultaneously, and m groups of LSIs were sequentially driven within a recording time of a line.

Thus, the number of heating elements driven simultaneously was easily varied by data applied to the enable shifter terminals. As a result, high-speed printing was achieved. Another feature of this printer was temperature control for heating elements, owing to the LSI's double-latch function. At a certain moment, the image signal data for a certain line is transferred to latch A, and the data for the previous line stored in latch A is latched into latch B. The heating elements are driven among the log pulse width $t_1 + t_2$ in a state of (B, A) = (0, 1), otherwise they are driven among the short pulse width $t_2$ in a state of (B, A) = (1, 1). The pulse width control in comparison with data in the previous line can prevent the heating elements from overheating. As a result pictures are printed more clearly, even in high speed driving of the thermal head. Consequently high-speed recording at a rate of 2.5 m/line was successfully achieved without overheating of the head.

Figure 11-3 shows the operation of the thermal head, which is used currently in several models of Panasonic fax machines. Figure 11-4 shows the driver circuitry and Figure 11-5 shows the timing chart. A description of the circuit operation follows.

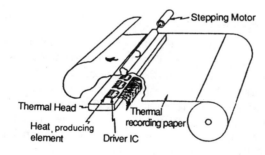

**Figure 11-3** Composition of Receive-Record Section in Current Panasonic Fax Machines

## Circuit Operations

There are 27 driver ICs aligned horizontally on the thermal head, and each one of these ICs can drive 64 heat-emitting resistors. This means that one line is at a density of 64 × 27 = 1728 dots = (8 dots/mm) (see Figure 11–4).

White-black (white = 0, black = 1) data in one line increments is synchronized at IC37 pin (76) (DMARCK) and sent from IC37 pin (72) (HEADDT) to the shift register. The shift registers of the 27 ICs are connected in series, and on shift of 1728-dot increment, all the shift registers become filled with data, and a latch pulse is emitted to each IC from IC37 pin (73) (HEDLCH). With this latch pulse, all the contents of shift registers are latched to the latch registers. Thereafter,

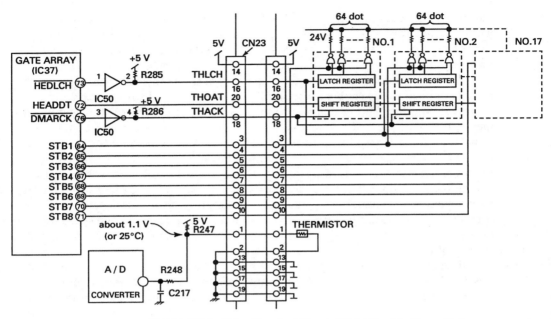

**Figure 11-4**   Drive Circuit of Thermal Print Head in Figure 11-3

through the addition of strobe from the IC37 pins 64 ~ 71, only dot of location of black (=1) among latched data activates driver, and current passes to the heat-emitting body to cause heat emission. Here the strobe of eight lines STB1 to STB8 impresses 9.22 ms, as required for one-line printout, for each 1/8th of IC27 unit (3 or 4 unit) each time interval divided into eight equal increments.

The sequence is as shown subsequently. Moreover, in the case of strobe width, the resistance value of the thermistor inside the thermal head is constantly detected by the A/D converter (IC29), and values from the ROM (IC23, 24) table corresponding to temperatures eliminate temperature changes of density through setting by CPU (IC22).

When the thermal head is not used, the +24-V power supply for the thermal head driver is not impressed to protect the IC.

## Paper for Thermal Printers

An important consideration in the use of fax machines with thermal printers is the right choice of paper. The best paper will have the right amount of chemicals and coatings to produce a high-quality image of lasting qualities. Many factors influence the copy quality and its stability relative to fading. Two of them are base stock color

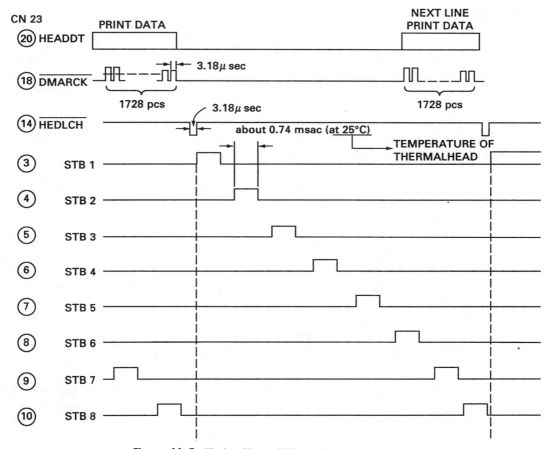

**Figure 11–5** Timing Chart of Thermal Printer Shown in Figure 11-3

and weight. Most high-quality paper is bright white in color. It must not be too heavy to avoid jamming and be easy to cut. Nor should it be too light to last or cause handling problems. Thermal response of the paper is another important characteristic. Print heads vary in their operating temperatures. Often a paper, which matches the thermal head of the machine being used, can be found by trying different ones. Surface smoothness is another important quality. Thermal papers need to be very smooth because of the large amount of paper, which passes by the print head.

The roll diameters of better papers are matched to specific fax machines. It is better to use them than general diameters, which match a number of machines, to avoid jams and paper feeding difficulties.

## LASER PRINTERS

The second most popular type of printer used in facsimile machines is the laser printer. It uses plain paper sheets, which are cut to size rather than a roll of paper as in the case of thermal printers. It has been found almost entirely in high-end machines (see chapter 7), but efforts have been made to reduce its cost to bring it into midrange machines.

A detailed description of the operation of a laser printer in a high-end fax machine is given in chapter 7. As shown in Figure 11-6 the following basic steps occur in a laser beam printer in one form:

1. *Static charging*—A high voltage is applied to a charging electrode to place a negative charge on a selenium drum.
2. *Exposure*—The image is exposed to light from a laser to erase the negative charge.
3. *Development*—Negatively charged toner from a reservoir attaches to the photo drum.
4. *Transfer*—The toner clings to the latent image, produced by the laser, and is transferred to the recording paper.
5. *Excoriation*—The electric charge of the precharged recording paper is erased and the toner is peeled from the drum.
6. *Fixing*—The toner is fixed with the heat and pressure of the fuser.

In the printer described in chapter 7, the reciprocating mirror shown in Figure 11-6 is replaced by a polygon mirror, driven to rotate in a predetermined direction at a constant speed in the printer.

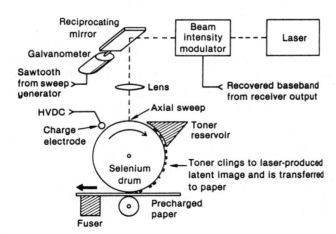

**Figure 11-6** Basic Diagram of Laser Printer © *1980 IEEE [3]; reprinted with permission.*

## TRANSFER-TYPE THERMAL PRINTERS

There are many transfer-type thermal printers in which ink is applied by thermal transfer to paper that has surface irregularities. For example, one type of such printers uses a ribbon including a releasing layer and a highly condensed ink material while another uses a force other than or in addition to that generated by ink adhesion to transfer ink from the ribbon to the transfer paper (for example, magnetic force or air force). In the former type, the ink material tends to adhere only or mainly to the convex or projecting portions of the surface irregularities in the paper, whereas depressions tend to be covered with ink mainly because of the ink's cohesion force. This limits the choice of the ink material because of the need to control the cohesion force, which tends to be highly dependent on the ink's temperature. Accordingly, it can be difficult for such a machine to make full-color images. Further, such a machine can impose restrictions on the construction of the thermal head. In a device of the later type, printers using a magnetic force can encounter difficulties in full-color printing because the magnetic material tends to be dispersed in the inking material. Printers using an air force can be relatively expensive because the base film of the ink sheet comprises a porous material. Good effects can be obtained in such printers when high pressure is applied to the printing head, but this can limit the service life of the head. An improved printer is described below.

Referring to Figures 11–7 and 11–8, a cartridge (1) is affixed to a driving wire or tape (2), which is trained on pulleys (3-1 and 3-2). The pulleys are rotatably mounted at predetermined positions to a printer schematically illustrated at (15). A driving means, such as a motor (16) driving pulley (3-1), moves wire or tape (2), and thus cartridge (1), to the left and to the right relative to a first platen roller (4) (as seen in Figure 11–8). A main image-transfer station (17) is defined at the nip between cartridge (1) and the first platen roller (4). Transfer paper (5) is moved up

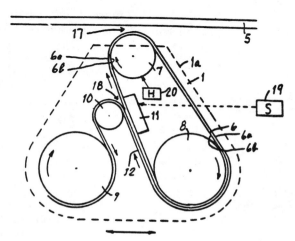

**Figure 11–7**  Cartridge for Thermal Transfer of Image onto Transfer Paper in Accordance with This Invention (U.S. Patent No. 4,740,798)

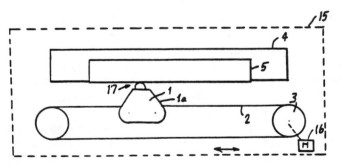

**Figure 11-8** Cartridge of Figure 11-7 as Used in Thermal Printer

(or down) through main transfer station (17) (i.e., perpendicularly to the plane of Figure 11-9).

Cartridge (1) contains, in a housing (1a), a ribbon (6) that is supplied from a supply in the form of a supply roller (8) and has a front or ink side (6a) and a back or substrate side (6b). Fresh ribbon (6) is paid out from supply roller (8), which rotates clockwise, and forms a first ribbon run as it moves up along the left side of supply roller (8) (as seen in Figure 11-7), with its front side (6a) facing to the left, passes between an intermediate image-transfer station (18) defined between a thermal printhead (11) and a second pressure member in the form of a second platen roller (10), loops around a first pressure member in the form of a first pressure roller (7), then moves down along the right side of supply roller (8) and again loops over supply roller (8) and over the roll of fresh ribbon (6) thereon. Ribbon (6) then starts a second ribbon run as it again goes up along the left side of supply roller (8) (and to the left of the first ribbon run up along the left side of supply roller (8)), passes between thermal printhead (11) and the second platen roller (10), and thus through the intermediate transfer station (18), loops over the second platen roller (10), and is taken up and wound on a take-up roller (9). Each of rotatable rollers (7 to 9 and 1) and printhead (11) is mounted to cartridge housing (1a).

Note that the front or ink side (6a) of ribbon (6) faces transfer paper (5) at the main transfer station (17), and that the back or substrate side (6b) of the ribbon in the first run is pressed against printhead (11) at the intermediate transfer station

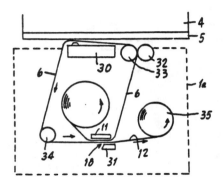

**Figure 11-9** Thermal Printer Using Another Embodiment of This Invention

(18). Note further that at the intermediate transfer station (18) the front or ink side (6a) of the second (left) run of ribbon (6) faces the second platen roller (10), whereas the back or substrate side (6b) of this second run of ribbon (6) faces and makes contact with the front of ink side (6a) of the first run of ribbon (6) (the run that loops over both the supply roller (8) and pressure roller (7)). In this arrangement, the second run of ribbon (10) services as an intermediate transfer member or medium (12) as described subsequently.

In operation of the device described earlier, ribbon (6) is paid out from supply roller (8) and moves along the first ribbon run through the nip between thermal printhead (11) and the second platen roller (10) at the intermediate image transfer station (17), where the nonimage portions of ribbon (6) are heated by the action of the thermal printhead (11), to which electrical control signals are applied as known in the art. The printhead (11) can be a multielement, matrix thermal printhead of the type known in the art. The electrical signals, which can be supplied to the printhead (11) from a source (19) that is external to cartridge (1), energize selected heater elements to transfer the nonimage portions of the ink from ribbon (6) to the intermediate transfer medium (12) at the intermediate transfer station (18). Since the front, inked side (6a) of ribbon member (6) along the first run contacts the back, substrate side (6b) of the second run of ribbon (6) at that position, ink material corresponding to the nonimage portions is transferred to the back side (6b) of the ribbon that is along the second ribbon run (i.e., the ribbon run that is leftmost in Figure 11–7). The back side (6b) of this second run of ribbon thus serves as an intermediate transfer medium (12), onto which are deposited, by thermal transfer, the nonimage portions of the inked side (6a) of the ribbon moving along the first ribbon run. Accordingly, only the image portions of the inked side (6a) remain on the first run of ribbon (6) after the action thereon of the thermal printhead (11). Subsequently, ribbon (6) moves along the first run toward the pressure roller (7) and its inked side (6a) contacts transfer paper (5), which is in the nip between pressure roller (7) and the first platen roller (4) (i.e., at the main image-transfer station (17)). At this image-transfer station, the image portion of the ink material is transferred by thermal transfer to transfer paper (5), and the pressure force generated by the pressure of pressure roller (7) against the first platen roller (4) helps the ink material flow into recesses of the surface irregularities in transfer paper (5), to thereby assure good ink coverage and ink-to-paper adhesion. This flow into recesses can be improved further if the ink material includes wax components designed to facilitate the flowing phenomenon. To improve the transfer rate, pressure roller (7) can be heated, as by a heater (20), to a temperature near the melting point of the ink material. Such heating is preferable but not necessarily required.

After this main image-transfer operation, ribbon (6) again loops over supply roller (8) and then starts along the second ribbon run, to serve the function of intermediate transfer medium (12) at the intermediate image-transfer station (18), that is, at the nip between printhead (11) and the second platen roller (10), where the back side (6b) of the ribbon in the second run faces and contacts the front side (6a) of the ribbon in the first run. After the intermediate thermal transfer (of nonimage portions of the ink) at the nip between printhead (11) and the second platen roller (10), the ribbon continues its second run by looping over the second platen roller, and by being taken up and wound on take-up roller (9).

Because the first pressure members (7) is a rotatable pressure roller in this embodiment, no abrasion difficulties are encountered at the main image-transfer station (17) even when high pressure is applied between the first platen roller (4) and the pressure roller (7). Accordingly, it is possible in this embodiment of the invention to cause particularly effective transfer of ink into recesses of the surface irregularities of the transfer paper (5). Usually, the ribbon member (7) includes a base or substrate layer of polyethylenetelefutalate, and a layer of ink material thereon. Image-transfer sensitivity for the intermediate image-transfer at station (18) is improved when the back side (6b) of the base layer is made rough, with surface irregularities, such that material having a high melting point and high cohesion force can be used. When such material is used the ink transferred at the intermediate and main transfer station tends to bridge recesses into which it is unable to flow, to thereby improve the quality of the image on the transfer paper (5) and allow more effective transfer action.

If slippage (relative movement) occurs at the intermediate image-transfer station (18) between the first and second runs of ribbon (6), that is, between the fresh ribbon (6) and the intermediate transfer medium (12), the edges of the ribbon that continue along the first run toward pressure roller (7) can pick up ink material that should have remained on the intermediate transfer medium (12). Such ink material picked up by the edges of ribbon (6) could then be deposited on transfer paper (5) at the main image-transfer station (17), contaminating the image thereon. To prevent such contamination, the width of the pressure member can be made less than that of ribbon (6). In this embodiment, 0.5-mm-wide margins at each edge of the ribbon (6) extend beyond the width of the pressure member (7) and are not pressed thereby against the transfer paper (5). Furthermore, as an additional measure for preventing such contamination, the width of the ink material layer of ribbon (6) is less than that of base layer, to leave non-inked margins along both edges of the front side of ribbon (6).

As is understood from the aforementioned explanation, the step of applying an image signal to a thermal printhead is separated in time and space from the step of applying pressure against the ribbon and the transfer paper for image transfer. Accordingly, relatively high pressure can be applied to the ribbon and the transfer paper in the main image-transfer step, with the result that an uneven surface of the paper can be made temporarily even to facilitate effective image transfer.

In this embodiment, the back side of the ribbon already used at the main image-transfer station (17) serves as the intermediate transfer medium at station. A separate intermediate transfer medium can be used instead in an alternate embodiment of the invention, however.

Printer (15) includes additional components such as a mechanism (not shown) to space cartridge (11) from platen (4) and transfer paper (5) when no printing is to be carried out (e.g., in a back stroke of the printhead). It should be clear that the printer is timed such that the operation of the printhead (11) and the movement of ribbon (6) through the intermediate image-transfer station (18) are synchronized with the movement of cartridge (1) in its printing stroke along platen (4) such that the image portions of the inked side left on the ribbon after the action of printhead (11) will reach the main image-transfer station (17) at the desired position of the cartridge relative to platen roller (4).

Figure 11–9 illustrates another embodiment of the invention, in which elements that correspond to parts of the embodiment of Figures 11–7 and 11–8 bear the same reference numerals. In Figure 11–9 the first pressure member, at the main image-transfer station (17), is a second printhead (30), used in place of the pressure roller (7) of the first embodiment. The second pressure member, used at the intermediate image-transfer station (18), is a stationary platen plate (31), used in place of the pressure roller (10) of the first embodiment. The second printhead (30) can use a single heating element, as the ribbon (6) carries only the image portion of the ink layer at the main transfer station (17). The second printhead (11) can be made of abrasion resistant material, and can be inexpensive, as its entire surface facing the ribbon (6) can be heated. In other respects the second embodiment can be the same as the first or, as illustrated in Figure 11–9, the cartridge can comprise a supply roller (32), from which fresh ribbon (6) is paid out and passes through the intermediate image-transfer station (18), at which the nonimage portions of the ink layer at the front side (6a) of the ribbon (6) are transferred to the intermediate transfer medium (12) (the back side of (6b) of the run of ribbon (6) which has already passed through the main image-transfer station (17)). The ribbon (6) then continues up along the right side in Figure 11–10, then passes through the nip between a roller (32) (which can be driven by a motor, not shown) and a backup roller (33), then passes through the main image-transfer station (17), where the image portions of the ink remaining on the ribbon (6) are transferred to paper (5), then continues down along the left side

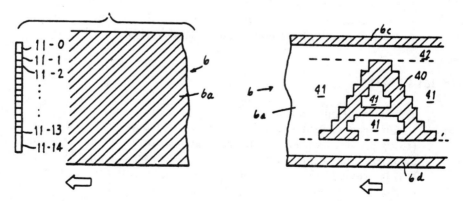

**Figure 11–10** (a) Portion of Ink Side of Ribbon That Has Passed through Intermediate Thermal Image Transfer Station but before Main Image Transfer Operation; (b) Portion of Fresh Ribbon and Its Spatial Relationship to Exemplary Thermal Print Head at Intermediate Image Transfer Station

of Figure 11–10, turns to the right over a roller (34), passes through the intermediate image-transfer station (18), where its back side serves as the intermediate transfer medium (12), and is taken up by a take-up roller (35). The cartridge illustrated in Figure 11–10 can be in a cartridge housing (1a), and can move relative to platen (4) in the manner discussed in connection with cartridge (1) in the first embodiment.

Figure 11–10a, illustrates the front side (6a) of a portion of ribbon (6) moving toward the printhead (11), which comprises heating elements (11-0 to 11-14) and is at the intermediate image-transfer station (18). The front side (6a) at this time is covered with the ink layer (in this exemplary embodiment). The end elements (11-0 and 11-14 of printhead) are energized (heated) at all times, whereas the intermediate elements (11-1 to 11-13) can be energized or not (heated or not) selectively, in accordance with an image signal. If the image signal is for the letter A, then this portion of the ribbon can be as illustrated in Figure 11–10b after passage through the intermediate image-transfer station (18). Because the printhead (11) is shorter than the width of the ribbon, two margins of ink material (6c and 6d) remain in the ribbon. Because of image signal applied to the heating elements (11-1 to 11-13), ink material remains at the image area (40), but has been transferred to the intermediate transfer medium (12) from the areas (41), which are within the dashed lines. Because of the constantly energized heating elements (11-0 and 11-14), the ink material has been removed from the strips (42 and 43). Note that the constantly energized heating elements (11-0 and 11-14) allow for satisfactory operation even when the printhead (11) and the ribbon (6) are somewhat misaligned in the vertical direction in Figure 11-11, by leaving a strip of non-ink areas (42 and 43) on each side of the image. Thus, if the first pressure member (the roller (7) in the first embodiment or the second printhead (30) in the second embodiment) has a width (in the vertical direction in Figure 11–10a), which is greater than the height of the image portion (40) but less than the distance between marginal ink strips (6c and 6d), no ink material other than the image portion (40) is likely to be transferred to the paper (5) even when there is some vertical misalignment between the ribbon (6) and the first pressure member (7 or 30) at the main transfer station (17).

## INK-JET PRINTERS

The conventional ink-jet recording apparatus using electrostatic force and air streams is described as follows, referring to Figure 11–11. In Figure 11–12, a body (13) is provided with an air nozzle plate (2) formed of an insulating material. The air nozzle plate (2) has a plurality of air discharge channels (1). An ink nozzle plate (14) is provided in parallel with the air nozzle plate (2) and has a plurality of ink discharge channels (4) that are arranged facing the plurality of air discharge channels (1), respectively.

Convex part (17), projecting in the direction of the air discharge channel (1), is formed around the ink discharge channel (4). Between the convex parts (17) neighboring each other, a projection (5) is formed on the ink nozzle plate (14) to stabilize

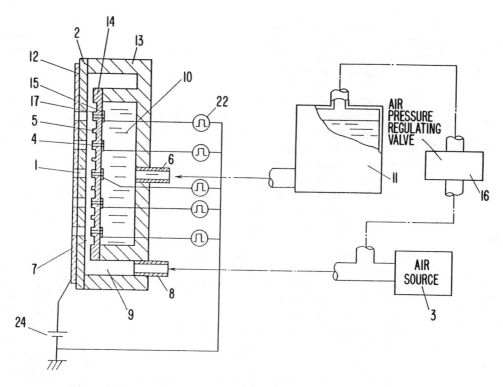

**Figure 11-11** Sectional View of Conventional Ink-Jet Recording Apparatus

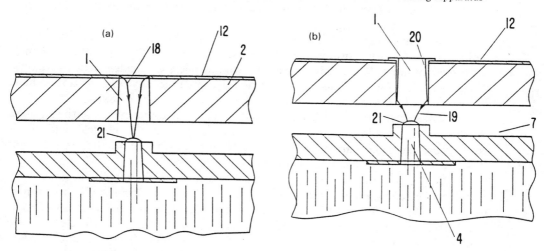

**Figure 11-12** (a) Partly Enlarged View of Conventional Ink-Jet Recording Apparatus Showing Normal Ink Jets; (b) Partly Enlarged View of Conventional Ink-Jet Recording Apparatus Showing Electric Field When Ink-Jet Volume Decreases

air flow. Air flows into an air supply passage (8) from an air source (3), is made uniform in a circular air chamber (9), and further flows into an air passage (7) between the air nozzle plate (2) and ink nozzle plate (14), and finally flows out from the air discharge channels (1).

The air expands at the air discharge channel (1) and therefore a sharp air pressure gradient appears in a space between the ink discharge channel (4) and the air discharge channel (1). An ink chamber (10) neighboring the ink discharge channels (4) is connected to an ink tank (11) through an ink supply passage (6). Ink in the ink tank (11) is applied with pressure by the air pressure of the air source (3), the air pressure being regulated by an air pressure regulating valve (16).

The reason for the air pressure regulation is that it is necessary to maintain a meniscus of ink formed at the ink discharge port (4) static by nearly equalizing the air pressure near the ink discharge channel (4) to the ink pressure of the ink discharge channel (4), or the ink tank (10), when the ink-jet recording apparatus is not driven.

Bias electric source (24) is connected to a common electrode (12) provided around the air discharge channels (1) and a plurality of signal sources (22) are connected to control electrodes (15) provided on the surface of the ink nozzle plate (14) facing the ink chamber (10), around the ink discharge channels (4). Because the ink is conductive, the sum of the bias voltage and the signal voltage is applied between the common electrode (12) and ink of the ink discharge channel (4). The meniscus of ink formed at the ink discharge channel is extended toward the air discharge channel (1) by the electrostatic force produced by the voltage.

Further, because there is the sharp pressure gradient in the space between the ink discharge channel (4) and the air discharge channel (1), when the ink meniscus of the ink discharge channel (4) is the proper length, the ink meniscus jets out from the air discharge port (1).

The conventional ink jet recording apparatus has the problem that ink jet volume decreases when atmospheric (room) temperature is 25°C and relative humidity is 60% or more. Reasons for the ink jet volume decrease are described as follows. Figure 11–12a shows the electric field when ink jets normally. The air nozzle plate (2) is made of photosensitive glass with a dielectric constant of 6.54.

Conversely, the dielectric constant of air is about 1 and therefore the strength of the electric field in the air is larger than that of plate 2. The electric field that is strong and therefore particularly contributes to the extension of the ink meniscus (21), is shown by electric line of force (18).

The electric line of force (18) is produced through the air discharge channel (1), from the common electrode (12) to ink meniscus (21). Because the direction of the electric line of force (18) and the direction of ink jetting are the same, the electric field effectively extends the ink meniscus (21). Figure 11–12b shows the electric field when ink jet volume decreases. When the relative humidity is 60% or more, water (moisture, vapor) (20) is adsorbed into the wall of the air discharge port (1).

The specific resistance of the water is $2.5 \times 10^7 \, \Omega$ cm, namely, conductive, so that the voltage of the water (20) becomes equal to that of the common electrode

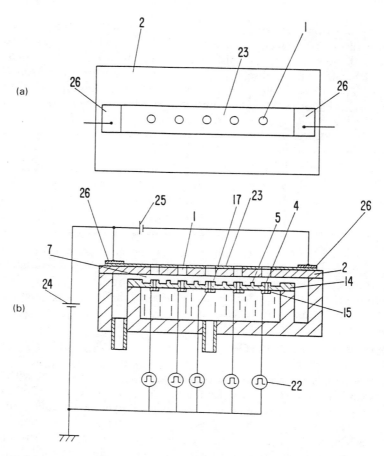

**Figure 11–13** (a) Plan View of Improved Ink Jet Printer; (b) Sectional View of Improved Ink Jet Printer

(12). In Figure 11–12b, the line of electric force (19), which indicates the strong electric field, is produced between the ink meniscus (21) and the water (20) that is nearer to the ink meniscus (21).

In such a case, the direction of ink jet and the direction of the line of electric force are not equal to each other, and therefore the force of the electric field is not concentrated. As a result, the ink meniscus (21) is not efficiently extended and the ink-jet volume decreases.

Further, because the electric field is not stable, the ink volume varies. The reason why the water (20) is adsorbed is described as follows. Considering the air discharge channel 1 with air flowing therethrough, the air pressure decreases in the air discharge channel (1) and air volume expands when the air is 0.12 kg/cm² in the air passage (7) exists to the atmosphere (0 kg/cm²). When the air rapidly expands, the air absorbs heat from the wall of the air discharge channel, and therefore the temperature of the wall of the air discharge channel decreases. Because the temperature of the wall of the air discharge channel is lower than or equal to the flowing air, the wall of the air discharge port (1) tends to adsorb water from the atmosphere. Table 11-1 shows conditions of temperature and humidity where the ink volume decreases, varies and becomes unstable in a thermohygrostat.

**TABLE 11-1**

| Atmosphere temperature | Relative humidity in the room |
|---|---|
| 20°C | 65% or more |
| 25°C | 60% or more |
| 30°C | 55% or more |
| 40°C | 60% or more |

The air flowing out from the air discharge channel (1) is air from the room supplied from the air source (3), which is, for example, a diaphragm-type air pump. Therefore, when the relative humidity of the room is 55% to 65% or more, the volume of the adsorbed water (20) increases, the ink-jet volume decreases and the ink jetting becomes unstable.

## AN IMPROVED INK JET PRINTER

An ink jet printer, improved to prevent variation in ink volume with room humidity, was patented in 1990 by Akami and other inventors. Figure 11-13(a) shows a plan view and Figure 11-13(b) shows a sectional view of an embodiment of this invention.

A common electrode (23) serving also as a heat device, comprising a rectangular resistance element is attached on an air nozzle plate (2) surrounding a plurality of air discharge channels (1) disposed in a straight line. A terminal of common electrode (23) is connected to a positive terminal of a bias power source (24) and to a positive terminal of a heat power source (25).

The other terminal of the common electrode (23) is connected to a negative terminal of the heat power source (25). The common electrode (23) serves as a common electrode for applying a bias voltage and as a heating device. It is connected to the power sources (24) and (25), utilizing silver paste (26). Other elements constituting the ink jet recording apparatus of this invention are similar to the conventional ink jet recording apparatus shown in Figure 11-11. The common electrode (23) is formed by depositing Cr 1000A thick on the air nozzle plate (2) by utilizing an electron beam evaporation method. The width of the common electrode (23) is 2mm and the length of common electrode is 19mm. It is formed by using a mask such that a 30 ohm resistance is obtained. The common electrode (23) has a voltage applied by the heat power source (25) to heat it. The heat increases the temperature of the air nozzle plate (2). For example, when the room temperature is 25°C and the air flows, 3.5 volts is necessary to make the temperature of the air nozzle plate 32°C.

# CHAPTER 12

# *Paper Cutters*

Paper cutters are available on many machines, especially those in the midrange and those at the top of the line. They avoid the disadvantage of having to cut the sheets apart externally after copies are received and eliminate long rolls of fax messages piling up on the floor. The operation of the paper cutter as provided in Panasonic's Model KX-F220 is described subsequently.

Following that description the problems experienced with paper cutters are covered as related to an invention by Mitsubishi covered by U.S. patent no. 4,967,285, issued to Mitsubishi on October 30, 1990. Some details are also given from an earlier U.S. patent # 4,646,162 issued to the Ricoh Corporation on February 24, 1987.

## CUTTER OPERATION

The cutter and cutter position switch life is about 300,000 times.

### Driving Operation of Cutter

1. The cutter is in the wait status with the cutter position switch ON as shown in Figure 12–1 (strictly speaking, the position of the motor after the cutter position switch is turned ON and the motor rotated 48 steps).
2. As the driving gear is rotated by the motor as shown in Figure 12–2, the cutter blade is lowered and the paper cut.

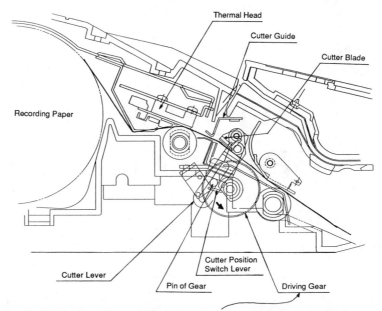

(The section with which the cutter position switch lever is in contact is D-shaped so that the cutter position switch lever can detect the position of the document. The driving gear is equipped with a pin which is inserted in the cutter lever.)

**Figure 12–1**   Paper Cutter of Panasonic KX-F220 in Wait State

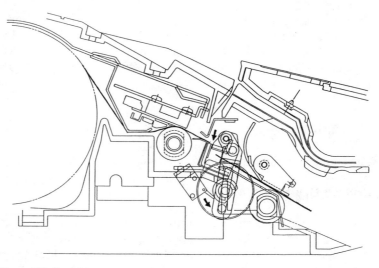

**Figure 12–2**   Paper Cutter of Figure 12–1 When Blade Is Lowered and Paper Is Cut

3. The driving gear keeps rotating, lowering the cutter blade to a lower position (Figure 12–3).

4. The driving gear rotates further on and the cutter blade moves closer to the wait status position (Figure 12–4).

5. The motor stops in the wait status as shown in Figure 12–1.

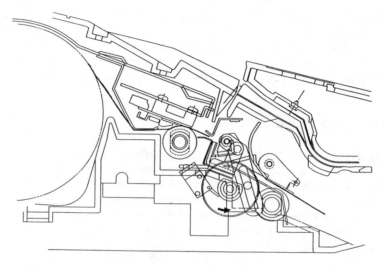

**Figure 12–3**  Cutter Blade of Figure 12–2 Moved to Lower Position

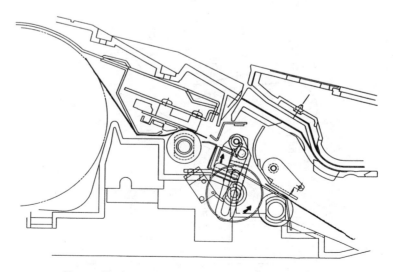

**Figure 12–4**  Cutter Blade Moves Closer to Wait State

The driving operation of the cutter is executed several times.

Paper cutters have introduced time delays in the reception of documents due to backlash and have required factory adjustments leading to increased costs. These factors have led to inventions whose aim has been to reduce time delays and eliminate factory adjustments wherever possible. The invention described on the following pages is an example of such efforts.

Generally a separate motor is used to drive the paper cutter. However, there have been designs where the read and write motors move the paper cutter without a separate motor. One such design is described toward the end of this chapter.

The invention to be described first relates to a method in which recording paper such as thermosensitive recording paper wound on a roll is cut off by a cutter after recording is performed on a one-sheet area of the paper.

## COMPENSATING FOR BACKLASH

In Figure 12–5, numeral 1 denotes a roll-wound thermosensitive recording paper provided in a prescribed housing portion and platen roller (2) is for feeding the recording paper. Thermosensitive head (3) has a heating portion (3a) in the face of the platen roller and is put in contact with the roller under prescribed pressure so as to record information on the recording paper. Electric motor (4) has gear train (5) comprising gears (5a to 5d) to transmit the torque of the motor (4) to the platen roller to rotate it at a lower speed than the motor. Cutter (6) is for cutting off the recording paper after the information is recorded on one-sheet of paper.

The operation of the conventional facsimile apparatus will be described with reference to Figure 12–5, Figure 12–6, which is a time chart, and Figure 12–7, which

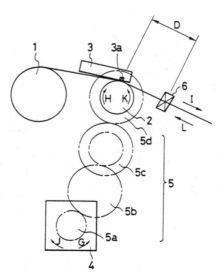

**Figure 12–5**  Side View of Conventional Recording Paper Cutoff Method

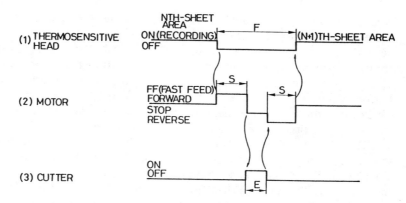

**Figure 12-6** Time Chart of Conventional Recording Paper Cutoff Method

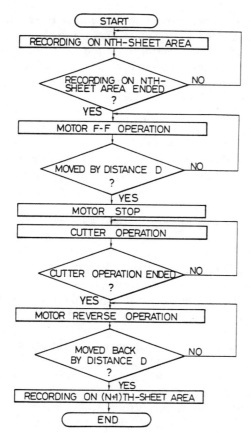

**Figure 12-7** Flow Chart of Conventional Recording Paper Cutoff Method

is a flow chart. In Figure 12–6, A designates the timing of the recording by the thermosensitive head (3), B designates the operation of the motor (4), and C designates the operation of the cutter (6). In Figure 12–6, S denotes the time that it takes for the recording paper (1) to move through the distance D (which is shown in Figure 12–5) from the heating portion (3a) of the thermosensitive head (3) to the cutter (6). Period E represents the time of the operation of the cutter, and F represents the time of the stoppage of the recording by the head (3). When the motor (4) is rotated forward in a direction G shown in Figure 12–5 (in Figure 12–6 shown as FORWARD), the platen roller (2) is turned in a direction H through the gear train (5) so that the recording paper (1) is fed in a direction I. At the same time, the thermosensitive head (3) is turned on so that information is recorded on the nth-sheet area of the paper (1). The paper is then fast fed forward by the distance D (in Figure 12–7, as shown as F–F) for a portion of the time F so that the trailing edge of the nth-sheet area of the paper is stopped at the cutter (6). After the stoppage of the motor (4) is confirmed, the cutter (6) is put into operation to cut off the recording paper (1). Subsequently, the motor (4) is rotated backward in a direction J (in Figure 12–6, shown as REVERSE) so that the platen roller (2) is turned in a direction K through the gear train (5) so that the recording paper is pulled back by the distance D in the direction L. The motor (4) is then set to rotate forward in the direction G so that the recording paper (1) is fed in the direction I. At the same time, the thermosensitive head (3) is turned on so that information is recorded on the $(n+1)$th-sheet area of the recording paper (1). The time F of the stoppage of the recording, as illustrated in Figure 12–6, is expressed as follows:

$$F = S + E + S$$

The conventional operation of the thermosensitive head (3), the motor (4), the cutter (6) and the other interacting elements is regulated, for the sequence shown in Figure 12–6 by a control circuit including a microcomputer or the like not shown in the drawings. Figure 12–7 is a flow chart illustrating the steps of the conventional paper cutting method as described earlier.

Figure 12–8 is a side view of a major part of another conventional facsimile apparatus. In Figure 12–8, numerals 7a and 7b designate timing pulleys, and 8 is a timing belt for rotating a platen roller (2) through the timing pulleys (7a and 7b) by the rotation of a motor (4). Except the platen roller drive mechanism of the apparatus, the arrangement of Figure 12–8 is the same as that shown in Figure 12–5.

The operation of the apparatus shown in Figure 12–8 will be described with reference to Figure 12–9, which is a time chart. In Figure 12–9, T denotes the time of the stoppage of recording by thermosensitive head (3). When the motor (4) is rotated forward in a direction V shown in Figure 12–8 (in Figure 12–9, shown as FORWARD) the platen roller (2) is rotated in a direction H through the timing pulleys (7a and 7b) and the timing belt (8) so that thermosensitive recording paper (1) is wound on a roller is fed in a direction I. At the same time, the thermosensitive head (3) is turned on so that information is recorded on the nth-sheet area of the paper (1). After the information is recorded on the nth-sheet area of the paper (1),

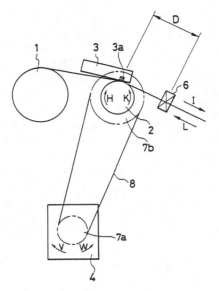

**Figure 12–8** Side View of Major Part of Another Conventional Fax Apparatus in which Another Conventional Recording Paper Cutoff Method Is Practiced

the recording of information on the (n + 1)th-sheet area of the paper is started. As the recording of the information on the (n + 1)th-sheet area of the paper (1) continues, the nth-sheet of paper (1) moves forward by the distance D from the heating portion (3a) of a thermosensitive head (3) to a cutter (6). The motor (4) is stopped as well as recording on the (n + 1)th-sheet. The cutter (6) is thereafter put into operation to cut off the recording paper (1). The thermosensitive head (3) is then turned on so that the recording of the information on the (n + 1)th-sheet area of the recording paper (1) is resumed. The time T of the stoppage of the recording, as illustrated in Figure 12–7, is expressed as follows:

$$T = E$$

In the facsimile apparatus as shown in Figure 12–5, the recording on the (n + 1)th-sheet area of the recording paper (1) is started after the completion of the recording on the nth-sheet area, and after the nth-sheet area is cut off. This procedure is to ensure that the recorded image on the (n + 1)th-sheet area of the paper is not disturbed owing to the backlash of the gear train (5). Backlash of the gear train results from the paper being pulled forward in direction I by the cutting action of cutter (6). When recording resumes, the motor (4) moves gear (5c) a distance, equal to the amount of gear (5d) was rotated forward, before engaging gear (5d) and advancing the paper. This distance is equal to the distance between the teeth of gears (5d and 5c). The time required to move this distance results in blank spaces or overlapping recordings on the (n + 1)th-sheet. For that reason, the trailing edge of the nth-sheet area of the recording paper is once quickly moved to the cutter (6), and cut off thereby. The leading edge of the (n + 1)th-sheet area of the paper is then moved back toward the thermosensitive heat (3), as shown in Figure 12–7. Fast feeding, stopping and reversing paper (1) results in lengthening the time from the end of the recording on the nth-sheet area of the paper (1) to the start of the recording of the (n + 1)th-sheet area. Therefore, it takes a long time to perform communication to the facsimile apparatus through a telephone line. High communication costs result from this problematic method of cutting off a recorded area of paper (1).

In the conventional facsimile apparatus shown in Figure 12–8, because the torque of a gear is transmitted to the platen roller (2) through the timing pulleys (7a and 7b) and timing belt (8), the recorded image on the (n + 1)th-sheet area of the recording paper (1) is not disturbed by backlash. For that reason, the time from the end of the recording on the nth-sheet area of the recording paper (1) to the start of the recording on the (n + 1)th-sheet area thereof is shorter, as shown in Figure 12–9. Therefore, it takes a shorter time to perform communication to the facsimile apparatus of Figure 12–8 through a telephone line. Because the tension of the timing belt needs to be adjusted in installing the electric motor, however, the facsimile apparatus of the type shown in Figure 12–8 has a problem in that the efficiency of its manufacturing is low.

This invention is directed toward solving the preceding problems. Accordingly, it is an object of the present invention to provide a recording paper cutoff method for a facsimile apparatus, in which the time from the end of the recording on the nth-sheet of recording paper to the start of recording on the (n + 1)th-sheet area thereof is shortened to reduce the cost of communication with the apparatus through a telephone line.

It is another object of the present invention to provide a recording paper cutoff method for a facsimile apparatus, in which, although the recording on the (n + 1)th-sheet area of the recording paper is started continuously from the end of recording on the nth-sheet area and temporarily stopped in order to cut off the nth-sheet area from the (n + 1)th-sheet area, the recorded image on the (n + 1)th-sheet

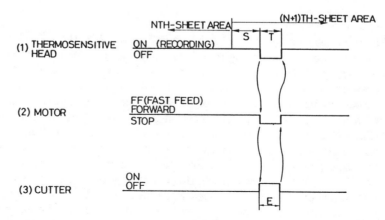

**Figure 12–9**  Timing Chart of Conventional Recording Paper Cutoff Method Shown in Figure 12–8

area is not disturbed when the recording on the area is resumed after the temporary stoppage.

It is yet another object of the present invention to provide a recording paper cutoff method for a facsimile apparatus, in which the total time of communication with the apparatus is shortened in a simple and less expensive manner.

The previously mentioned and other objects and novel features of the present invention will be apparent from the description herein and the associated figures. The figures are only for purposes of description, and not for limiting the scope of the present invention.

To accomplish the above-described objects, the recording paper cutoff method according to one embodiment of the invention comprises a step in which the torque of an electric motor is transmitted to a platen roller through a gear train so that the recording on the (n + 1)th-sheet area of the recording paper wound as a roll is performed continuously from the end of recording on the nth-sheet area thereof; another step in which the boundary between the nth-sheet area and the (n + 1)th-sheet area has reached the position of a cutter, the recording on the (n + 1)th-sheet area is temporarily stopped and the backlash of the gear train is compensated for by rotating the motor backward; another step in which the recording paper is cut off by the cutter; another step in which the backlash of the gear train is compensated for once again by rotating the motor forward after the cutoff of the paper by the cutter; and a further step in which the recording on the (n + 1)th-sheet area is resumed.

In the recording paper cutoff method of the aforementioned embodiment, the backlash of the gear train is compensated for by the backward and forward rotation of the motor immediately before and after the cutoff of the recording paper by the cutter so that the recording paper is prevented from being disturbed at the time of the cutoff by the cutter and at the time of the resumption of the recording on each sheet area of the paper. In other words, the recording paper is not disturbed, although a previously recorded paper is cut off by the cutter while recording on a subsequent sheet area of the paper is stopped and resumed. As a result, the recorded image on each sheet area of the recording paper does not have blank spaces or overlapping recordings. In addition, the time of communication to the facsimile apparatus through the telephone lines is shortened to reduce the cost of the communication.

Figure 12–10 is a time chart of a recording paper cutoff method that is one embodiment of this invention. Figure 12–11 is a flow chart of the method of this embodiment. The method of the present invention is applied to a facsimile apparatus shown in Figure 12–12, which is substantially the same as the facsimile apparatus shown in Figure 12–5. Facsimile apparatus (10) additionally comprises a suitable control unit (7) that uses a microcomputer for regulating the electric motor (14), the cutter (16) and the other related elements to implement the method of this invention.

As illustrated in Figure 12–10, after information is recorded on the nth-sheet area of thermosensitive recording paper (1) wound as a roll, the recording of information on the (n + 1)th-sheet area of the paper is initiated immediately thereafter

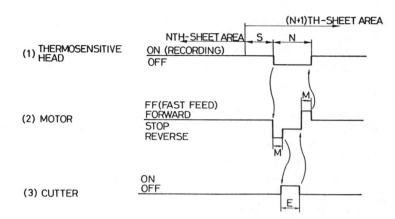

**Figure 12–10**   Timing Chart of Recording Paper Cutoff of This Invention (U.S. Patent No. 4,967,285)

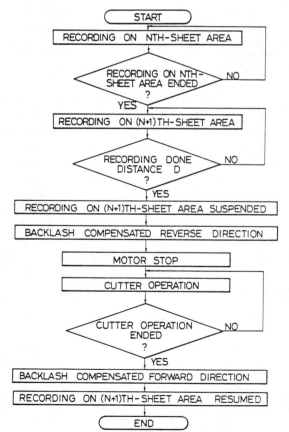

**Figure 12–11**   Flow Chart of Recording Paper Cutoff Method of Embodiment Shown in Figure 12–10

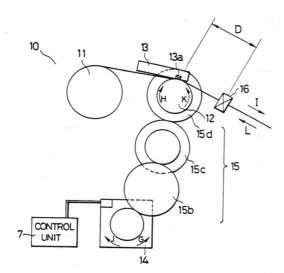

**Figure 12–12**　Side View of Novel Control Method for Cutting Sheet of Recording Paper According to This Invention

and continues until the recording on the nth-sheet area of the paper (11) reaches the distance D from the heating portion (3a) to the cutter (16). Recording of the (n + 1)th-sheet is then interrupted. The motor (4) is then rotated backward in a direction J, as shown in Figure 12–5, for the short time M to compensate for the backlash of the gear train (15). The backlash compensation period M is typically about 10 ms. The cutter (16), is then put into operation to cut off the recording paper (11). Because the backlash of the gear train (15) is compensated for before the cutoff of the recording paper (11), the gear (15c) engaged with gear (15d) is in the backward direction, and the paper is not pulled in a direction I. After the paper (11) is cut off by the cutter (16), the motor (14) is quickly driven in a direction G for the short time M to compensate for the backlash of the gear train (15) again, thus engaging gears (15c and 15d) in the forward direction. This enables the gear (15c) to engage gear (15d) immediately in the forward direction. The thermosensitive head (13) is then turned on so that the recording on the (n + 1)th-sheet area of the paper (11) is resumed. The time N of the stoppage of the recording, as illustrated in Figure 12–10 is expressed as follows:

$$N = M + E + M$$

Because backlash compensation time M is very small (about 10 ms as noted earlier) compared with cutting time E, it can be ignored and equation 3 is transformed into N = E, wherein E is approximately 1–2 s. It is understood through the comparison of the equations 1 and 3 that the time of the recording stoppage is greatly shortened in the recording paper cutoff method in the embodiment described. In addition, it is to be understood that the time N of the stoppage of the recording is nearly equal to that of T expressed by the equation 2.

In the previously described embodiment, the backlash of the gear train (15) is compensated for immediately before and after the cutting of the recording paper (11) by the cutter (16) so as to prevent the recorded image on the (n + 1)th-sheet area of the paper from being disturbed. In a modification of the aforementioned embodiment, however, the backlash of the gear train (15) is compensated for only immediately after the cutoff of the thermosensitive recording paper (11) by the cutter (16). At that time, the electric motor (14) is rotated backward in the direction J for a short time P, typically about 10 ms, so that the paper is pulled back in a direction L. The recording on the (n + 1)th-sheet area of the paper (11) is then resumed. As illustrated by the time chart in Figure 12–13, the control unit (7) regulates the thermosensitive head to record information on the nth-sheet and then to immediately initiate recording information on the (n + 1)th-sheet, as indicated by the time period S. After the boundary between the nth-sheet and the (n + 1)th-sheet travels distance D to cutter (16), recording is interrupted, the motor is stopped and cutting operation is initiated, as indicated by the time period E. The gear (15d) is rotated backward by pulling the paper in direction I, and then the motor is rotated forward a short time M to compensate for backlash of gear train (15).

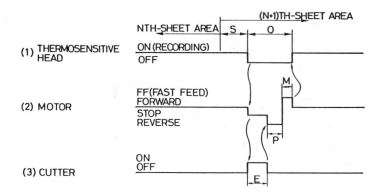

**Figure 12–13**  Timing Chart of Recording Paper Cutoff Method in Another Embodiment of This Invention

In this embodiment, the backlash is not compensated for before cutting, which will cause a small gap between printed lines on sheet (n + 1). This is acceptable in most circumstances, however. The step of compensating gear train backlash after the paper has been cut is necessary, however, to prevent recording lines on sheet (n + 1) from being superimposed when recording is resumed.

Figure 12–14, is a flow chart showing the manner in which control unit (7) regulates the Figure 12–12 apparatus to compensate for gear train backlash only after the paper is pulled by the cutting operation. The time of the stoppage of the recording, period D, is greatly shortened in the modification as well as the previously described embodiment. Although thermosensitive paper wound on a roll is

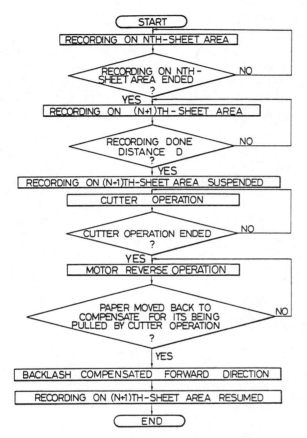

**Figure 12-14** Flow Chart of Recording Paper Cutoff Method of Figure 12-13

used in the previously described embodiment, the present invention is also applicable to plain paper wound on a roll that is to be subjected to recording by a recording head.

According to the present invention, the timing of the recording is regulated by the control unit (7) so that when the boundary between the nth-sheet area and (n + 1)th-sheet area of the recording paper (11) has come to the location of the cutter (16) during the recording on the (n + 1)th-sheet area, the recording on the (n + 1)th-sheet area is temporarily stopped and the paper is cut off. The backlash of the gear train (15) is compensated for immediately before or after the cutoff of the recording paper (11), and the recording on the (n + 1)th-sheet area is then resumed. As a result, the time of communication to the facsimile apparatus through a telephone line is shortened to reduce the cost of the communication, and each image recorded on the paper is protected from disturbance. In addition, the recording paper cutoff method can be practiced with the facsimile apparatus without altering its basic construction through which the platen roller (12) is driven by the gear train (15).

## CUTTER WITHOUT SEPARATE DRIVE MOTOR

Referring to Figures 12–15 to 12–17 a driving arrangement installed in the facsimile apparatus is shown. The platen roller (40) is rigidly mounted on a shaft (60) that is journalled to a side panel (58) of the apparatus body. A dual pulley (62) is also securely mounted on the shaft (60) and comprises a first pulley (62a) and a second pulley (62b) that is smaller in diameter than the first pulley (62a). A reversible motor

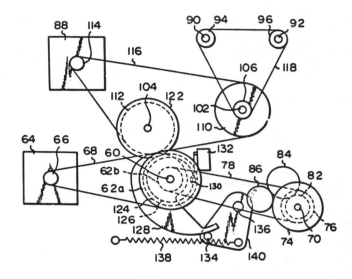

**Figure 12–15**  Side Elevation of Driving Device in Fax Machine Using Only Two Motors to Drive Read and Write, and Paper Cutter Operations

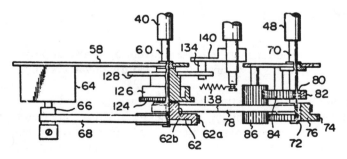

**Figure 12–16**  Partial Plan View of Drive Mechanism for Write System

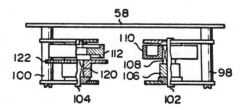

**Figure 12–17**  Partial Plan View of Drive Mechanism for Read System

(64) is mounted on the side panel (58) to serve as a drive source for the write system. A belt (68) is passed over a motor pulley (66), and the larger pulley (62a) of the dual pulley (62). The discharge rollers (48) are mounted on a shaft (70), which is also journalled to the apparatus body. A pulley (76) formed with gear teeth (74) is mounted on the shaft (70) through a one-way clutch (72) and linked with the smaller pulley (62b) by a belt (78). A gear (82) is mounted on the shaft (70) through a one-way clutch (80) and operatively associated with the teeth or gear (74) through idle gears (84) and (86).

Reversible motor (88) is mounted on the side panel (58) of the apparatus body as a drive source for the read system. Pulleys (94) and (96) are rigid on shafts (90) and (92), which carry the conveyor rollers (16) and (18), respectively. Support members (98) and (100) extend from the side panel (58) and support shafts (102) and (104), respectively. A shaft (106) and a pulley (110) are mounted on the shaft (102) with a one-way clutch interposed between the pulley (110) and the shaft (102). Mounted on the shaft (104) is a pulley (112). A belt (116) is passed over the motor pulley (114) and pulleys (110 and 112), while a belt (118) is passed over the pulleys (94, 96, and 106).

A gear (122) is mounted on the shaft (104) through a one-way clutch (120). A gear (124) meshes with the gear (122) and is rotatably mounted on the shaft (60). The gear (124) carries a disk (126) and a cutter cam (128) integrally therewith, and one after the other in the axial direction thereof. The disk (126) is formed with a recess (130) in which a switch (132) is engageable for detecting a position as will be described. Designated by the reference numeral (140) is a cutter actuator, which is pivotable about a fulcrum (136) and constantly urged by a spring (138) in a cutting direction. A cam follower (134) is studied on the cutter actuator (140) to be actuated by the cutter cam (128).

In operation, as the motor (64) rotates counterclockwise, or forwardly in this embodiment, the platen roller (40) is rotated counterclockwise via the motor pulley (66), belt (68) and pulley (62a) to feed the recording paper (32). Under this condition, the cutter cam (128), which is free to rotate relative to the shaft (60), does not follow the rotation of the shaft (60). When the motor (64) rotates clockwise or reversely, it causes the platen roller (40) to rotate in the same direction, thereby pulling back the paper (32). Concerning the discharge rollers (42), they are always rotated counterclockwise because the one-way clutches (72 and 80) are individually arranged to transmit a torque to the shaft (70) only when their associated gears (74 and 82) rotate counterclockwise. That is, the discharge rollers (48) are rotated counterclockwise by the pulley (76) during forward rotation of the motor (64) and by the gear (74), idle gears (86 and 84) and gear (82) during reverse rotation of the motor (64).

As to the motor (88), the forward rotation is the clockwise rotation. During forward rotation of the motor (88), the conveyor rollers (16 and 18) are rotated forwardly via the motor pulley (114), belt (116), pulleys (110 and 106), belt (118) and pulleys (94 and 96), thereby feeding a document. The one-way clutch (120) is constructed to prevent the gear (122) from being rotated by the forward rotation of the shaft (104). On reverse rotation of the motor (88), the torque is transmitted to the pulley (110) and not to the shaft (102) owing to the presence of the one-way clutch (108), whereby the conveyor rollers (16 and 18) are kept unmoved. However, The gear (122) is rotated counterclockwise to cause the cutter cam (128) to rotate clockwise via the gear (124). Then, the cam follower (134) on the cutter actuator (140) is abruptly released from the cutter cam (128) so that the cutter actuator (140) is bodily moved clockwise by the spring (138) from the position shown in Figure 12–15. The movable edge (44) of the cutter (42) cuts the paper (32). Continuing to rotate, the cutter cam (128) returns the cam follower (134) to the initial position (Figure 12–18) with its lobe, whereon the motor (88) is deenergized. The return of the cam follower (134) to the initial position is sensed by the cooperating switch (132) and the recess (130) of the disk (126).

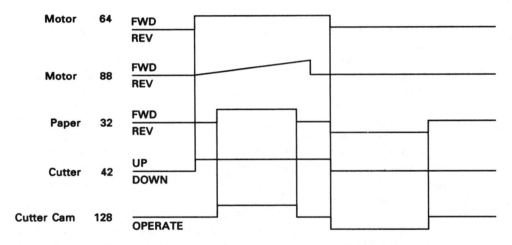

**Figure 12–18**   Timing Chart Showing Operation of Paper Cutter

The operation of the driving device described earlier will be better understood from the timing chart shown in Figure 12–18. After the completion of a recording operation, the movement of the paper (32) continues until it reaches the cutter (42). As soon as the paper (32) is stopped, the motor (88) starts a reverse rotation to actuate the cutter (42) to cut the paper (32). The motor (88) continues to rotate in reverse after cutting of the paper (32) to return the cutter (42) to the initial position. The cut length of the paper (32) to return the cutter (42) to the initial position. The cut length of the paper (32) is discharged to the tray (50), whereas the rest of the paper (32) is pulled back until the leading end becomes positioned just below the platen roller (40). The paper (32), therefore, allows no wasteful blank area to develop in the leading end portion thereof.

Thus, in accordance with the embodiment shown and described, the use of two motors (64 and 88) eliminates the need for an exclusive drive source for the cutter (42), whereas the forward and reverse rotations of the motors (64 and 88) are employed as a trigger to omit on-off clutches heretofore relied on. The device requires a minimum number of one-way clutches and, therefore, achieves a simple construction.

The motor (64) serves to advance the paper when rotated forwardly and to pull it back when rotated backwardly, whereas the motor (88) serves to advance a document when rotated forwardly and to actuate the cutter when rotated reversely. This sets up a substantially even distribution of loads acting on the drive sources and, thereby, allows them to work with maximum performance.

The drive sources are designed to accommodate the maximum loads. Nevertheless, owing to the even distribution of loads the drive sources can be selected with the maximum efficiency eliminating noise or the like owing to sharp buildup, which might result from overloading.

In summary, it will be seen that the present invention provides a driving apparatus for a facsimile apparatus that uses two drive sources to attain a simplified construction resulting in uniform loads acting on the drive sources to promote desirable drive.

Various modifications will become possible for those skilled in the art after receiving the teachings of the present disclosure while departing from the scope thereof.

Some of the components mentioned above, not shown in Figures 12-15 to 12-17, may be found in Figure 1-9 where an overall drawing of this machine is shown.

# CHAPTER 13
## Error Correction Mode

Before the CCITT recommendations for error control in 1989, there was no established error control technique for facsimile transmissions. The CCITT made an investigation of error control for G3 transmissions and summarized two different options in its 1989 Blue Book.

One option is called error limiting and applies only to one-dimensional MH coding. The intent of this option is to limit the effect of an error to half of a scan line instead of an entire scan line. Its value has not yet been proven in practice.

The second option, a half-duplex HDLC selectively repeating ARQ concept, has been more widely accepted and has been incorporated into many fax machines. An example of an implementation of this technique by the Ricoh Corporation is covered on the following pages. It is found in U.S. patent no. 4,975,783, issued to Ricoh Corporation on December 4, 1990.

## ECM MODE OPERATION

The ECM is a mode in which image information is transmitted in blocks that are constituted by a plurality of data frames in conformance with a high-level data link control (HDLC) procedure, and when a receiving side facsimile machine (hereinafter simply referred to as a destination) detects a transmission error a transmitting side facsimile machine (hereinafter simply referred to as a source) retransmits a data frame in which the error is detected. An error correction code is transmitted with the image information in frames, and the transmission error is detected by using the error correction code.

For this reason, to enable retransmission of the requested data frame from the source, it is necessary for the source to temporarily store one block of image information that is transmitted. In addition, when one received block of image information contains an error, the destination must receive the retransmitted frame data that corresponds to the frame data in which the error was detected. Hence, the destination must also temporarily store the received image information so that one block of image data may be constituted using the retransmitted frame data that contains no error.

Accordingly, the facsimile machine having the ECM is provided with an ECM buffer memory for temporarily storing one block of image information. For example, the ECM buffer memory has a memory capacity of 64 kb, which is normally sufficient to store an image information amounting to one page of document.

When the facsimile machine having the ECM is receiving a transmission, a plotter may break down, a paper jam may occur in the plotter, and the plotter may run out of recording paper during a recording of an image. When this nonrecordable state of the plotter occurs in a facsimile machine, which is not provided with a so-called store and forward (SAF) image memory, the reception process of the destination is discontinued by transmitting to the source a disconnect (DCN) signal, or a procedural interrupt negative (PIN) signal, each of which is a line disconnect instruction. Conversely, in the case of the facsimile machine provided with the so-called SAF image memory, the received image information is stored in the SAF image memory, but the DCN signal or the like is transmitted to discontinue the reception process when the memory capacity of the SAF image memory becomes insufficient to store all the image information.

In the preceding case, one block of the received image information is temporarily stored in the ECM buffer memory. When the reception process is discontinued, however, the content of the ECM buffer memory is erased at the same time. For this reason, there is a problem in that the received image information amounting to one page of document is erased without ever being recorded on the plotter.

Generally, the image memory for storing the image information is of a type that erases (or clears) the content thereof when the supply of power is cut off. Thus, when the image information that is not yet recorded is stored in the ECM buffer memory but the power supply to the facsimile machine is cut off owing to a power failure or the like, the image information stored in the ECM buffer memory is erased.

Conventionally, when the power supply is cut off, the facsimile machine records and outputs after the supply of power is resumed a report indicating that the power supply was cut off, so that the operator is informed of the erasure of the received image information stored in the SAF image memory. Conventionally, however, there is a problem in that the operator is not informed of the erasure of the image information stored in the ECM buffer memory owing to the cutoff of the power supply, and the operator has no means of knowing this erasure of the image information stored in the ECM buffer memory. Accordingly, it is a general object of the present invention to provide a novel and useful facsimile machine in which the problems described earlier are eliminated.

Another and more specific object of the present invention is to provide a facsimile machine having an error correction mode in conformance with CCITT recommendations. These recommendations comprise modem means coupled to a transmission path for modulating image information that is transmitted to the transmission path and for demodulating image information which is received from the transmission path. Image information is transmitted and received in blocks respectively having a predetermined format. A predetermined number of frames of information with error correction codes for use in detecting an error in image information is included. The following elements comprise the system:

- Communication-control means coupled to the modem means for controlling communications to and from the transmission path;
- Scanning means for scanning a document that is to be transmitted and for outputting the image information of the scanned document image as a transmitting image information;
- Recording means for recording an image described by received image information onto a recording sheet;
- First-memory means for temporarily storing the transmitting image information and the received image information in blocks;
- Second-memory means and display means for displaying a message;
- System-control means for controlling operations of the communication control means, the scanning means, the recording means and the display means.

The system control means includes the following:

- Means for supplying the image information read out from the first memory means to the recording means when the recording means is in a recordable state and for temporarily storing the image information readout from the first-memory means in the second memory means when the recording means is in a nonrecordable state and the second memory means has an empty region;
- Discontinuing means for discontinuing a reception process by disconnecting from the transmission path when the recording means is in the nonrecordable state or when no empty region is available in the second memory means;
- Means for displaying on the display means a message indicating that image information is stored in the first memory means when the reception process is discontinued;
- Means for supplying the image information readout from the first memory means to the recording means to record an image when the recording means resumes the recordable state after the reception process is discontinued.

Still another object of the present invention is to provide a facsimile machine having an error correction mode in conformance with CCITT recommendations and a system control means including the following:

- Means for discriminating whether or not image information is stored in the memory means when a supply of power to the facsimile machine is cut off and thereafter resumed;
- Means for supplying to the recording means a report indicating that a power supply cutoff occurred.

With such a facsimile machine, it is possible to inform the operator of erased image information when the image information is erased because of a power supply cutoff.

Figure 13–1 shows a facsimile machine according to this invention. The facsimile machine generally comprises a scanner (1), a plotter (2), an encoder-decoder (3), an ECM buffer memory (4), and image memory (5), a network control unit (6), a modem (7), a communication control unit (8), an operation and display device (9), a system memory (10), and a system controller (11).

The scanner (1) reads a document image and outputs an image information having a predetermined resolution. The plotter (2) records an image information on a recording sheet (paper). The plotter (2) is provided with known devices for detecting nonrecordable states thereof such as when the plotter (2) runs out of the recording sheet, a paper jam occurs in the plotter (2) and when the plotter (2) breaks down.

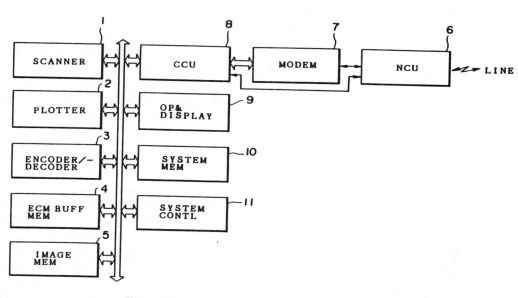

**Figure 13–1** System Block Diagram of Fax Machine with ECM Mode

The encoder-decoder (3) encodes an image information that is to be transmitted to a destination facsimile machine and decodes an image information that is received from a source facsimile machine.

The ECM buffer memory (4) temporarily stores one block of image information that is transmitted and received when making a communication in the ECM. The image memory (5) is the so-called SAF image memory, and stores image information when making a transmission of memorized information or when making a reception of memorized information. The network control unit (6) carries out predetermined call-out and call-accept operations by making a line connection, sending a destination telephone number as a selection signal and detecting a call in.

The modem (7) modulates the image information that is transmitted to the destination and demodulates the image information that is received from the source. The modem (7) also transmits various procedure signals of the transmission control procedure. The communication control unit (8) controls the network control unit (6) and the modem (7), and carries out a facsimile transmission according to the predetermined transmission control procedure.

The operation and display device (9) includes a display for displaying states (or modes) of the facsimile machine and a manipulation part having keys for instructing predetermined transmission and reception processes to the facsimile machine.

The system memory (10) stores various information required for the transmission and reception processes. A portion of the system memory (10) is constituted by a static RAM, which is backed up by a battery. Various communication information such as the destination telephone number, the communication mode, the line density of the received image, an information of receive terminal identification (hereinafter simply referred to as an RTI information), the compression mode, the size of the received image, and the communication result of the facsimile communication being made is stored in a memory region of the static RAM. This memory region also stores management information on image information files, which are stored in the ECM buffer memory (4) and the image memory (5).

The system controller (11) is constituted by a microcomputer. The system controller controls various parts of the facsimile machine to carry out a predetermined operation on the facsimile machine.

## THE RECEPTION PROCESS

Figure 13–2 shows a reception process carried out by the system controller (11) of the facsimile machine shown in Figure 13–1 in the ECM. In Figure 13–2, a step 101 connects the facsimile machine to a line when a call in is detected. This step 101 includes a process of discriminating the communication mode by carrying out a predetermined transmission control procedure. In this embodiment, the communication mode is detected as being the ECM, and a step 102 successively receives the image information. Then, a step 103 decodes the received image information and temporarily stores the decoded image information in the ECM buffer memory (4).

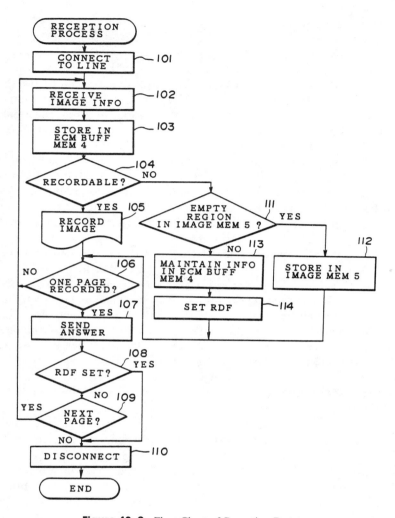

**Figure 13–2** Flow Chart of Reception Process

Next, a step 104 discriminates whether or not the plotter (2) is in a recordable state. When the discrimination result in the step 104 is YES, a step 105 successively reads the image information from the ECM buffer memory (4) one line at a time and transfers the read image information to the plotter (2) so as to record the received image one line at a time. A step 106 discriminates whether or not the recording of one page is ended. The process returns to the step 102 when the discrimination result in the step 106 is NO.

Conversely, when the discrimination result in the step 106 becomes YES, a step 107 sends a procedure signal indicative of the reception result as an answer. For example, when a transmission error is detected in the received image information by use of an error correction code that is received therewith, a partial page request (PPR) signal is sent to make a retransmission request. In addition, when discontinuing the reception process such as when it is impossible to continue receiving the image information, a DCN signal or a PIN signal is sent to end the reception process. For the sake of convenience, it will be assumed that the image information is correctly received and a message confirmation (MCF) signal is sent. In this embodiment, when it is impossible to continue receiving the image information, the step 107 sets a reception discontinuance flag RDF.

A step 108 discriminates whether or not the reception discontinuance flag RDF is set. When the discrimination result in the step 108 is NO, a step 109 discriminates whether or not a next page will be transmitted. When the discrimination result in the step 109 is YES, the process returns to the step 102 so as to similarly carry out the reception process with respect to the image information related to the next page.

When the discrimination result in the step 109 is NO, a step 110 disconnects the line by carrying out a predetermined transmission control procedure. Hence, the reception process is ended and the facsimile machine enters a waiting state.

Conversely, the plotter (2) may run out of the recording sheet, a paper jam may occur in the plotter (2), and the plotter (2) may break down during the reception of the image information. When the plotter (2) is in the nonrecordable state and the discrimination result in the step 104 is NO, a step 111 discriminates whether or not an empty region exists in the image memory (5). When the discrimination result in the step 111 is YES, a step 112 stores the image information within the ECM buffer memory (4) into the empty region of the image memory (5) instead of transferring the image information to the plotter (2). Thereafter, the reception process is carried out similarly to the above by advancing to the step 106.

The image memory (5) stores the image information of the document image which is to be transmitted as an image information file also when making a transmission of memorized information. For this reason, the image memory (5) may not have an empty region for storing the received image information.

When the image memory (5) does not have an empty region and the discrimination result in the step 111 is NO, a step 113 maintains the image information stored in the image memory (5) as an image information file so as not to erase this image information, and also maintains the image information stored in the ECM buffer memory (4) as it is. But because it is impossible to continue receiving the image information in this case, a step 114 sets the reception discontinuance flag RDF and the management information on the image information files maintained in the ECM buffer memory (4) and the image memory (5) are stored in a memory region of the static RAM, which is within the system memory (10) and is backed up by the battery.

When the reception discontinuance flag RDF is set and the reception of one page of image information is ended in the step 106, the step 107 sends a PIN signal, for example, so as to discontinue the reception process. In this case, the discrimination result in the step 108 is YES, and the process advances to the step 110 to immediately disconnect the line and enter the waiting state.

As described earlier, various communication information such as the destination telephone number, the communication mode, the line density of the received image, the RTI information, the compression mode, the size of the received image, and the communication result of the facsimile communication being made is stored in the memory region of the static RAM of the system memory (11). When the reception process is correctly ended without being discontinued, the various communication information stored in the static RAM is erased.

## THE WAITING PROCESS

Figure 13–3 shows a process carried out by the system controller (11) of the facsimile machine shown in Figure 13–1 in the waiting state thereof. In Figure 13–3, a step 201 discriminates whether or not the plotter (2) is in the recordable state. When the discrimination result in the step 201 is NO, a step 202 displays a message (or warning) on the operation and display device (9) by detecting the cause of the non-recordable state of the plotter (2). For example, when the plotter (2) is in the nonrecordable state owing to a paper jam, the message displayed on the operation and display device (9) may state "PAPER JAM—PLEASE REMOVE RECORDING SHEET."

Next, a step 203 discriminates whether or not the reception discontinuance flag RDF is set. The process returns to the step 201 when the discrimination result in the step 203 is NO.

Conversely, when the discrimination result in the step 203 is YES, a step 204 displays a message on the operation and display device (9) to indicate that there is an image information stored in the ECM buffer memory (4). For example, this message may state "ECM FILE EXISTS." Thereafter, a step 205 discriminates whether or not the plotter (2) is in the recordable state.

The operator attends to the maintenance of the plotter (2) by reading the message displayed on the operation and display device (9). In other words, the operator removes the paper jam or supplies the recording sheets, for example, depending on the message displayed on the operation and display device.

When the plotter (2) resumes the recordable state by the maintenance, the discrimination result in the step 205 become YES. A step 206 discriminates whether or not the image information stored in the image memory (5) by the step 112 shown in Figure 13–2 exists, that is, whether or not a received image information file exists. When the discrimination result in the step 206 is YES, a step 207 successively reads out the stored image information from the image memory (5) and records the image information on the plotter (2).

After the step 207 or when the discrimination result in the step 206 is NO, a step 208 discriminates whether or not the image information maintained within the

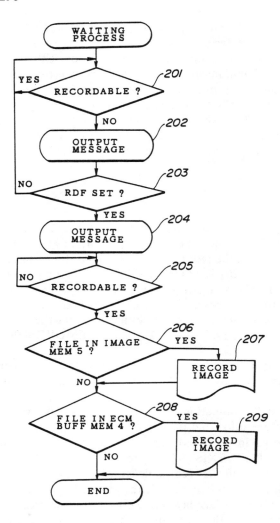

**Figure 13-3**  Flow Chart of Waiting Process

ECM buffer memory (4) by the step 113 shown in Figure 13-2. exists, that is, whether or not a received image information file exists. When the discrimination result in the step 208 is YES, a step 209 successively reads out the stored image information from the ECM buffer memory (4) and records the image information on the plotter (2). Conversely, the process is ended after step 209 or when the discrimination result in the step 208 is NO.

When the supply of power to the facsimile machine is once cut off, the image information files stored in the ECM buffer memory (4) and the image memory (5) are erased. Figure 13-4 shows a process carried out by the system controller (11) of the facsimile machine shown in Figure 13-1 when the power supply is once cut off and thereafter resumed.

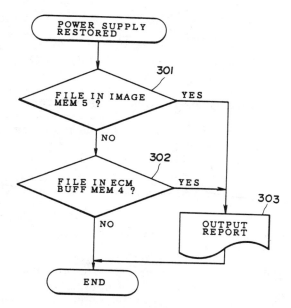

**Figure 13–4** Flow Chart of Process When Power Is Restored

## RESUMPTION OF POWER SUPPLY

In Figure 13–4, when the power supply to the facsimile machine is resumed, a step 301 discriminates whether or not an image information file was stored in the image memory (5) when the power supply was cut off, based on the file management information stored in the memory region of the static RAM within the system memory (10). When the discrimination result in the step 301 is NO, a step 302 discriminates whether or not an image information file was stored in the ECM buffer memory (4).

When the discrimination result in the step 301 or 302 is YES, a step 303 records on the plotter (2) an information related to the stored image information file so as to output a power supply cutoff report. The process is ended after the step 303 or when the discrimination result in the step 302 is NO.

## POWER SUPPLY CUTOFF REPORT

Figure 13–5 shows an embodiment of the power supply cutoff report which is output from the facsimile machine. In Figure 13–5, a indicates a title of the report, b indicates an output date, c indicates a date and time when the power supply cutoff occurred, and d indicates a message indicating that a power supply cutoff has occurred. In addition, e indicates a file number of the image information file stored in the image memory (5), and f indicates a type of the image information, where

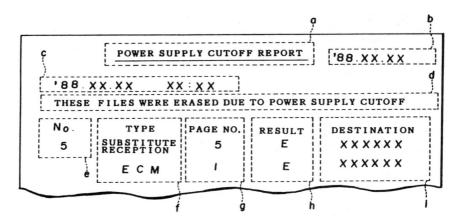

**Figure 13-5** Power Supply Cutoff Report Output by Fax Machine

"SUBSTITUTE RECEPTION" indicates a received image information file within the image memory (5), and "ECM" indicates an image information file within the ECM buffer memory (4). Furthermore, g indicates a page number of the image, h indicates a result of the reception process, where "E" indicates that an error has occurred owing to the power supply cutoff, and i indicates a destination telephone number.

Therefore, according to this embodiment, when the plotter (2) becomes non-recordable during the image information reception process, a substitute reception is made by storing the received image information in the image memory (5), but the reception process is discontinued when there is no more empty region within the image memory (5). In this case, the image information stored in the ECM buffer memory (4) is not erased but maintained, and a message is displayed to indicate that the ECM buffer memory (4) contains the image information. Conversely, when the plotter (2) becomes recordable after displaying the message, the image information is read out from the ECM buffer memory (4) and recorded on the plotter (2).

When the power supply to the facsimile machine is cut off, the image information in the ECM buffer memory (4) will be erased. Hence, when the operation and display device (9) displays the message indicating that the ECM buffer memory (4) contains the image information, the operator can make sure not to cut off the power supply when attending to the maintenance of the plotter (2). Accordingly, it is possible to always record the received image information which is stored in the ECM buffer memory (4).

When the power supply to the facsimile machine is cut off and thereafter resumed, the power supply cutoff report which is output makes an indication when there exists an image information file within the ECM buffer memory (4) or the image memory (5), which is erased. As a result, the operator is informed of the erased image information.

Conventionally, there is a power supply cutoff report which indicates only the content of the image information file within the image memory (5). But in this embodiment, it is possible to also indicate the content of the image information file within the ECM buffer memory (4) with ease.

## ECM ERASURE REPORT

In the preceding embodiment, the image information files within the ECM buffer memory (4) and the image memory (5) are indicated on a single power supply cutoff report. It is possible, however, to output independently the content of the image memory (5) as a power supply cutoff report shown in Figure 13–6 and the content of the ECM buffer memory (4) as an ECM erasure report shown in Figure 13–7. By independently outputting the power supply cutoff report and the ECM erasure report, it is possible to output only one of the reports that is required. Further, the

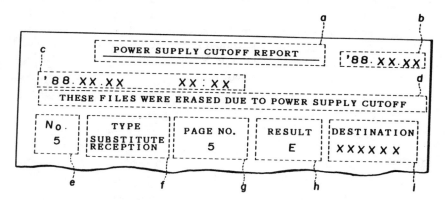

**Figure 13–6**  Power Supply Cutoff Report from Image Memory

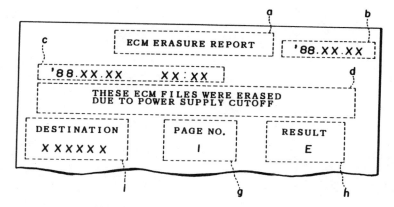

**Figure 13–7**  ECM Erasure Report from ECM Buffer Memory

content of the report can be readily understood by the operator by merely looking at the title a.

The embodiment described heretofore is applied to the facsimile machine that is provided with the SAF image memory (image memory, 5). In the case of a facsimile machine that is not provided with the SAF image memory, however, the step 113 shown in Figure 13–2 is carried out immediately when the discrimination result in the step 104 becomes NO. In addition, the processes related to the image memory (5), that is, the steps 206 and 207 shown in Figure 13–3 and the step 301 shown in Figure 13–2 are omitted. As a result, it becomes possible to always record the content of the ECM buffer memory 4 similarly as in the case of the described embodiment.

Furthermore, according to the process shown in Figure 13–3, the content of the image memory (5) is recorded when the plotter (2) becomes recordable. It is of course not essential to do so, however. Moreover, by outputting the power supply cutoff report or the like when the power supply is resumed even when no image information file to be output exists, it becomes possible to inform the operator of the time when the power supply was cut off.

The steps 202 and 204 shown in Figure 13–3 need not display the message in characters, and the message may be displayed by a lamp such as a light emitting diode (LED), or a sound or voice.

# CHAPTER 14

# *Modems*

Along with scanners and printers, modems are key components in facsimile machines. After the data provided by the scanner has been compressed or encoded, it is sent to the modem. The modem converts this digital data into a serial format and modulates a carrier with it. Most fax machines in use today incorporate modems that have the capability of transmitting and receiving at a maximum rate of 9600 bits per second (bps). This rate is twice that of the G3 CCITT standard rate of 4800 bps. Before transmitting a document the modem performs a test called modem training. This test is to check the ability of the modem to communicate over the telephone circuit in use. It can slow the data rate if necessary to make the communication possible. In the G3 standard there are three slower data rates: 7200, 4800, and 2400 bps. These data rates, however, are not the actual rates at which the data is being sent over the telephone line, as explained subsequently.

## DATA RATE VERSUS BD RATE

Bd rate is the number of times per second that the modem modulates the carrier. The carrier can be modulated by changing its amplitude, frequency, or phase. If a Bd rate of 500 were modulated onto a carrier, its amplitude, frequency, or phase would change up to 500 times per second depending on the type of modulation used. In this case the data rate and the Bd rate are equal. The data rate can be higher than the Bd rate, however. More than one bit can be sent at a time.

With binary, two bits can have four possible combinations: 11, 10, 01, 00. If four phase shifts were used to send this data, they could be 45°, 135°, 225°, and 315°. Each phase shift would represent two bits of data rather than one. The result would be that the data would be transmitted at twice the Bd rate. The V.29 modem uses quadrature modulation (QAM). It uses two different amplitudes and eight different phase shifts: 0°, 45°, 90°, 135°, 180°, 225°, 270°, and 315°. Taking these together 16 different four-b combinations may be transmitted; such as, 1111, 1110, 1101, 1100 . . . 0000. By transmitting 4 b per Bd simultaneously, the modem can transmit 9600 bps at 2400 Bd.

The maximum baud rate is limited by bandwidth, which in the case of the telephone network is about 2700 Hz. Thus, with a 2700-Hz bandwidth, the maximum Bd rate would be 2700 Bd. The frequency range of the telephone network is 300 to 3000 Hz, so the bandwidth is about 2700 cycles. So by using the quadrature amplitude modulation described above, 9600 b per second at a Bd rate of 2400 can easily pass through the public telephone network.

The terms V.29 and V.27 ter are CCITT terms used to identify the characteristics of the modem used in G3 equipment. The V.29 characteristics are optional under the CCITT guidelines, whereas V.27 ter is the standard.

The modulation format of the G3 mode is as shown in the following table:

| Transmission mode | V.29 | | V. 27 ter | | V.21 |
|---|---|---|---|---|---|
| Modulation mode | 16-pt QAM | 8-pt QAM | 8-pt PhM | 4-pt PhM | FSK |
| Communication speed (bps) | 9600 | 7200 | 4800 | 2400 | 300 |
| Modulation speed (Bd) | 2400 | 2400 | 1600 | 1200 | 300 |
| Carrier frequency (Hz) | 1700 | | 1800 | | 1850/1650 |
| Equalizer | Built-in adaptation-type automatic equalizer | | | | — |

## EVOLUTION OF MODEM DEVELOPMENT

The conversion of digital signals to analog signals (modulation) and the reverse (demodulation) may be done through the use of analog circuits and components such as, resistors, capacitors, and coils. Modems, which were designed around 1960, used this approach. By the mid-1970s, integrated circuits in the form of operational amplifiers came into the picture. By using such analog semiconductors, as shown in Figure 14-1, it was possible to make smaller and lower-cost modems.

In the 1980s serial command dialing using a microprocessor was introduced by Hayes Microcomputer Products. With PCs, the advantages of serial autodialing was such that these modems soon replaced the earlier generation of modems, although they still used operational amplifier technology as shown in Figure 14-2. During the past five years, the operational amplifier function and associated components have been incorporated into specialized integrated circuits. Such specialized ICs connected with the microprocessor as shown in Figure 14-3, minimized the

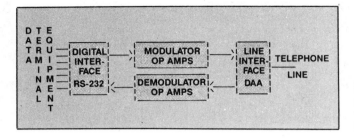

**Figure 14–1**  Modem Design using Analog Components (circa 1975); reprinted with permission of *Telecommunications*® Magazine © October 1990 [13].

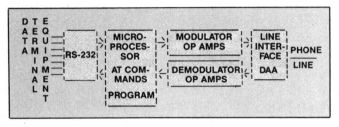

**Figure 14–2**  Applying Microprocessors to Modems; reprinted with permission of *Telecommunications*® Magazine © October 1990 [13].

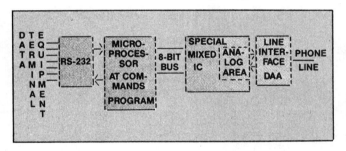

**Figure 14–3**  Specialized ICs in Modems; reprinted with permission of *Telecommunications*® Magazine © October 1990 [13].

number of external components and simplified the task of the designer. The specialized ICs have been responsible for the price reductions of modems in recent years and may produce the lowest-cost modems. They have been limited by the amount of complexity, however, that can be put onto a single specialized integrated circuit. As the demand for increased speed and performance has risen, it has not been possible to implement this type of design into a single chip.

## DIGITAL SIGNAL PROCESSING

The next generation of modem technology is based on digital signal processing as shown in Figure 14–4. In this design the memory used by both the microprocessor and the digital signal processor (DSP) is ROM. This memory is usually fabricated as part of the DSP chip to provide the lowest-cost form of program storage. The

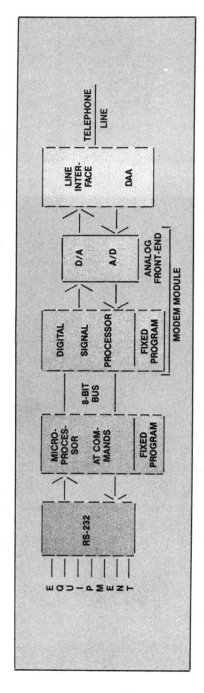

**Figure 14–4** Digital Signal Processing (DSP) in Modems; reprinted with permission of *Tele-communications*® Magazine © October 1990 [13].

potential of DSP modem architecture is limited significantly, however, through the use of ROM for program storage.

Flexibility is the real advantage of using DSP. It depends on how the flexibility is used, however, whether the manufacturer or the user derives the benefit. The use of the DSP allows the basic modem functions to be accomplished by a programmable microprocessor (Figure 14–5). The advantages of doing so are that additional modulation-demodulations can be provided for only the cost of the memory required to store the program and changes to the modulation and demodulation can be made without hardware changes. Also, compatibility problems can be resolved without changing the hardware.

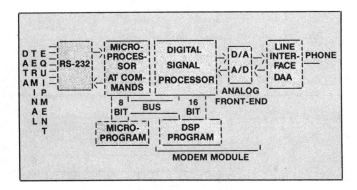

**Figure 14–5** DSP with Programmable Microprocessor in Modems; reprinted with permission of *Telecommunications*® Magazine © October 1990 [13].

The design of modems is closely linked to the various standardizations for digital communications, which have been promulgated by the CCITT. Two new standards, Microcom Networking Protocols (MNP), which has not been adopted by the CCITT, and V.42 and V.42 bis, which has been adopted by the CCITT, provide for performance enhancement. The CCITT V.42 recommendation defines an error correction scheme and V.42 bis defines a new data compression scheme that offers a 4:1 compression ratio. A 2400-bps modem essentially operates at 9600 Bd when equipped with V.42 bis and a 9600-bps modem attains effective speeds of 38,400 bps.

Rockwell was the first manufacturer to announce a modem chip set for the V.42- and V.42-bis standards. One of the chips integrates an analog front end (AFE) and a DSP core. The other chip includes a microcontroller, which implements the error correction and data compression. One of Rockwell's fax chips is their R96DFX Monofax, which requires no external components to support HDLC (high-level data-link control) framing and DTMF. It also supports the ECM (error-correction mode) described in chapter 13. Since the early 1980s Rockwell has had the fax-modem-chip business to itself, but others are coming into the picture. One of their competitors, Yamaha, has had particular success in the fax-board market with their YM7109, which is also a DSP chip.

## YAMAHA YM7109 ONE-CHIP MODEM

The YM7109 LSI (Figures 14–6 and 14–7) is a one-chip modem for half-duplex synchronous data transfer at 9600 bps, 7200 bps, 4800 bps, 2400 bps, and 300 bps (CCITT V.29, V.27 ter, V.21 and V.21 ch2). With its built-in programmable dual-tone originating function and programmable tone detection function, this LSI is designed for use with a public telephone line network and is ideal for modem applications for G3 facsimile machines. The YM7109 is also designed to cope with long-training and short-training when transmission is carried out at 4800 bps or 2400 bps (CCITT V.27 ter), thereby making itself suitable for modem-used telecommunications with PCs under the system recommended by the Ministry of Posts and Telecommunications.

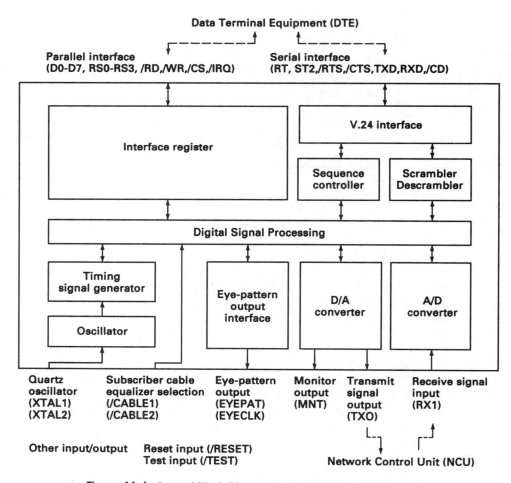

**Figure 14–6**   Internal Block Diagram of Yamaha YM7109 Modem Chip

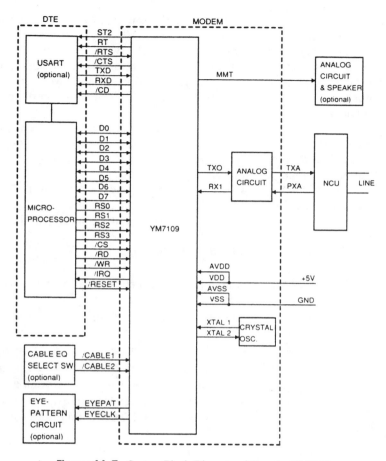

**Figure 14–7**   System Block Diagram of Yamaha YM7109

In addition, the YM7109 is equipped with function for modulation into full duplex (CCITT V.21 and BELL 103) and a 75 bps (CCITT V.23 backward channel) transmission function. It can thus also be used as the modem for telecommunications by personal computer or as a CAPTAIN adapter.

The YM7109 also has a built-in interface register that can connect to the data bus of a microprocessor, allowing reading and writing to and from that data bus. By accessing this interface register via a parallel interface, you can set the operating mode, set various parameters, read status flags, transfer the data to be transmitted or received, operate the modem and so on. The transfer of the transmit and receive data as well as modem operation can also be performed via a serial interface. The YM7109 is fabricated in a 40-pin dip unit. Because of its low-power consumption thanks to CMOS, the full capability of the LSI can be facilitated with 5-V battery power supply. FAXSIM software is a collection of modules especially designed to assist in the development of integrated facsimile products using Yamaha's YM7109 modem chip.

The package contains a collection of low-level function blocks, a diagnostic tool kit and a set of sample applications programs to send and receive G3 fax. The modules and applications are designed to operate on IBM™ PC, XT, and AT class computers in conjunction with Yamaha's fax evaluation card included as part of the package.

All of the preceding software modules are written in the C programming language, and are supplied with source code, and make files and documentation. The package was designed and developed with Borland's Turbo C™ integrated development environment, version 1.5 or higher.

Although the FAXSIM software operates on the IBM PC family of computers, it is easily adapted to most any host microprocessor. The C source code clearly demonstrates correct methods for operating the chip and can save significant design and development time.

The low-level modules include the following:

*YAMODEM.OBJ*—Handles modem chip DSP configuration, line conditioning, and modem RAM access

*FAX.H*—Has complete set for template definitions for the modem's registers and interfaces

*DTMF.OBJ*—Handles DTMF tone encode and decode operations

*DAA.OBJ*—Manages the telephone line access; provides connect, disconnect, ring detection, auto-answer, and pulse-dialing services

*HDLC.OBJ*—Implements V.21 HDLC framed transmission and reception routines essential to G3 FAX communications

The diagnostic tool kit includes the following:

*HUFFMANW.TBL*—ASCII CCITT T.4 one-dimensional coding tables

*BUILDG3D.EXE*—Builds G3 decoding tables

*BUILDG3E.EXE*—Builds G3 encoding tables

*BITPRINT.EXE*—Utility to dump a G3 encoded file as a bit sequence segmented as T.4 codes

*HDLCCOMP.EXE*—Compiler for precomputing the T.30 response frames such as DCS, DIS, MCR, and so on

*HDLCPRN.EXE*—Disassembles HDLC frames built with HDLCCOMP.EXE.

*V21WATCH.EXE*—Uses YAMAHA's YM7109 evaluation board to monitor fax calls and record the T.30 protocol interaction between two fax machines

FAXSIM* contains a set of sample applications to demonstrate the composition, transmission, and reception of FAX messages in a paperless workstation environment.

*SENDFAX.EXE*—Transmits G3 coded documents to a designated telephone number

*RECVFAX.EXE*—Receives G3 fax files and saves them on a receive spool disk

*DOCTOFAX.EXE*—Converts ASCII documents to G3 fax using a 12-point font

*FAXEGA.EXE*

*FAXCGA.EXE*

*FAXVGA.EXE*—Allows viewing of contents of a G3 fax spool on display

*FAXPRINT.EXE*—Prints out the contents of a fax document on an EPSON compatible printer

*DIAL.EXE*—Dials a telephone number, demonstrating DTMF coding

*DTMFSHOW.EXE*—Answers telephone and displays touch-tone sequences to the display

## MODEM CIRCUIT OPERATION IN PANASONIC MODEL KX-F80 MACHINE

The modem (IC27) has all the hardware satisfying the CCITT standards mentioned previously (Figure 14–8). When the gate array IC26 (G6) is brought to low level, the modem (IC27) is chip selected, and resistors inside the IC are selected by select signals from CPU (IC3) A0-A4, commands are written through data bus, and through readout, all processing is controlled at the CPU (IC3) according to CCITT procedures. Here the signal INT dispatched IRQ (58) to the CPU (IC3) and gate array IC17 is output when preparation for acceptance of transmission data is OK and when demodulation of reception data is complete; the CPU (IC3) implements postprocessing.

This modem (IC27) has an automatic application equalizer. With training signal 1 or 2 at time of G3 reception, it can automatically establish the optimum equalizer. With CABS1 and CABS2, the equalizer in the modem (IC27) can be set up from outside. When the distance to the station is long or transception does not occur properly, correction of 0.0 km, 1.8 km, 3.6 km, and 7.2 km is possible with user setting. (See port description of gate array IC26.)

---

*FAXSIM is a trademark of Yamaha Corp. of America. IBM is a registered trademark of IBM Corp. IBM XT and AT are trademarks of International Business Machines Corp. Turbo C is a trademark of Borland Corp.

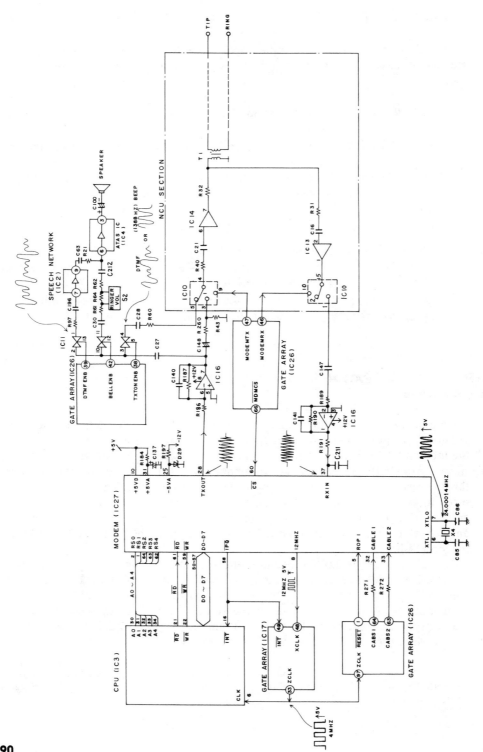

**Figure 14-8** Modem Circuit Operation in Panasonic's Model KX-F80 Fax Machine

Also, the modem (IC27) generates an internal clock of 24,00014 MHz by means of an external crystal oscillator (X4), and a 12-MHz clock is output at pin 8 by internal frequency division. This clock enters at pin 48 of the gate array (IC17), further frequency division is executed in the gate array (IC17), and an 8-MHz clock is output at pin 33 as the basic clock for CPU (IC3) and gate array IC26. The functions of the modem (IC27) and the signal path are shown subsequently.

## Facsimile Transmission

The digital image data on the data bus is modulated in the modem (IC27) and sent from pin 28 via amplifier IC16 (6 and 7), and the NCU section to the telephone line.

$$IC27(28) -> R186 -> IC16(6)(7) -> C148 -> R260 -> NCU \ Section$$
$$[IC10(3)(4) -> R40 -> C21 -> IC14(6)(7) -> R32 -> T1] -> TEL.Line$$

## Facsimile Reception

The analog image data that is received from the telephone line passes through the NCU section and enters pin 37 of the modem (IC27). The signals that enter pin 37 of the modem (IC27) are demodulated in the board to digital image signals, then placed on the data bus.

In this case, the image signals from the telephone line are transmitted serially. Hence, they are placed on the bus in 8-b units. Here, the internal equalizer circuit reduces the image signals to the long-distance receiving level.

It is designed to correct the characteristics of the frequency band centered about 3 kHz and maintain a constant receiving sensitivity. It can be set in the service mode.

$$TEL.Line -> NCU$$
$$Section[T1 -> R31 -> C16 -> IC13(2)(1) -> IC10(15)(1)]$$
$$-> C147 -> R189 -> IC16(1)(1) -> R191 -> IC27(37)$$

## DTMF Transmission (Monitor Tone) and Line-Send Beep for ATAS

The DTMF signal generated in the modem (IC27) is output from pin 28, then passes through the analog switch IC11 pins (3 and 4) and the NCU section to the telephone line.

During speakerphone operation, the monitor tone is output from the analog switch IC11 pins (2 to 1) through speech network IC2 pins (7–9) and the ATAS IC4 pins (6 to 3) power amplifier to the speaker.

DTMF and beep line send

$$IC27(28) -> R186 -> IC16(6)(7) -> C27 -> IC11(3)(4) -> IC28 -> R\ 60 -> NCU$$
$$Section\ [IC10(5)(4) -> R40 -> C21 -> IC14(6)(7) -> R32 -> TEL.Line$$

DTMF monitor tone

$$IC27(28) -> R186 -> IC16(6)(7) -> IC11(2)(1) -> R97 -> C196 ->$$
$$IC2(7)(9) -> C63 -> R21 -> IC4(6)(3) -> C100 -> Speaker$$

## Call-Tone Transmission

The call signal that is generated in the modem (IC27) passes through analog switch IC11(10–11) and ATAS IC4(6–3) to the speaker.

$$IC27(28) -> R186 -> IC16(6)(7) -> C27 -> IC11(10)(11) -> C30 -> R61 -> R64 -> R62 -> C212 -> IC4(6)(3) -> C100 -> Speaker$$

S2(Ringer VOL SW)

## Busy–Dial-Tone Detection

The path is the same as for fax receiving. When it is detected, the carrier detect bit of the register in the modem (IC27) becomes 1, and this status is monitored by the CPU (IC3).

# APPENDIX A
# *Paper-Size Equivalency Approximation*

| U.S. standard | A size | B size |
|---|---|---|
| Statement<br>5.5″ × 8.5″<br>(140 × 216 mm) | A5<br>5.8″ × 8.3″<br>(148 × 210 mm) | B6<br>5.0″ × 7.2″<br>(128 × 182 mm) |
| Letter<br>8.5″ × 11″<br>(216 × 279 mm) | A4<br>8.3″ × 11.7″<br>(210 × 297 mm) | B5<br>7.2″ × 10.1″<br>(182 × 257 mm) |
| Legal<br>8.5″ × 14″<br>(216 × 356 mm) | No close<br>equivalent | No close<br>equivalent |
| Computer<br>10″ × 14″<br>(254 × 356 mm) | No close<br>equivalent | B4<br>10.1″ × 14.3″<br>(257 × 364 mm) |
| Ledger<br>11″ × 17″<br>(279 × 432 mm) | A3<br>11.7″ × 16.5″<br>(297 × 420 mm) | No close<br>equivalent |

# APPENDIX B

# *Telephone Line and Product Testing*

Facsimile machines and computer-based facsimile devices depend upon telephone lines and networks for their channels of communication. Therefore, it is important to check them to be sure that they are not impairing the transmission or reception. Various telephone line and network testers have appeared on the market. Two examples of analyzers and testers that are being used by facsimile service personnel at this time are described below. Also, the type of tests which they perform as related to facsimile machine operation are covered.

## THE VNA-70A VOICE NETWORK ANALYZER

The first example is the Model VNA-70A voice network analyzer offered by Metro Tel. An outline of its front panel is shown in Figure B–1, which indicates A. On/off/volume Control, B. Telephone line jack, C. Butt set/CPE jack, D. Setup switch, E. Test mode switch, F. Ohms switch, G. Audio monitor speaker, H. Display screen, I. Battery charging jack, and J. Dial pulse level select.

### Telephone Line Testing for Fax Operation

The telephone line should be connected to the Line jack on the VNA-70A. The Mode switch should be in the Test position, the Setup switch in the BRDG position

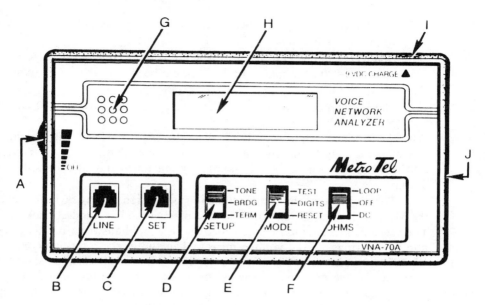

**Figure B–1** Outline of VNA-70A Front Panel

and the Ohms switch in the Off position. The Fax machine should be connected to the Set jack.

With the Fax machine idle, i.e., neither sending nor receiving, the following observations should be noted:

1. DC line voltage should read between 42 and 53 volts. A reading outside of this range usually indicates a telephone line problem.

2. DC line current ideally should read zero. However, due to noise, it may read +00.5 or −00.5. Any reading greater than this amount may indicate a DC leakage problem in the Fax machine.

3. The dB and Frequency sections of the screen will not display meaningful information at this time unless there is excessive noise or tones on the line. Presence of noise above the −25 dB level could impair Fax operation. By turning up the volume of the monitor speaker the noise or tones can be heard and verified.

Following these tests, the handset of the Fax machine should be lifted and the display screen of the VNA-70A should be observed as follows:

1. DC volts should read between 4 and 18. If the reading is less than 4 volts a problem may exist in the Fax machine, but it is more likely that the phone line is excessively long or has a bad connection.

2. DC current should read between 15 and 90 milliamperes. If below 15 milliamperes a bad connection is likely.
3. Dial tone can be heard by adjusting the volume control on VNA-70A. A level between −20 dBm and −12 dBm should be seen in the upper right-hand corner of the display.
4. The Frequency section of the display should read between 350 and 440 Hz.

With the Mode switch of the VNA-70A in the Digits position, the Touchpad on the Fax machine may be tested. Each number is pressed and checked for its display on the VNA-70A screen. Auto-dialing Fax machines may also be tested using the display.

The response of the Fax machine to ringing signals may be tested by returning the Mode switch to the Test position and placing the Fax handset back "on-hook." The Fax machine should then be called and it should answer after the programmed number of rings. If the voltage measured in the upper right-hand section of the VNA-70A display screen is greater than 25 VAC, the Fax machine should respond. A lower voltage may indicate a faulty phone line. The tests discussed provide a general indication of telephone line quality. Major deviations from the values given indicate potential telephone line problems that could impair Fax performance.

## Testing between Fax Machines

With the VNA-70A connected as in the above procedures, a call should be initiated from the local fax machine to the remote one. Observe that after dialing the last digit, the local Fax machine will send a 1100 Hz tone for $\frac{1}{2}$ second at a nominal level of −9 dBm. This cycle may repeat at 3 second intervals.

Audible ringback should be heard in the monitor speaker. Two seconds after answering, the receiving machine should send a 2100 Hz tone for 3 seconds at a level of −9 dBm. This tone should be received at the local machine at a level greater than −44 dBm. Indications below these levels on the dBm section of the VNA-70A's display means that there is excessive line loss.

The remote machine should now send data tones to the local machine. The lower right-hand section of the VNA-70A display will indicate frequencies between 1550 and 1750 Hz. During this period a single burst of 1850 Hz should be seen. These tones are sent at a nominal level of −9.0 dBm and should be received at a level greater than −44 dBm at the local machine. These tone exchanges will continue until the two machines are synchronized. After synchronization, another series of tones at the same frequencies and levels will be exchanged as the image information is passed from one machine to the other. At the end of this period, both machines will disconnect simultaneously.

If all of the above indications are normal and documents cannot be transmitted in one or both directions, one or both of the Fax machines is at fault.

## THE 1045A TELEPHONE PRODUCT TESTER

The second example is the Model 1045A telephone product tester, a B&K Precision product, sold by Maxtec International Corporation. An outline of its front panel is shown in Figure B-2. This panel contains 1. Power switch, 2. Dialed number display, 3. Low ringer level/reset button, 4. Normal ringer level button, 5. Polarity norm/ rev test button, 6. Single/aux button, 7. Telephone test jack #2, 8. Telephone test jack #1, 9. Voice/dial level OK indicator, 10. Handset cord test jacks, 11. Handset cord test jacks, 12. Single line indicator, and 13. Telephone cord test jacks.

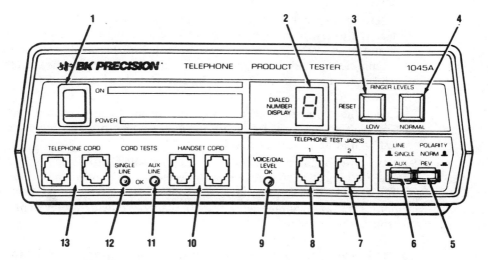

**Figure B-2** Outline of 1045A Front Panel; reprinted with permission by Maxtec International Corporation

### Fax Machine Test

This Telephone Product Tester can simulate a telephone exchange and two telephone lines for testing fax machines. The steps to be taken are as follows:

1. Toggle the Power switch on. The Dialed number display indicator lights when the tester is on.
2. Plug the fax machine's AC power cord into an AC outlet.
3. Plug the telephone plug of the fax machine to be tested into Telephone test jack #1. Plug a second fax machine known to be in working order into Telephone test jack #2.
4. Release Single/aux switch to the single (out) position.

5. To cause the fax machine being tested to answer a call, take the handset of fax machine #2 "off hook." Press the Normal ringer level button. The fax machine being tested should answer the call. If it fails to do so, it should be repaired or replaced.

6. Leave the fax machine in the answering mode and keep the fax machine plugged into Telephone tester jack #2 still "off hook." Press the Reset/low ringer level button. The fax machine should answer the call. If the fax machine, under test, will not answer the call in this step but did so in Step 4, the machine cannot be used in long line situations. It should be repaired or replaced.

7. After the fax machine being tested answers the call, the service person should hear the tones (or observe the message) indicating that it is ready to receive from the handset earpiece (or message panel) of the fax machine plugged into Telephone test jack #2. When the fax machine gives the tone (or message) to send a document, insert the test document into the sending fax machine and transmit it.

8. Check the document received by the fax being tested to ensure that no problems exist. If the received document is not satisfactory, the fax machine under test should be repaired or replaced.

9. Transpose the fax machine telephone cords plugged to Telephone test jacks #1 and #2 (plug the fax machine being tested into #2 and the good fax machine into #1). Perform steps 4 through 7 to check the answering and receiving capabilities of fax machine being tested. If any problems are evident, repair or replace the machine.

The Model 1045A performs a number of other tests, such as Cord test, Dial test, and Ring test, all of which are explained in detail in the Manual furnished with this tester. Since they do not relate specifically to Fax machine testing, they are not covered in detail above.

Figure B-1 and related text are presented through the courtesy of Metro Tel, 250 S. Milpitas Boulevard, Milpitas, CA 95035. Figure B-2 and the related text is presented through the courtesy of Maxtec International Corporation, 6470 W. Cortland Street, Chicago, IL 60635.

# *Glossary*

**Analog facsimile**  Facsimile transmission in which the signals are kept in analog form throughout the system and are not digitized in any part of it.

**Automatic document feeder**  A part of a facsimile machine from which sheets of a multipage document are sequentially fed into the scanner.

**Bandwidth compression**  A technique to reduce the bandwidth needed to transmit a given amount of facsimile information in a given time.

**Baud (Bd)**  A unit of signaling speed. The speed in baud is the number of discrete signal elements per second.

**Bit**  An abbreviation for a binary digit. The smallest unit of information in a binary system. A one or zero condition.

**Bit rate**  The speed at which bits are transmitted expressed in bits per second (bps).

**Charge coupled device**  A photosensitive device used to scan documents in facsimile machines to convert black and white information into electrical signals. Because of its small size a long optical path is needed.

**Compatibility**  A matching of facsimile transceiver characteristics that results in the transmission and reception of acceptable copy.

**Compression ratio**  The ratio of the total bits used to represent original copy to the total number of encoded bits for the copy.

**Contact-type scanner**   A scanner in which the photosensitive portion extends over the full width of the document to be transmitted. It is also close to the document and does not need a long optical path.

**Data compressor reconstructor**   A VLSI device used to encode-decode page data using modified Huffman or modified READ algorithms.

**Digital facsimile**   Facsimile in which digital coding techniques are applied to reduce redundancy as in Groups 3 and 4.

**Document facsimile**   That type of facsimile in which the original copy is reproduced primarily in black and white.

**Echo suppressor**   A device used to suppress or attenuate echoes on long distance telephone lines or sea-bottom cables.

**Encoder**   A device for coding a signal, usually in binary form, to represent individual characters or groups of characters in a message.

**End-of-line (EOL)**   A sequence of digital symbols introduced at the end of a scanning line to establish synchronization of decoding and for error detection. Used in Group 3 facsimile systems.

**Error correction mode (ECM)**   A mode in which image information is transmitted in blocks constituted by a plurality of data frames in accordance with a high-level data link control (HDLC) procedure.

**Facsimile transceiver**   An apparatus that sends and receives facsimile signals.

**Frequency shift keying (FSK)**   Frequency modulation method in which the frequency is made to vary at significant instants, such as binary 1 for one frequency and shift in frequency to represent binary 0. The facsimile V.21 modem uses this method.

**Group 1**   Analog facsimile equipment conforming to the CCITT recommendation T.2. An A4 page is sent in 6 min over a voice-grade telephone line using frequency modulation with 1300 Hz corresponding to white and 2100 Hz corresponding to black. North American 6-min equipment did not conform to the CCITT standard; 1500 Hz was used for white and 2400 Hz for black. Consequently, it was not compatible with the CCITT standard of the time.

**Group 2**   Analog facsimile equipment conforming to the CCITT recommendation T.3. An A4 page could be sent in 3 min over voice-grade telephone lines using 2100 Hz AM-PM-VSB.

**Group 3**   Digital facsimile equipment conforming to CCITT recommendation T.4. An A4 page can be sent in 30 s or less time over a voice-grade telephone line.

**Group 4**   Digital facsimile equipment conforming to CCITT recommendation T.5 and T.6, which uses Public Data Networks and their procedures for essentially error-free reception. Group 4 may also be sent on the public switched telephone network provided an appropriate modulation is applied.

**Halftone image**   An image that has been converted from a continuous tone image into a two-tone image, while retaining the appearance of a continuous tone image.

**Handshake**   The exchange of a predetermined signal for control when a connection is established between two modems. Facsimile machines do handshaking before any page data is transmitted.

**Horizontal resolution**   The number of picture elements per inch or per millimeter in the horizontal direction.

**Hub machine**   A facsimile apparatus used as a central communications device for a group of people, typically a number of departments in a large company. A rub machine is often connected to smaller special-purpose facsimile machines within the same office.

**Ink-jet recording**   The type of recording in which ink particles are directly deposited on the record sheet.

**Jitter**   An irregular error in the position of the recorded spot along the recorded line.

**K factor**   The number of facsimile scanning lines in a set used for coding.

**Line-to-line correlation**   Correlation of image information from line to line as scanned. Used in two-dimensional coding (modified READ).

**Modem**   A contraction of modulator-demodulator. The modulator is used for transmitting and the demodulator is used for reception. Such operation takes place for communication between facsimile equipment over the telephone line.

**Modified Huffman coding**   A one-dimensional run length digital coding scheme for white and black runs. The shortest length code words represent the most probable run lengths. Used in Group 3 facsimile.

**Modified READ Coding**   A two-dimensional optional digital coding scheme for Group 3 facsimile.

**Modified Modified READ Code**   A two-dimensional coding scheme for Group 4 facsimile.

**Network control unit (NCU)**   A PCB that interfaces the facsimile machine with the telephone circuit, sometimes called a coupler.

**Paper cutter**   A mechanical device, in a fax machine, used to cut received documents into individual pages.

**Pel**   A picture element that contains only black and white information.

**Photographic facsimile**   That type of facsimile in which the original copy is reproduced faithfully with graded tonal densities.

**Protocol**   The defined procedure necessary to initiate and maintain communications.

**Random access memory (RAM)**   A memory that has its stored information available when addressed in any order.

**Redundancy reduction**   Coding for the elimination of redundant information in the picture signal, which need not be transmitted.

**Ring**   One of the pair leads in a two-wire telephone system. This wire is usually red and is considered to be the return line.

**Read-only memory (ROM)**   A memory that is preprogrammable, cannot be changed, and can only be read.

**Scanner**   That component of a facsimile machine that systematically translates densities of the original into a signal waveform.

**Store and forward**   The storing of messages into memory at a local terminal to be transmitted when desired.

**Thermal printing**   A type of recording produced by signal-controlled thermal action.

**Thermal transfer printing**   A type of printing that uses heat from a thermal print head to transfer marking from a carbon ribbon or overlay sheet to another sheet.

**Tip**   One of the pair leads in a two-wire telephone system. It is usually green and is the high side of the line.

**Transmission time**   The elapsed time between the start of transmission and the detection of the end-of-message signal.

**Voice grade line**   A telephone line suitable for the transmission of voice, analog data, or facsimile with a frequency range of 300 to 3000 Hz.

# *Abbreviations*

**ADF**—Automatic document feeder

**CCD**—Charge coupled device

**CED**—Called station identification

**CCITT**—Consultative Committee for International Telephone and Telegraph

**CFR**—Confirmation to receive

**CNG**—Calling tone

**CSI**—Called subscriber identification

**DCN**—Disconnect

**DCR**—Data-compressor reconstructor

**DCS**—Digital command signal

**DIS**—Digital identification signal

**DMAC**—Direct memory access controller

**DMU**—Data memory unit

**DR**—Data reducer

**DRAM**—Dynamic random access memory

**DRU**—Drive and registration unit

**DSB**—Document sensor board

**DTMF**—Dual-tone multifrequency

**ECM**—Error correction mode

**EOL**—End of line

**EOM**—End of message

**EOP**—End of procedure

**EPROM**—Electronically programmable read-only memory

**FCU**—Facsimile control unit

**FIFO**—First-in, first-out

**FTT**—Fail to train

**I/O**—Input/output

**LB**—Line buffer

**LCD**—Liquid crystal display

**LD**—Laser diode

**LDDR**—Laser diode driver

**LED**—Light-emitting diode

**LSD**—Laser synchronization detector

**LSI**—Large-scale integration

**MBU**—Memory board unit

**MCF**—Message confirmation

**MH**—Modified Huffman

**MIF**—Modem interface

**MPS**—Multipage signal

**MR**—Modified read

**MTF**—Modulation transfer function

**NCU**—Network control unit

**NSF**—Nonstandard facilities

**OPU**—Operator unit

**PABX**—Private automatic branch exchange

**PD**—Pulse dialing

**PIN**—Procedural interrupt negative

**PIP**—Procedural interrupt positive

**PIS**—Procedure interrupt signal

**PPR**—Partial page request

**PSTN**—Public switched telephone network

**PSU**—Power supply unit

**QAM**—Quadrature amplitude modulation

**RTI**—Remote terminal identification

**RTN**—Retrain negative

**RTP**—Retrain positive

**SAF**—Store and forward

**SBU**—Scanner board unit

**SIO**—Serial input/output

**SMDR**—Scanner Motor Driver

**TCR**—Transaction confirmation report

**TFT**—Thin film transistor

**TTI**—Transmit terminal identification

**UIB**—Upper interface board

**VPU**—Video processing unit

# *References*

## TRAINING MANUALS AND SERVICE LITERATURE

Panasonic Service Manual and Technical Guide KX-F80
Panasonic Service Manual and Technical Guide KX-F120
Panasonic Service Manual and Technical Guide KX-F220
Ricoh Fax 105 Field Service Manual
Ricoh Fax 1000L Service Training Manual
Ricoh Fax 1000L Field Service Manual
Sharp Service Manual—No. 1 Facsimile—Model F0-230

## ARTICLES, PAPERS, AND PATENTS

1. Akami, K., Oda, G., Iwasaw, T., and Miura, M., "Ink Jet Recording Apparatus," U.S. Patent No. 4,975,718; filed 9/2/88, granted 12/4/90.
2. Bodson, D., Schaphorst, R. A., and Urban, S. J., "Gray Scale Pictures Via Group 3 Facsimile," *IEEE Communications Magazine,* September 1989, pp. 42–47.
3. Costigan, D. M., "Facsimile Comes Up to Speed." *IEEE Communications Magazine,* May 1980, pp. 30–35.
4. Hamano, T., Takenouchi, M., Ozawa, T., Fuse, M., and Nakamura, T., "Elongate Thin-Film Reader," U.S. Patent No. 4,419,696; filed 12/10/81, granted 12/6/83.
5. Higashi, A., Kurita, M., Ohwada, H., Tamako, K., Hagiusara, T., and Sugihara, K., "A Standard Multipurpose Fax Processor." *IEEE Transaction on Consumer Electronics,* 37, no. 3, August, 1991.

6. Huffman, D. A., "A Method for the Construction of Minimum Redundancy Codes," *Proceedings of the IRE,* September 1952, pp. 1098–1101.

7. Hunter, R., and Robinson, A. H., "International Digital Facsimile Coding Standards," *Proceedings of the IEEE,* 68, no. 7 (July 1980) pp. 854–67.

8. Ijuin, K., Otsuki, S., Nakano, Y., and Ogushi, H., "Facsimile Apparatus Having a Thermal Image Recording Head Retractable from a Recording Position," U.S. Patent No. 5,014,135, filed 7/5/90, granted 5/7/91.

9. Ino, M., Kohata, M., Itagaki, M., Nagata, T., and Tanaka, H., "Linear Solid State Image Sensor," U.S. Patent #4,977,304, filed 2/6/90, granted 12/11/90.

10. Kakinuma, H., Kasuya, Y., Sakamoto, M., and Watanabe, T., "Direct-Contact-Type Image Sensor," U.S. Patent No. 4,887,166; filed 5/20/88, granted 12/12/89.

11. Kobayashi, K., "Advances in the Facsimile Art," *IEEE Communications Magazine,* February 1985, pp. 27–35.

12. Koichi, E., Jeng, T., Roth, R., and Lam, L.M., "Facsimile Remote Diagnostic System," U.S. Patent No. 4,965,676; filed 2/28/89, granted 10/23/90.

13. Kretchmer, K., "Digital Signal Processing Creates the Next Generation of Modems," *Telecommunications,* October 1990, pp. 43–46.

14. Matsura, Y., and Koseki, Y., "Facsimile Machine Having a Page Printing Function," U.S. Patent No. 4,933,771t; filed 11/4/88, granted 6/12/90.

15. Scharen-Guivel, J. H., and Carlson, A. A., "Facsimile: An Old Technology with a Fresh Digital Look," *Data Communications,* January 1982, pp. 65–74.

16. Shimotono, S., "Communication Adapter Device for Use with a Facsimile Device Combined with a Computer," U.S. Patent No. 4,964,154; filed 1/13/89, granted 10/16/90.

17. Shinoazaki, A., "Transfer-Type Thermal Printing Device," U.S. Patent No. 4,740,798; filed 9/9/86; granted 4/26/88.

18. Sue, T., "Driving Device for Facsimile Apparatus," U.S. Patent No. 4,646,162; filed 2/9/84, granted 2/24/87.

19. Tabuchi, H., "Method of Compensating for Backlash Caused after Cutting off Recording Paper in Facsimile Apparatus," U.S. Patent No. 4,967,285; filed 11/9/89, granted 10/30/90.

20. Takaoka, T., "Facsimile Machine Having Error Correction Mode," U.S. Patent No. 4,975,783; filed 6/28/89, granted 12/4/90.

21. Tokumaru, Y., Nakai, M., Ota, M., Ikeda, M., Furukawana, H., and Hasegawa, M., "A Powerful 32 Bit Thermal Printing Head Driver LSI," *IEEE Transactions on Consumer Electronics,* CE-28, no. 1 (August 1982), pp. 351–57.

22. Yasuda, Y., "Overview of Digital Facsimile Coding Techniques in Japan," *Proceedings of the IEEE,* 68, no. 7 (July 1980), pp. 840–45.

23. Yoshinouchi, A., Itoh, M., Tsuchimoto, S., Tarui, K., and Nishigaki, S., "Contact-Type Image Sensor," U.S. Patent No. 4,942,481; filed 7/11/88; granted 7/17/90.

24. ———. "A Direct-Contact-Type Amorphous Silicon Image Sensor," *Proceedings of a Symposium on Advances in Amorphous Silicon Devices,* Society of Electrophotography of Japan, May 24, 1985, pp. 53–56 (in Japanese).

25. ———. "Contact-Type Image Sensors with Short Light Paths—The Key to Smaller OA Equipment," *Nikkei Mechanical,* December 1, 1985, pp. 71–78 (in Japanese).

26. ———. "Direct-Contact-Type Image Sensors," *Nikkei Electronics,* no. 434 (1987), pp. 207–21 (in Japanese).

# *Index*